Rhetorical
Strategies
and Genre
Conventions
in Literary
Studies

Rhetorical Strategies and Genre Conventions in Literary Studies

Teaching and Writing in the Disciplines

Laura Wilder

Southern Illinois University Press
Carbondale and Edwardsville

Library of Congress Cataloging-in-Publication Data
Wilder, Laura, 1971–
Rhetorical strategies and genre conventions in literary
studies : teaching and writing in the disciplines /
Laura Wilder.
    p. cm.
Includes bibliographical references and index.
ISBN-13: 978-0-8093-3093-5 (pbk. : alk. paper)
ISBN-10: 0-8093-3093-8 (pbk. : alk. paper)
ISBN-13: 978-0-8093-3094-2 (ebook)
ISBN-10: 0-8093-3094-6 (ebook)
1. English language—Rhetoric—Study and teaching.
2. Interdisciplinary approach in education. I. Title.
PE1404.W5335 2011
808'.0420711—dc23   2011034949

Contents

Acknowledgments

The research and arguments presented in this book have been influenced, nurtured, and made possible by several communities of scholars, students, instructors, and friends. I am enormously indebted to the many instructors and students who gamely consented to participate in my research over the past decade at various institutions. This book would not have been possible without their generous willingness to let me peek into their teaching and writing practices and their candor in speaking with me.

Equally, this book would not have been possible without Joanna Wolfe's collegiality, logistical assistance, and expertise. I am so glad Joanna found my initial forays into uncovering the rhetorical practices of literary scholars pedagogically useful. Our collaboration on the study discussed in chapter 4 was an enormously rewarding experience. All my subsequent thinking on making disciplinary discourse conventions explicit has been influenced by our two minds working through the attendant complexities of this together.

In addition to Joanna, I owe gratitude to many others I met at the University of Texas at Austin who supported the early stages of this research. Davida Charney first persuaded me that this project was feasible and then made it possible with her steadfast encouragement and her unparalleled methodological and rhetorical instruction. I am also indebted to Linda Ferreira-Buckley, Rosa Eberly, Diane Schallert, Jacqueline Henkel, Brian Bremen, Vimala Pasupathi, and Cory Lock.

Marie Secor provided important early encouragement and critique, and my intellectual debts to her and Jeanne Fahnestock are clearly substantial. My own undergraduate literature professors at the University of Florida and my first writing students at Montgomery County Community College, Pennsylvania, are also due humble thanks as they were the first to witness my trials and errors in addressing the rhetorical and pedagogical problems this book engages.

I am also grateful for the support and camaraderie of my colleagues at the University at Albany, State University of New York. Steve North and Randall Craig provided important mentorship. I am grateful for kindnesses big and small performed by Branka Arsić, Rick Barney, Jeffrey Berman, Ronald Bosco, Don Byrd, Lana Cable, Pat Chu, Helen Elam, Jennifer Greiman, jil hanifan, Mike Hill, Pierre Joris, Eric Keenaghan, Kir Kuiken, James Lilley, Ineke Murakami, Tomás Noel, Martha Rozett, Helene Scheck, Ed Schwarzschild, Paul Stasi, Lisa Thompson, Barry Trachtenberg, Mary Valentis, and David Wills. The students in my Writing across the Curriculum seminar (Lucas Hardy, Jon Coller, Debbie Rowe, Silvia Chung, and Robyn Long) helped me understand the varied terrain of the larger enterprise. Thanks also to Lucas Hardy for his transcription work.

Albany's current and former community members have also sustained me through to completion of this project. I extend special gratitude to Elisa Albert, Lee Franklin, Gene Garber and Bobby Garber, Megan Ingalls, Marci Nelligan, Lauren Sallata, and Dariana Williamson.

My family has been enormously supportive in every way. Ann Wilder, Michael Wilder, Tracey Burdick, Nancy Benjamin, Robert Benjamin, and Jeremy Benjamin have modeled for me perseverance, ingenuity, and cooperation at every turn with good humor and love. I dedicate this book to my mother, Ann, and father, Michael, with unending love and gratitude.

And to Bret Benjamin, with whom I have weathered many storms, enjoyed genuine laughter, shared *all* the struggles of this work, and found home, thank you does not suffice. Your righteous, calm, deep commitment moves me every day. With you I welcome Jolie Ann who may turn everything upside down and inside out but sets everything right.

My research and writing were generously supported by the Spencer Foundation, Yale University's Whitney Humanities Center Griswold Fund, the University at Albany's College of Arts and Sciences Faculty Research Award Program, and the New York State/United University Professions Dr. Nuala McGann Drescher Affirmative Action/Diversity Leave Program.

Grateful acknowledgment for permission to reprint is extended for "'The Rhetoric of Literary Criticism' Revisited: Mistaken Critics, Complex Contexts, and Social Justice," *Written Communication*, 22, no. 1 (January 2005): 76–119, reprinted in revised form in chapter 1 by permission of Sage Publications, Inc., copyright © 2005 by Sage Publications, Inc., all rights reserved.

Rhetorical
Strategies
and Genre
Conventions
in Literary
Studies

Introduction

Writing, as the now commonplace view in rhetoric and composition holds, takes place in specific social contexts that are at once constricting and generative for writers. But writing instruction in the United States has not always been informed by this view. Influenced by poststructuralist critiques of authorial autonomy and wishing to better understand the social contexts in which students write, early participants in the emergence of rhetoric and composition as a discipline called for research that makes explicit the conventions of academic discourse, especially those conventions considered transparent and tacitly transmitted. Shaughnessy (1977) is frequently cited as the originator of this call, later echoed by Bizzell (1982), Kinneavy (1983), Bartholomae (1985), Freed and Broadhead (1987), and MacDonald (1989). MacDonald argued such research can help students "adapt their writing to the shifting demands made upon them in different parts of the academy" (p. 411). Writing in the Disciplines (WID) researchers sought to answer these calls and have explored the ways disciplines shape and are shaped by the rhetorical practices of their members. Analyses of professional genres from the natural, social, and engineering sciences have revealed that their conventions are far from static and serve persuasive purposes (Bazerman, 1988; Dowdey, 1992; Fahnestock, 1999; Gross, 1988; Halloran, 1984; MacDonald, 1994; C. R. Miller, 1992; C. R. Miller & Selzer, 1985; Prelli, 1989). Additionally, observational studies of "experts" and "novices" have shed light on how disciplinary enculturation influences composing and reading processes (Beaufort, 2007; Berkenkotter, Huckin, & Ackerman, 1988; Blakeslee, 1993, 1997; Charney, 1993; Geisler, 1994; Haas, 1994; Herrington, 1985, 1992; Myers, 1985; Prior, 1998; Rymer, 1988; Winsor, 1996). These rhetorical analyses, process analyses, and longitudinal studies have themselves helped to shape an understanding among rhetoric and composition scholars of the socially negotiated nature of knowledge and academic authority. However, literary studies, a discipline that like rhetoric and composition lays claim to texts as its object of study, presents a uniquely challenging case for this line of research.

WID's Neglect of Literary Studies

The proximity of literary studies to rhetoric and composition may explain some of the nature of this challenge. Generally speaking, scientific and professional discourse further afield from rhetoric and composition's own place in the humanities occupied much of the early attention of WID researchers. This is understandable since from this perspective there is so much to learn about these discourses. Not surprising then, the few early examinations of literary scholarship from a WID perspective (Bazerman, 1981; Fahnestock & Secor, 1988, 1991; MacDonald, 1987, 1989, 1994) tended to treat this discourse primarily as a foil for illuminating the contrasting rhetorical character of scientific discourse.

Changing understandings of the relationship between literary study and instruction in the nearly ubiquitous composition course for first-year college students provided added motivation for WID researchers to look anywhere but literary studies in their early examinations of disciplinary discourse. Though literature once commonly provided the "content" about which first-year students composed in these courses, a recognition that not all rhetorically effective writing follows the conventions of literary criticism motivated decisions to remove literary texts from first-year composition syllabi, a shift that began in the 1970s (Gamer, 1995). Replacing literature on syllabi were often sample texts from across the curriculum and outside the academy in such areas as public policy or journalistic writing. Reasons offered for these modifications include a shift in the course's goals from consuming texts to producing them and the need to provide texts as models of the various kinds of writing students will produce during and after college (Lindemann, 1993). Additionally, many undergraduate Writing across the Curriculum (WAC) and WID initiatives began to require coursework beyond first-year composition that included writing instruction in a student's chosen major field. The shift in composition pedagogy away from writing about literature to public writing and writing in various disciplines can be seen as both sparked by and necessitating further research into the discourses practiced outside English departments. Simply put, composition instructors, long housed and trained in departments of English, had a lot to learn about the kinds of writing practiced in other disciplines and arenas. Bazerman (1988) acknowledged this when he began his influential rhetorical investigation of science, *Shaping Written Knowledge*, with the explanation that his research was initially motivated by his charge to prepare university students "to write academic essays for their courses in all disciplines" (p. 3). MacDonald (1994) similarly prefaced *Professional Academic Writing in the Humanities and Social Sciences* by describing the research questions that emerged for her out of her experiences as "a teacher of 'basic writing' students" and an administrator of a WID program (p. vii).

The turbulent political tensions between rhetoric and composition and literary studies during the former's emergence as a distinct field may partially explain yet another reason for writing researchers' inattention to literary studies. Just as WID research and the move away from writing about literature in first-year composition began, some compositionists proposed transforming literary studies, rather than analyzing and helping students acclimate to this disciplinary discourse community. Apparently motivated by desires to solve the recurrent "problems" instructors see in students' attempts to write about literature, they made calls to radically alter the curriculum of traditional literature courses. For instance, Wentworth (1987) suggested the problems caused by a teacher's unstated assumption of the "inherent value" in writing about literature and a student's propensity to "circumvent a direct response . . . by retelling the story, the poem, the novel, or the play in question" (p. 155) could be solved by transforming the literature class into a composition class that uses literature as a springboard of ideas for writing personal narratives and rewriting literature in different settings or from different points of view. Similarly, Fulwiler (1988b), extending a practice of the new composition classroom, recommended that literary texts should be treated as models for literature students to consult when composing their own poems and stories, and the anthology he coedited with A. Young, *When Writing Teachers Teach Literature: Bringing Writing to Reading* (1995), seems to have been compiled in this radically revisionary spirit. Thus in the disciplinary turf wars played out in English departments at this time, these compositionists vied for a form of turf taking through transformation of the writing assignments and purposes of existing literature courses.[1]

The Challenge Literary Studies Presents WID

If the shifting demands of different disciplines present noteworthy challenges for undergraduates, then presumably the demands of specialized, scholarly literary study would present no lesser challenge to students than those they encounter in other corners of the academy. McCarthy's (1987) "A Stranger in Strange Lands: A College Student Writing across the Curriculum" notably depicted difficulties a biology major faced in interpreting the expectations of his literature professor. Similarly, Herrington (1988) observed that students in an undergraduate literature class varied in their abilities to infer the methods for reading and writing "like an English major" that the course implicitly encouraged. If a goal of WID is to help students understand the shifting demands placed upon them in different parts of the academy, literary studies deserves the attention of WID researchers.

Further, because of their long association with writing instruction, undergraduate literature courses may challenge some of the characterizations of disciplinary enculturation supported by previous WID research of other disciplines. This research (see especially Geisler, 1994; Russell, 2002) provides an image of traditional approaches to undergraduate disciplinary instruction as one of a researcher-scholar dispensing content knowledge from a lectern to undergraduates while withholding rhetorical process knowledge, practices many WAC and WID initiatives have attempted to revise. But in the literature classrooms McCarthy and Herrington described, students were asked to write a great deal, and they received plentiful feedback on their writing from their professors. Literary instruction may thus usefully complicate and expand WID researchers' understandings of disciplinary enculturation, especially because it is routinely described as imparting general, rather than discipline-specific, critical thinking and writing skills.

Additionally, literary studies may present an interesting challenge to WID researchers' conceptions of rhetorical activities considered fundamental to scholarly discourse, such as knowledge building. Repeatedly rhetorical analyses of discourse in the sciences have traced how scientists position their texts in order to emphasize how they are contributing new knowledge to a field (Berkenkotter & Huckin, 1995; Blakeslee, 1993; Hyland, 2000; Kaufer & Geisler, 1989; Myers, 1985; Swales, 1990). However, those studies that have compared literary scholarship with scientific discourse have characterized literary studies as far less interested in the knowledge-building enterprise. Bazerman (1981) contrasted assumptions underpinning one article of literary criticism published in 1978 with those of a molecular biology article and a sociology article, finding the literary criticism to be more particularistic, idiosyncratic, and personal, in contrast to the project of communal knowledge that the scientific texts present. MacDonald's (1992, 1994) finding that scholarly discourse in the fields of psychology and history is more likely to highlight research methods and warrants than the discourse of Renaissance New Historicist scholars published in the 1980s further contributes to an understanding of literary criticism as an isolated enterprise that is "not knowledge-building" (1992, p. 556). And Fahnestock and Secor (1991) argued that the articles published in a selection of major scholarly journals in literary studies between 1978 and 1982 they analyzed functioned as epideictic or ceremonial rhetoric, which they contrasted with the action-oriented implications of scientific discourse. Instead of having significant consequences for the lives of those outside of the disciplinary discourse community, Fahnestock and Secor (1991) characterized works of literary criticism as conservative, self-celebratory sermons of an enclosed religious community.

These characterizations of the ends of literary study resonate with descriptions of the field's purposes provided by some literary scholars. For instance, in his widely influential *English in America: A Radical View of the Profession*, Ohmann (1996) declared a key distinction between literary and scientific study is that the goal of literary study "is not the accumulation of new knowledge" but "the fostering of literary culture and consciousness" (p. 13), and thus the profession's emphasis on scholarly publication is mismatched to its true purpose. In addition to fostering literary culture, another goal of literary study Ohmann advocated is the promotion of social justice through social change, and again he sees the professionalism of literary studies thwarting this goal. By acting to "enhance the professional self-image of their members," English departments are "conservative" and "serve the discipline and its traditions and respond to social change only within that framework" (p. 227).

However, Ohmann's and others' (Fleming, 2000) concerns about the pressures on literary scholars to both produce new publications and preserve the discipline indicate that they may work within constraints, expectations, and motivations similar to those within which scientists work. Inspired by the same influx of poststructuralist theory, interest among literary scholars in the disciplinary context of their work began to grow around the time rhetoric and composition scholars became intrigued with disciplinary discourse communities. Their self-reflexive histories and genealogies (Eagleton, 1983; Franklin, 1978; Frantzen, 1990; Graff, 1987; Mathieson, 1975; McMurtry, 1985; Parker, 1981; Scholes, 1998; Shumway, 1994; Vanderbilt, 1986) chart the shifting yet accumulative character of literary theory as well as the social and material conditions and motivations for pursuing literary study. They help us see that literary study as pursued today on college campuses is the product of rhetorical maneuvering to "count" as a research-based discipline, in particular arguments contending that literary study is as rigorous and disciplined as science. Although what we call "literature" has been produced and read for centuries, its treatment as an object of study in a university setting dates rather precisely to the late nineteenth century when, like nearly every other academic discipline, scholars organized professional societies, journals, conferences, and requirements for undergraduate majors and doctoral training.[2] One outcome of this burgeoning interest in disciplinarity among literary scholars has been a growing number of critiques of what is characterized as a still-potent emulation of science within literary studies. For instance, Sosnoski (1994, 1995) critiqued the modernist legacies of scientism and objectivity lurking within disciplinary practices in literary and cultural studies.

This image of literary studies' entrenched disciplinarity and emulation of science does not match well the conclusions of the few WID-inspired examinations of literary scholarship. Further, because these previous WID studies were conducted in the 1970s and 1980s just as the influence of poststructuralist theory and political activism began to be felt in English departments, their analyses warrant a second look with more recent samples of discourse. Since Bazerman, MacDonald, and Fahnestock and Secor first looked at them from a WID perspective, the rhetorical practices of literary scholars may have changed in conjunction with their apparent increased sense of self-conscious disciplinarity. This book seeks to investigate these possible changes, taking this discourse on its own terms rather than treating it primarily as a foil for scientific discourse. Likewise, the potential for literary studies to challenge previously established characterizations of the processes of enculturation into disciplinary discourse communities motivates my examination of discourse practices at the "margins" of the discipline and the center of undergraduates experiences of "general education."

Is There a Community in This Discourse?

Since Bizzell's (1982) call to "help poor writers" by explaining "that their writing takes place within a community" and by demystifying the conventions of this "academic discourse community" (p. 230), WID research has relied heavily on the concept of "discourse community" to explain the rhetorical practices of academic disciplines. Rhetorical explanations of genre tend to hinge on the concept. C. R. Miller (1984) concluded her influential essay "Genre as Social Action" with the claim that "for the student, genres serve as keys to understanding how to participate in the actions of a community" (p. 165). Swales (1990) intertwined the concepts by making ownership of genres a defining feature of discourse communities, and Berkenkotter and Huckin (1995) intertwined them by making ownership by discourse communities a defining feature of genre.

However, calls to abandon the concept have emerged. Compositionists have justifiably been suspicious of characterizations of their work as acculturating first-year college students into "*the* academic discourse community." One reason is that the growing body of WID research greatly calls into question the existence of a monolithic academic discourse community and instead reveals profound differences between not only the humanities and the sciences but also differences at the finer-grained level of disciplines and subspecialties. Another is the concern that the discourse community concept, even when treated less monolithically, can be "co-opted" to perform gatekeeping functions by seeing the genre conventions dominant at one moment in a discipline's history as stable standards by which students' performances can be sorted (Cooper, 1989). Another of the recurrent criticisms of the concept is that it suggests too strongly that consensus and unity of purpose are necessary components of discourse communities (Cooper, 1989; Harris, 1989; Roberts-Miller, 2003). Drawing on R. Williams's (1983) definition of "community" in *Keywords*, which claims that the term "seems never to be used unfavourably" (p. 76), Cooper (1989) and Harris (1989) questioned the stability and lack of conflict implied by the term *discourse community*, especially because this runs counter to their perceptions of the discursive interactions of academics and other similarly socially situated writers. Similarly, Prior's (1998) WID research has led him to argue against the usefulness of the concept of discourse community because he sees it as being predominantly treated as static and structuralist with little room for agency. According to Prior, "writing researchers have generally conceptualized disciplinarity in basically structuralist terms, seeing discourse communities as abstract, autonomous, spatialized structures of objects and rules, and disciplinary enculturation as transmission of those structures to largely passive novices" (p. 138), whereas his research has led him to see "heterogeneity and particularity more than uniformity and generality" (p. 139).

Seeking to avoid these problems associated with the concept of discourse community, some rhetoricians have been recently drawn to theories of networks (Prior, 1998) and activity systems (Bawarshi, 2003; Russell, 1995; Russell & Yañez, 2003; Winsor, 1999) to explain the social action of genres within disciplines. While their applications of these theories have yielded enormously useful insights—many of which I seek to use or build upon in this book—my research has led me to believe that though the discourse community concept requires some refinement, its explanatory power for researchers and teachers is too great to support abandoning it. I favor retaining the concept of discourse community—over proposed alternatives such as "network" and "activity system"—despite the criticism it has received, in fact *because* of such criticism. *Discourse community* is a useful term for describing the social and socially constructed fabric of perceived semi-stable connections and common goals that influence and are influenced by the rhetorical practices of a stratified and increasingly diverse group. The discursive exchanges of its members exist amidst, and because of, unequal configurations of power within the community. The concept of discourse community is useful for describing this phenomenon and, I argue, for helping individuals (including both instructors and students) become aware of their positioning within multiple discourse communities and make informed choices about their rhetorical practices within the constraints of these positions.

A revised concept of *discourse community* thus explicitly acknowledges concerns regarding power dynamics, hierarchy, and gatekeeping precisely because these concerns point to real tendencies that we need to be aware of as instructors, students, and researchers—as those who at times find ourselves in positions to wield power within particular discourse communities and as those who at times also find ourselves alienated at a community's periphery. An understanding of disciplinary discourse communities as static and impenetrable runs counter to available evidence, which supports an understanding of disciplinary conventions as in flux and capable of being transformed by relative newcomers to the community. The static view also emphasizes acculturation as a process of sorting and excluding rather than informing and including. Undeniably acculturation performs both these functions; however, a number of studies (Herrington, 1985, 1988, 1992; McCarthy, 1987) suggested instructors may have some impact on the degree to which their practices promote either emphasis. Rather than romanticizing community,[3] I believe instructors, researchers, and students are more than capable, as exemplified by the criticism the concept has already received, of marking the ways in which communities exclude as well as include, undercut radical change in favor of a conservative status quo, and reward sweeping changes that alienate members of an old guard. In his reevaluation of the discourse community concept, Swales (1998) similarly observed that a "functioning" discourse community need not be congenial, democratic, consensual, or free of prejudice (p. 204). In contrast, *network* and *activity system*, with their mechanistic connotations, would seem to further obscure such darker social aspects of the work of genres.

Another virtue *discourse community* has over proposed alternatives is its pedagogical utility and potential support for transferring students' learning to new contexts. Johns (1997) found the concept of discourse community particularly useful because students could readily apply the concept; opening discussion with the genres relevant to discourse communities in which they already participate helped students "to grasp the complexity of text production and processing and the importance of understanding the group practices, lexis, values, and controversies that influence the construction of texts" (p. 54) in contexts with which they have less familiarity. Pointing to evidence that "transfer of learning is aided when there is meta-cognitive awareness of overarching principles or schemata which can be applied to new problems" (p. 524), Beaufort (1997) argued that "the notion of discourse community can be a useful heuristic to give to students, along with heuristics such as rhetorical analysis and genre analysis, in order to solve problems when confronted with new writing tasks" (pp. 524–25).[4]

However, a revised understanding of *discourse community* must address criticism that the concept is too vague (Harris, 1989) and seek to resolve some of the radically different ways it has been applied. Definitions of *discourse community* (Bartholomae, 1985; Beaufort, 1997; Devitt, 2004; Freed & Broadhead, 1987; Hyland, 2000; Swales, 1990) often sharply conflict in regard to how tied they are to sociolinguists' concept of a localized "speech community." For instance, though Freed and Broadhead (1987) indicated that a professional discipline such as rhetoric and composition may be a discourse community, they appeared to equate the term with *speech community*, and more frequently their examples of discourse communities were groups who meet regularly face-to-face, such as a single composition class and an accounting firm. Similarly, Devitt (2004) posited that members of discourse communities "must have contact with one another" (p. 40) and "share substantial amounts of time together in common endeavors" (p. 42). For Devitt, being "physically together . . . might be required for the closeness of a community" (p. 44), and thus a professional organization like the Conference on College Composition and Communication or an institutional structure like an English department qualifies as a discourse community.[5] Thaiss (2001) seemed to go even further in this direction, questioning the aptness of labeling "so-called disciplines" as discourse communities when "the proliferation of subspecialties . . . render communication among 'colleagues' almost nil" (p. 315). Stressing instead the importance of instructors' individual and local classroom goals, he proposed that for writing researchers and administrators, a more meaningful concept may be "writing in the course" rather than "writing in the disciplines" (p. 316).

In contrast, Swales (1990) pointedly distinguished discourse communities from speech communities by highlighting how "literacy takes away locality and parochiality" (p. 24), allowing members to communicate with less-imme-diate connections in space and time. He further differentiated them by stress-ing a discourse community's distinct sociorhetorical characteristics such as its sharing of goals and need to recruit new members. While his later study of the textual life of one university building led Swales (1998) to develop an understanding of "place" discourse communities, whose members "regularly work together" (p. 204) in the same location, it was in "focus" discourse com-munities that Swales (1998) saw the more "prestigious . . . structurations" (p. 201) occurring. C. R. Miller's (1994) concept of rhetorical community built on Swales's (1990) understanding of discourse community by proposing that such communities are "virtual rather than material or demographic" (p. 73). By this she meant that such a community is "a discursive projection, a rhetorical construct. . . . the community as invoked, represented, presupposed, or devel-oped in rhetorical discourse" (p. 73). She thus claimed rhetoricians have been in error in "looking for community demographically and geographically—in classrooms, civic task forces, hobby groups, academic conferences" (p. 74).

These differing conceptions of discourse community have influenced writ-ing research, encouraging, for instance, researchers to describe a particular classroom as either a discourse community unto itself or as a scene relevant to the exploration of a larger disciplinary community. They have also similarly influenced pedagogical and curricular decisions, encouraging instructors to see establishing a discourse community within their writing classroom as a goal or to see preparing students for entering a larger, already established discourse community as a goal. Although Swales and C. R. Miller's "virtual" understanding requires some refinement, an understanding of disciplinary discourse communities as overarching discursive projections and rhetorical constructs that members use to conceptually understand and link their activities is greatly useful. We need to understand both the conceptual projections of discipline that Thaiss (2001) dismissed as unreal and the particular, local, and diverse instantiations of these projections. That so many of the faculty Thaiss has worked with "routinely evoke their concept of 'the discipline' as part of the rationale for their [teaching] methods" (p. 318) suggests that there is something powerfully controlling *and* enabling in this concept—an essential point of Foucault's (1972) "Discourse on Language." A revised understanding of *discourse community* should be useful to researchers and teachers in describing the material, social, and rhetorical effects of disciplines. Though many if not all of these effects and constructions are felt and carried out at the local level, to be usefully distinct from *speech community* or even simply *community*, the discourse community concept should incorporate Swales's and C. R. Miller's insights on the virtual, atemporal, and ideological relationships that literacy supports.

C. R. Miller's (1994) conception of rhetorical community as a rhetorical construction and discursive projection helps us understand the social dynamic of rhetorical practices that scholars might describe as connecting them more to other members of their discipline than to other members of their local campus, yet the work of Prior (1998), Casanave (1995), Chin (1994), and Roozen (2009, 2010) helps us understand the idiosyncratic ways in which these rhetorical practices can be represented, shared, and performed in specific campuses. Qualitative research by Chin (1994) and Casanave (1995) has revealed the impact specific local contexts and material resources had for graduate students learning to become participating members of professional discourse communities. Likewise, studies by Casanave (1995), Prior (1998), and Roozen (2009, 2010) have stressed that the experiences, identities, and personal interests that graduate students bring to their beginning work in a discipline greatly complicate the image of one-way transmission of disciplinary enculturation that Cooper (1989) worried the discourse community concept encourages. Casanave (1995) found that international and minority graduate students in a sociology program through "resistance, rebellion, co-operation, [and] suggestions" (p. 94) influenced their professors to modify their courses in order to meet their needs and that such influence may ultimately "help define the broader field and change it over time" (p. 94). Prior (1995) traced how a graduate student in sociology came to deeply influence and change the thinking of her professor through repeated written response and revision interactions. The changes in thinking that the graduate student persuaded her professor to make were motivated significantly by the graduate student's personal, family experiences. Roozen (2009, 2010) explored ways in which two English MA students' encounters with the disciplinary discourse of literary studies are mediated by their previous encounters with the work of other disciplines such as graphic arts and by their participation in extracurricular activities such as church groups and fan fiction.

These studies ask us to revise simplistic understandings of disciplinary enculturation involving a one-way transmission of views, values, practices, and knowledge and see how the diverse communities to which new members already belong may influence and shape established members' rhetorical constructions of the discipline. Such flux and "cross-pollination" suggests that this construct, though powerful, is not fully homogenizing. In fact, as Burke's (1973) famous parlor metaphor attempted to capture, one of the defining features of disciplinary discourse community may be heterogeneity of viewpoints and *agon*. C. R. Miller (1994) described the "fundamentally heterogeneous and contentious" (p. 74) character of rhetorical communities this way:

> It is the inclusion of sameness and difference, of us and them, of centripetal and centrifugal impulses that makes a community rhetorical, for rhetoric in essence requires both agreement and dissent, shared understandings and novelty, enthymematic premises and contested claims, identification and division. (p. 74)

Perfect consensus would remove the need for further connection, collaboration, contention, and argument that such a community uses discourse to perform.

In addition to being inaccurate, understandings of discourse communities as fixed in consensus may also lead to detrimental outcomes for instructors and students. Arguments that would limit the concept of discourse community to the temporally and physically proximate often posit the pedagogical goal of creating a discourse community within particular classrooms. These arguments thus articulate an understanding of discourse community as a sought-after ideal rather than a descriptive term for recurrent patterns of social organization and formation. As a result, a great many classrooms are seen as not meeting the ideal. For instance, Chiseri-Strater (1991) proposed that "community should imply a place where the norms of behavior and rituals and routines of language are implicit to all its members, not just to those in control. . . . Rather than having *community* serve as a default term, I think it should be reserved for places that make an effort to initiate students into their institutions, disciplines, or classrooms" (pp. 143–44). Even if this idealized image of classrooms were instantiated more frequently—and Russell's (2002) historical research coupled with WID ethnographies like McCarthy's (1987) indicates that few university classrooms in the past century would meet this ideal—limiting use of the term to only those ideal composition or WAC classrooms may serve to reify stiflingly benign connotations associated with "community." I argue that concerns regarding the coerciveness of community consensus arise most prominently when understandings of *discourse community* are limited to the walls of a single classroom. Roberts-Miller (2003) described the capacity an instructor has to inadvertently exclude and silence the already culturally marginalized in the name of maintaining a cordial and civil classroom discourse community. Yet, shifting focus to see an individual classroom as a scene within a larger disciplinary discourse community radically shifts our understandings of the instructor's power within the scene. Suddenly the professor's views, lectures, and assignments are in fact contested by other members of the discourse community with equal or greater power, as well as by those with less disciplinary and institutional power but who are learning to use and transform the conventions of the community. If students could be aided to make such a shift in conceptualizing the scene of their classroom—and I believe explicitly sharing and modeling the revised understanding of *discourse community* I am proposing can help them do so—then the *agon* that already exists in the disciplinary discourse community can more genuinely include the voices of students. Thus while I imagine Chiseri-Strater and I might advocate for a number of similar classroom practices to promote student involvement and make explicit the values and purposes implicit in disciplinary genres, I do not follow her and others in calling for limiting our use of *discourse community* to describe only idealized classrooms.

Given this revised understanding of disciplinary discourse communities as instable, agonistic, and virtual, pressing questions remain about their definitional shape and depth. Previous definitions and critiques have wrestled with the question of the distinctness of the boundaries of discourse communities. If Prior (1998) and Casanave (1992, 1995) showed that graduate students can be barred from genuine participation in a disciplinary discourse community, they also showed that graduate students can participate in ways that profoundly influence the community. Similarly, Cooper (1989) claimed new PhDs and other new members of groups often have "a dominant influence in reformulating the values, goals, participatory mechanisms, discoursal expectations, and language of a group and in bringing in new knowledge and expertise to the group" (p. 216). But is such legitimate peripheral participation (Lave & Wenger, 1991) a possibility for undergraduate students participating in less obviously acculturating contexts, such as in required general education introductory coursework? T. P. Miller (1999) argued that many disciplinary innovations in English departments, such as cultural studies, "have been institutionalized in general education courses before becoming part of the course of the major" precisely because of "the generative possibilities" of "work at the boundaries of the field of study where the educated culture is called upon to explain itself to relative outsiders." This provocatively suggests that students in these courses who may never take another course in the discipline may nonetheless make a profound impact on the discipline's current debates and practices. By encouraging and modeling ways WID research can extend its gaze to include introductory, "gen. ed." classrooms, the research presented in this book sets out to interrogate this possibility, complicating and broadening previous understandings of the boundaries of disciplinary discourse communities.

Another important, related, and unresolved issue concerns the depth of epistemological and value commitments that legitimate participation in a disciplinary discourse community asks of individuals. One of Kent's (1991) objections to the concept of "discourse community" was his understanding that moving from one discourse community to another entails radically changing worldviews. However, both Swales (1990) and Casanave (1995) pointed to the potential for individuals, especially students, to try on, without full commitment, the personae discourse community membership entails. Both hold out hope for this possibility out of concern especially for international and minority students for whom a requirement to abandon a worldview to participate casts too great "a hegemonical shadow" (Swales, 1990, p. 30) over apprenticeship and education. Instead, they see it as possible for students to "perceive themselves as having power to resist, push back, toy, experiment, and, if necessary, continue looking" (Casanave, 1995, p. 108). Villanueva (2001), distinguishing accommodation from assimilation, argued that mimicry or *imitatio* can empower colonial subjects and minority students with a subversive complicity—he argued that "we all accommodate . . . in the conventions we adopt (or even mimic)" (p. 175). Similarly, Prior (1998) proposed distinguishing among three "modes of participation": passing, procedural display, and deep participation. My analysis in this book suggests nonetheless that adherence to shared values—and the belief that experts can distinguish passing from deep participation by evaluating written performances—is integrally implicated even in novice and peripheral participation in disciplinary discourse communities.

The research that follows in this book supports a growing body of WID research (Beaufort, 1997, 2007; Geisler, 1994; Herrington, 1985, 1992; McCarthy, 1987; Walvoord & McCarthy, 1990) that establishes connections between the rhetorical practices encouraged in particular classrooms and those practiced in larger "virtual" professional and academic discourse communities. Critiques of the supposed unity and stability of discourse communities coupled with histories of their discursive practices teach us that rhetorical analyses used to characterize a discourse community's genres are necessarily blurred snapshots, always imperfectly pinning down conventions and topoi that are in flux. Nonetheless, *Rhetorical Strategies and Genre Conventions in Literary Studies: Teaching and Writing in the Disciplines* indicates such conventions are stable enough to be described and of use not only to writing researchers but also to writers. The conservative nature of disciplinary discourse communities ensures to a degree this stability, while the imperative of disciplinary communities to construct new knowledge and recruit new members equally ensures a counterbalancing pressure of instability and change.

Rhetorical Theories of Invention and Convention

A fruitful way to navigate the controversies surrounding the discourse community concept may come through a more thoroughly rhetorical understanding of convention. Critics of instruction aimed to support students' entrance into disciplinary discourse communities often adhere to an understanding of disciplinary discourse conventions rooted in formalist current-traditional theories of rhetoric that emphasize arrangement and style but that neglect invention (see Fulwiler, 1992; Knoblauch & Brannon, 1983; Mahala, 1991; Spellmeyer, 1989). This tendency leaves the impression that learning and knowledge building are divorced from disciplinary rhetorical practices—a distinction not unlike the division between dialectic and rhetoric disputed by the Sophists. In contrast, the twentieth-century scholarly recovery of ancient rhetoric has revived a richer, fuller rhetorical theory with invention—or what we might call creativity (McKeon, 1987)—at its center. This treatment of invention as within the realm of rhetoric is consonant with poststructuralist theories of social construction (Carter, 1988; LeFevre, 1987; C. R. Miller, 2000). Concepts pivotal to this understanding of rhetorical invention are stasis theory and topoi, heuristic tools intended to help rhetors explore and construct new arguments that would be appropriate to the situation at hand. This understanding of decorum (*to prepon*) "is not a superficial or slavish matter but a force that must be highly attuned to situation and equally attuned to substance" (C. R. Miller, 2000, p. 142). Seen in this light, conventions may include far more than socially sanctioned textual surface features of style and arrangement. Instead, conventions associated with invention such as stases and topoi tie a rhetor's exigencies, choice of topics and approaches, and self-representation—essentially the heart of what she has to say and how she says it—to her relationship with a particular discourse community.

Stasis theory and topoi are themselves the product of social construction, as they were adapted and passed on by the Sophists, the early instructors and theorists of the evolving body of knowledge eventually called rhetoric. The codification of this theory in manuscripts such as Aristotle's *On Rhetoric* by no means stopped this process, as rhetorical theory continued to be rewritten and reshaped through the centuries, along the way lopping off previously central concepts like invention as modern views of rhetoric developed—the very views that poststructuralism has more recently come to challenge (C. R. Miller, 2000). The mid-twentieth-century recovery of a fuller ancient rhetorical theory by scholars such as Burke, Kinneavy, Perelman, Corbett, and Bitzer did not aim to apply these ancient concepts wholesale into very different contemporary contexts but instead continued the process of adaptation. For instance, contemporary genre theory, as C. R. Miller (1994) noted, can be found inchoate in the more limited ancient understandings of three possible genres: epideictic, deliberative, and forensic.

Stasis theory aims to help a rhetor characterize the issue or issues on which community members disagree in order to facilitate a rhetor's development of exigent and appropriate arguments. Thus while the name conjures the image of stillness—an issue on which two or more competing points of view rest—the theory is intended to help rhetors organize potential creative energies and advance arguments and possibly subsequent actions (Carter, 1988). Drawing from the largely forensic treatment of the stases intended to help educate young lawyers in the surviving evidence of Hermagoras's lost manuscript,

Hermogenes's *On Stases*, Cicero's *De Inventione*, and Quintilian's *Institutio Oratoria* (Nadeau, 1964),[6] contemporary rhetoricians tend to agree on the classification of five hierarchically addressed stasis issues, each of which can be formulated as a question:

- existence (Did it happen?) *Fact*
- definition (What is it?)
- evaluation (Is it good?)
- cause (What caused it?)
- proposal (What should we do about it?)

These questions serve as probes to identify and explore difference within a community, an analytic function, as well as tools for the generation of arguments, a productive function. As Carter (1988) explained, each stasis is associated with topoi that support finer-grained analysis and invention of copious arguments from which rhetors may choose the most appropriate and persuasive for the situation at hand.

Topoi, according to Aristotle's *Topics* and *Rhetoric*, are a source for the often-unstated premises of enthymemes, commonly understood as rhetorical syllogisms (C. R. Miller, 1987; Slomkowski, 1997). Metaphorically, they are both an inventional "place" for storing these starting points for arguments (perhaps related to the mnemonic practice of associating memorized material with imagined physical locations) and points of entry when attacking an opponent's argument. According to Alexander of Aphrodisias's commentary, Aristotle's student Theophrastus labeled an unpredicated topic as *parangelma* and used the term *topoi* to describe the values that are derived by taking a pro or con stance on parangelma (Slomkowski, 1997, p. 62). Later scholars reviving classical rhetoric, such as Perelman and Olbrechts-Tyteca (1969), Leff (1983), C. R. Miller (1987), and Fahnestock and Secor (1991), have adopted this meaning of the term, defining *topoi* (or *loci*) as commonly held "warrants" (Toulmin, 1964) or often-unstated premises that seek to connect with an audience's hierarchy of values. Aristotle's treatment of topoi as abstractions facilitates rhetors' use of them as heuristic tools to develop new arguments rather than simply repeat ready-made and fully formed commonplaces, as had been encouraged previously (D'Angelo, 1984) and would come to be again during the fifteenth century with the practice of commonplace books. The disappearance of treatments of topoi as heuristic tools for invention, which began not long after the Hellenistic period, signals a developing separation between rhetoric and the realms of invention and dialectic. Dialectic increasingly became associated with philosophy and specific subject realms such as history and politics that provided the "content" for rhetoric to merely make stylistically and formally palatable (Leff, 1983; C. R. Miller, 1987).

Special topoi (*idioi topoi* or *eide*), in contrast to the twenty-eight commonplaces (*koinoi topoi*) Aristotle lists in his *Rhetoric*, are commonplaces of particular rhetorical situations, warrants not necessarily shared by the larger society in which a particular discourse community operates. Aristotle devoted much of the first two books of *Rhetoric* to discussion of the importance of special topoi, since he observed that persuasion is "materially grounded in the resources of particular situations" (C. R. Miller, 1987, p. 64). As C. R. Miller (1987) described, the special topoi represent for Aristotle a sort of compromise between the promise of rhetoric as a broadly applicable and teachable subject, for which complexity must be reducible to useful precepts, and rhetoric as a field of research, where careful observation of discourse practices reveals the messiness of specificity and diversity. This sensibility resonated with those who undertook the mid-twentieth-century recovery of rhetoric. Perelman and Olbrechts-Tyteca (1969) discussed loci that are "agreements that are peculiar to the members of a particular discipline" and that "characterize certain audiences" (p. 99). Toulmin, Rieke, and Janik's textbook, *An Introduction to Reasoning* (1979), presents the use of particular warrants as connected to particular disciplines and fields such as "science and engineering," "law and ethics," "medicine," and "aesthetics and psychology," explaining that apprentices learn the backing for such particular warrants as they enter a profession (p. 63). Special topoi may be understood as a cluster of shared assumptions that allow each discipline to do its rhetorical work with an efficiency that would be absent if scholarly writers had to explain and defend all of their first principles and grounding assumptions in every argument. However, special topoi likely do far more rhetorical work than provide efficient means for constructing an argument's logos. Using them appropriately may subtly signal to other discourse community members that the writer has the credentials, or ethos, to make the argument worth regarding and tap into shared values, or pathos.

Contemporary rhetoricians have found stasis theory and especially topoi useful concepts for continuing Aristotle's pedagogical and research agenda. While classical treatises primarily intended for pedagogical purposes stressed the usefulness of stasis theory and topoi as inventional tools, contemporary rhetoricians have demonstrated that stasis theory and topoi can also be used "in reverse" as tools of rhetorical analysis. The work of the rhetorician in this instance is to interpret "after-the-fact" the audience's attitudes, values, and predispositions that a rhetor attempted to elicit, deliberately or not. For instance, topoi have been used by contemporary rhetoricians to analyze the public discourse surrounding the publication of controversial literary works (Eberly, 2000), popularizations of scientific discoveries (Fahnestock, 1986), and moments of social and political unrest (Eisenhart, 2006). Meanwhile, supporting Young's (1980) assertion that the explicit instruction in heuristic strategies the New Rhetoric offers is valuable to students, a number of pedagogical studies (Bilsky, McCrea, Streeter, & Weaver, 1953; Infante, 1971; Kirch, 1996) provides evidence that instruction in topoi can help students manipulate these inventional tools to explore and produce copious arguments.

Stasis theory and topoi have been particularly useful in WID research. As Fahnestock and Secor (1988) pointed out, the discourse of academic disciplines, unlike public discourse such as news media reports, tends not to address the full range of stasis issues in a given publication. Investigations of why particular audiences are addressed at particular stases can reveal the rhetorical function of disciplinary discourse. Similarly, because academics most often write for other academics, the concept of special topoi helps WID researchers explore the ways in which scholarly writers appeal to values shared among disciplinary discourse community members, thus highlighting the ways in which pathos functions in even the most seemingly objective academic discourses. They also provide a way for WID researchers to understand tacit knowledge (Sternberg, 1999; Wagner & Sternberg, 1985) rhetorically as procedural knowledge (Geisler, 1994), often passed along in apprenticeship relationships within communities of practice (Lave & Wenger, 1991; Wenger, 1999). Prelli (1989) and more recently Walsh (2010) have explored topoi customary in the sciences broadly conceived, C. R. Miller and Selzer (1985) examined the role special topoi play in engineering reports, Berkenkotter and Huckin (1995) charted the ways rhetoric and composition scholars invoked special topoi to establish ethos in abstracts submitted to their annual Conference on College Composition and Communication, and Prior (1998) traced the special topoi prevalent in graduate seminars in geography, American studies, and sociology. Topoi have even been demonstrated to be useful categories of analysis for examining hoaxes and spoofs of academic discourse (Secor & Walsh, 2004). Bartholomae's influential essay "Inventing the University"

(1985) strongly suggested that the findings of such research had a place in students' rhetorical educations when he argued that undergraduates need to be taught the "interpretive schemes" (p. 140) and "specifically acceptable gestures and commonplaces" (p. 143) of academic discourse communities, thus redefining the "problem" of "basic writing" as one of disciplinary socialization rather than one of students' cognitive deficits.

The Rhetoric of Literary Criticism

Stasis theory and special topoi would seem to be particularly useful for approaching discourse produced in disciplines in the humanities like literary studies where favored genres noticeably do not to follow rigid conventions of style or arrangement. For instance, neither the arrangement pattern of clearly demarcated introduction, method, results, and discussion sections nor the introductory "create a research space" moves that Swales (1990) charted in other disciplines appear in articles published in scholarly journals in literary studies (Balocco, 2000). To support his claim that "the production of any text, even the production of a text about a text, requires the application of special topics" (p. 375), Pullman (1994) sketched several possible special topoi of literary interpretation: "intention (or anti-intention), structure, context, influence, origin, significance, implication, sublimation, signs of ideological issues and conflicts, form and substance, ambiguity, indeterminacy, etymology, figurality" (p. 380). However, Pullman's evidence for the existence of these special topoi within literary scholarship was anecdotal and, as he acknowledged, he did not attempt to adequately distinguish which topoi were currently favored in the field's discourse and which may have receded in prominence.

Rhetorical analysis of a representative corpus of texts would be necessary for such a project, and the work of Fahnestock and Secor (1988, 1991; Secor, 1984) has thus far come the closest to fulfilling this goal. Analyzing scholarly articles drawn from the October 1984 *PMLA* (Secor, 1984), the January 1986 *PMLA* (Fahnestock & Secor, 1988), and a group of articles from "a selection of journals of established reputation" published between 1978 and 1982 (Fahnestock & Secor, 1991, p. 77), Fahnestock and Secor argued that the most frequent stasis issues that literary criticism addresses are existence, definition, and evaluation and that several special topoi bespeak these arguments' shared underlying assumptions. In "The Rhetoric of Literary Criticism" (1991), they identify five such special topoi and observe that these "special literary topoi invoke the shared assumptions of the community of literary scholars, and at the same time create that community" (p. 84). Distilling Fahnestock and Secor's characterizations, five special topoi of literary criticism are:

- **appearance/reality**. The critic points out a perception of two entities: one more immediate, the other latent; one on the surface, the other deep; one obvious, the other the object of search.
- **ubiquity**. The critic points out a form (a device, an image, a linguistic feature, a pattern) repeated throughout a work. Either many examples of the same thing are pointed out, or one thing is noted in many forms.
- **paradox**. The critic points out the unification of apparently irreconcilable opposites in a single startling dualism.
- **paradigm**. The critic fits a kind of template over the details of a literary text to endow them with order, elucidate a structure. A microparadigm topos describes a small structural unit in the text that becomes the center of ever-larger concentric applications, moving ultimately beyond the text under discussion, while a macroparadigm topos imports relationships from the world outside the literary text within the particular work. Often the critic juxtaposes two diverse works to elucidate some aspect of a text, or the critic may note a large social reality writ small in the individual text.
- *contemptus mundi*. The critic exhibits an assumption of despair over the condition of society. The critic tends to value works that describe despair, alienation, seediness, anxiety, decay, declining values, and difficulty of living and loving in our society. Similarly, the critic attempts to point out the unresolvable tensions and shadows in literature that at face value seem optimistic.

Fahnestock and Secor observed that these special topoi were tools the literary critics used upon texts as well as the warrants (i.e., "using this tool is good or appropriate interpretive methodology") that the critics as a professional discourse community shared. Consistently the use of these special topoi assumed values of complexity and nonreductive argumentation held by both the arguer and the audience. These values point to a crucial difference between literary studies and the sciences, where the principle of Occam's razor privileges the simplest explanations.

Because using the preferred stases and special topoi of literary criticism appropriately announces "one's membership in the community of literary scholars" (Fahnestock & Secor, 1991, p. 91), Fahnestock and Secor's descriptions of these conventions provide signposts that may start to help us trace the movement of rhetorical conventions over time in this disciplinary discourse community. They also provide signals that may announce a student's acquisition of key conventions of literary studies. Their descriptions provide a starting point, an inductive lens, that remains extremely useful to WID scholars examining literary studies. For instance, using think-aloud protocol analysis, Warren (2006) found that nine literature professors used the special topoi Fahnestock and Secor identified as a mixture of inventional tools and audience appeals when reading poems and preparing a professional conference paper. In a rhetorical analysis of the first volume, published in 1886, of *PMLA* (Wilder, 2006), I charted how research articles in this disciplinary community early on gravitated toward the existence and definitional stases, thereby distinguishing their work from the pedagogical proposals that also appeared for a short time in the early volumes of *PMLA* and establishing discourse conventions still seen in practice today in this discipline. However, I also found rather different topoi invoked by the late-nineteenth-century philologists who wrote these articles, confirming Fahnestock and Secor's (1991) claim that "the set of discipline-specific assumptions to which arguments appeal and from which they are generated are bound to evolve over time" (p. 91).

These rhetorical and process analyses create a tentative and loose schema for understanding the procedural rhetorical knowledge possessed by experts in this discipline. As is the case with other disciplines, research indicates that newcomers to the disciplinary discourse community do not automatically infer this knowledge. Think-aloud protocol analyses that compare the reading and writing practices of more established scholars in this field with those of beginning students reveal students' relative lack of strategies for exploring and producing multiple interpretations of literary texts (Earthman, 1992; Peskin, 1998). Several studies indicate that the pedagogical methods for imparting expert procedural knowledge to students in this discipline, as in other disciplines, tended to be largely implicit, with students' abilities to infer useful genre knowledge varying greatly. This appears to be the case with literature instruction at different education levels: high school (Beck, 2006), college (Doheny-Farina, 1989; Herrington, 1988; Langer, 1992; McCarthy, 1987; Schmersahl & Stay, 1992), and even graduate school (Sullivan, 1991), where concerns regarding disciplinary socialization would seem to be less acute.

This tendency has led Schilb (2002) to call for graduate instruction in literary studies that makes rhetorical analysis of features of its disciplinary discourse, particularly the special topoi Fahnestock and Secor (1991) identified, a central component of needed writing instruction. Wolfe (2003) anecdotally reported on her success basing an entire undergraduate "writing about literature" course around explicit instruction in these special topoi. Both Schilb and Wolfe stressed that such instruction can actually make straightforward disciplinary indoctrination less likely to occur because rhetorical analysis of topoi helps students see how disciplinary discourse changes over time and how scholars marshal some conventions in defiance of others. Both authors claim that calling attention to such embedded conventions helps students to make more conscious choices about their interpretive and rhetorical practices, whereas traditional patterns of intuiting rhetorical practices from model texts, professors' speech, and trial and error pose greater concerns related to indoctrination.

Because such claims are fiercely contested by those who contend that explicit instruction in disciplinary rhetorical practices is at best ineffective (A. Freedman, 1993a) and at worst uncritically accommodating of disciplinary hegemony (Herndl, 1993; LeCourt, 1996; Mahala, 1991; Malinowitz, 1998) and unethical (Spellmeyer, 1989), they deserve further scrutiny and research. Likewise, although Fahnestock and Secor's rhetorical analyses have provided extremely useful signposts for recognizing the contours of conventional discourse in a discipline that subscribes to few steadfast stylistic and formal conventions, their corpus now seems notably outdated. The landscape of literary studies has changed a great deal since the late 1970s and early 1980s when they conducted their analyses; it has been reshaped to such an extent by an influx of theoretical debate (poststructuralist, Marxist, psychoanalytic, feminist, among others) as well as broader social and historical transformations that its purposes, objects of study, and institutional configurations have all been called into question and impacted in ways that have been described by some in the field as revolutionary. Fahnestock and Secor (1991) themselves conceived of their analyses as "an invitation to further study, refinement, and correction" (p. 77), and they acknowledged that discourse practices within disciplines change over time. For a map of topoi and stasis practices that would be useful for to students of literature and WID scholars, analysis of a more recent, diverse corpus is needed.

Overview of Book: WID Research as Topographical Mapping

The research presented in this book seeks to fill this gap with rhetorical analysis of recent literary scholarship. But beyond a rhetorical analysis of scholarly texts by experts, I aim in this book to understand and clarify the ways history, hierarchy, enculturation, and even personal and cognitive development impact the situated practices of what we describe as disciplinary discourse communities. To do so, I use a mix of different research methods: rhetorical analysis of published scholarship, student papers, and textbooks and pedagogical materials; interviews of faculty and students; ethnographic observation; and intervention into pedagogical practices. I believe such methodological pluralism is necessary in order to untangle the web of cognitive, social, historical, institutional, individual, and disciplinary influences on situated discourse community practices and to see some of the ways this web is knotted together. Thus, among other claims, *Rhetorical Strategies and Genre Conventions in Literary Studies: Teaching and Writing in the Disciplines* makes a methodological argument pertinent to WID studies as well.

While my findings may be valuable to literature instructors and students, this book can be read as a case study of one discipline with implications for still-potent debates on the nature of discourse communities and the ethics and efficacy of various approaches to WAC and WID. Unlike the important cross-disciplinary surveys of disciplinary teaching and rhetorical practices conducted by Swales (1990), Walvoord and McCarthy (1990), and Thaiss and Zawacki (2006), I focus exclusively on one discipline with the intention of contributing to the knowledge these surveys helped produce by taking seriously the significance of specific disciplinary context that they helped to illuminate. In contrast to research from those WID-informed studies of a single discipline, such as Beaufort's (2007) examination of the socialization of a history major or Haas's (1994) of a biology major or Herrington's (1985, 1988, 1992) separate studies of chemical engineering, anthropology, and literature classrooms, I analyze not only the disciplinary enculturation of novices but also the complex terrain of their professors' rhetorical practices.

As I have worked to integrate the disparate parts of this research, connecting the tendencies I have observed both in the professional journal articles of scholars and in the successful essays of sophomore students, I have become increasingly appreciative of the spatial metaphors the ancient Greeks used to describe rhetorical practice. Because the rhetorical practices of the disciplines are not isolated from the larger culture, as critics of the concept of discourse community are right to point out, topoi prominent in one discipline may also figure within other disciplines as well as other nondisciplinary discourse communities. What may be more telling of a discourse community's rhetorical practices is not their "ownership" of a particular topos but the combination of several topoi that resonate with its members and the varying intensities to which these topoi are held.[7] That such rhetorical practices shift and change throughout a community's history further suggests some of the complexity and tenuousness of attempting to characterize a discipline's special topoi conventions. I have thus come to see the aptness of an analogy between attempting to rhetorically analyze a discipline's special topoi and the task of topographical mapmaking. Like the contours of a mountainous landscape, a discipline's characteristic special topoi vary in scale and intensity. Some erode over time, worn down by the pressures of new practices and perspectives; in turn, these new forces begin to form new peaks, new features for the topographical cartographer to attempt to locate. On the one hand, the boundaries that rhetorical mapmakers use to demarcate discourse communities clarify political and social relations with real consequences. On the other hand, such fixed boundaries mislead in their tendency to obscure the permeability and fluidity of the disciplinary landscape. The topographical map provides me a more complex and useful image of the rhetorical character of discourse communities than the two-dimensional schema of overlapping circles that has previously been posited (Beaufort, 1997; Bizzell, 1982) because it facilitates the conceptualization of hierarchy, time, and change. I believe a revitalization of the spatial metaphor for invention will prove useful for other WID researchers as well as for students.[8]

This book presents my attempt to map the topoi of discourse within one discipline. Chapter 1 updates and extends the previous rhetorical analyses of professional discourse in literary studies, noting how one discipline's discourse practices have changed over time. Although disciplinary special topoi do change, this change comes about through discourse community members' marshaling of some entrenched topoi against others, a process that demonstrates the simultaneously conservative and progressive potential of disciplinary conventions. Chapter 2 extends this work into the social context of the classroom, where I chart the presence of disciplinary special topoi in general education coursework intended to be nondisciplinary. My interviews with literature faculty and ethnographic observation of an introductory literature course reveal that through the multiple and competing rationales for and approaches to undergraduate literature instruction, a tacit adherence to disciplinary values tends to guide choices in course design and teaching style. Chapter 3 delves into the typically private and potentially idiosyncratic grading practices of literature professors. An image of these practices as more the product of communal disciplinary values than idiosyncrasy emerges from my discussions with several literature professors who were asked to evaluate the same student papers. Chapter 4 discusses an experimental study that investigates the effects of heightening students' awareness of the special topoi of literary studies; I present the results of this study in the context of debate among writing researchers and teachers on the ethics and efficacy of explicit instruction in genre conventions. I also suggest how a WID-informed "pedagogy of conventions" that demystifies procedural rhetorical knowledge can enrich the WAC goal of promoting deeply epistemic "writing to learn" opportunities. Chapter 5 presents these issues from students' perspectives. I discuss my longitudinal work with students who participated in the experimental study described in chapter 4. These students relate their perspectives on either the experimental or traditional "writing about literature" curriculum that they experienced and discuss how it fit within their experience of the undergraduate English major, shedding light on salient issues related to students' transfer of learning. They also help me interpret the results of that study in which they were participants. Lastly, chapter 6 discusses the resistances some literature professors have strongly expressed regarding the WID project of making disciplinary discourse conventions explicit to students; these include concerns that have not adequately been addressed in previous discussions of faculty resistance and point again to constraints of disciplinary power dynamics. If the arguments and analyses presented throughout the rest of this book and the larger WID project are to have any impact, these concerns must be heard and understood.

1

"The Rhetoric of Literary Criticism" Revisited: Mistaken Critics, Complex Contexts, and Social Justice

My topographical mapmaking begins in a site that most observers would characterize unhesitatingly as a forum for disciplinary discourse community exchanges: professional journals. Fahnestock and Secor (1991) turned to journal articles to describe the stasis and special topoi conventions of literary criticism. Though their analysis shared a tendency with early WID research to find literary scholars' discourse lacking in contrast to the perceived greater utility of scientific discourse, their work was unique among the few early WID investigations of literary studies in its large and diverse corpus of texts and attention to distinct disciplinary inventional strategies and value-based audience appeals. Their analysis provides an extremely useful map of stasis and special topoi conventions prominent in literary criticism published between 1978 and 1982. While significant theoretical and social changes have since transformed the landscape of literary studies, their work provides signposts and features that allowed me to develop an inductive analysis of another corpus, evaluating a more recent sample of discourse in the context of their findings.

The contrast between their findings and my analysis of the first issue of *PMLA* from 1886 is striking (Wilder, 2006). On the one hand, the stasis conventions of literary analysis appear already established in this philological scholarship's focus on questions of definition. Yet on the other hand, none of the special topoi Fahnestock and Secor found recurrent in literary criticism from the late 1970s, including in articles published in *PMLA*, are recognizable in this earlier publication. The recurrent topoi in the first *PMLA* work to connect and construct a disciplinary discourse community united in efforts mutually seen as worthwhile and overwhelmingly new. I saw these nascent conventions as establishing a forum where the philolgists' scholarship and teaching, which were new in the United States and controversial in their displacement of a classical curriculum, needed no justification and could develop isolated from questions of its worth. In wielding these conventions, the new philologists modeled their disciplinary structure and rhetorical practices on the sciences. In contrast, questions about the inherent value of literary scholarship appear to have been a non-issue in Fahnestock and Secor's sample.

More recently, however, rhetorical scholars have come to question the viability of the concept of disciplinary discourse communities because the expansion of membership, interests, and methods suggests that the supposed unity of disciplinary rhetorical practices is an illusion. Thaiss (2001) asserted that a discipline's subspecialties create such a cacophony of diverse interests and methods that genuine communication across them likely does not occur. Similar suspicion of this broader definition led MacDonald (1994) to restrict her analyses of disciplinary discourse to the more localized notion of speech communities, analyzing four articles by Renaissance New Historicists "who cited each other or were in other ways demonstrably participating in the same subdisciplinary discourse" (p. 201). She thereby avoided the "hopeless task" of attempting "to describe the discursive practices of literary academics" made so difficult because "the historical succession of unresolved conflicts within literary studies offers ample evidence that there are multiple discourses within a discipline" (p. 14). Yet as Thaiss (2001) described, scholars frequently refer to a projected, constructed image of a broader disciplinary community to justify actions and explain motivations. In my attempt to update Fahnestock and Secor's map with a rhetorical analysis of more recent discourse in literary studies, I took seriously these "relationships we carry around in our heads" (C. R. Miller, 1994, p. 75) and investigated the extent of common rhetorical practices across diverse subspecialties within a single discipline. Given the major transformations in literary studies over the past century and what are perceived to be enormous theoretical divides among individual scholars, do any collective values and assumptions on which this discipline builds its new discourse remain? Are there features common to a discourse community of literary scholars that transcend or run through the textual conversations of the subspecialties? Is there, in fact, still a discourse community in this discipline?

In order to investigate these questions, I analyzed twenty-eight articles (listed in table 1.1) drawn randomly from twelve prominent literary journals, including the same ten journals Fahnestock and Secor drew from, and published between 1999 and 2001 (for a fuller explanation of sample selection and analytic methodology, see Wilder, 2005). The lens through which I read this sample draws on categories first discussed by classical rhetoricians, and later by Toulmin (1964) and Perelman and Olbrechts-Tyteca (1969), to examine the "informal logic" and audience appeals frequently implicit in professional discourse due to the specialized nature of its community or readers. Like Fahnestock and Secor, I determined the stasis issues an article addresses and the special topoi it invokes, and by doing so attempted to analyze the attitudes, values, and predispositions of an audience entreated by a rhetor's discourse, deliberately or not (see the introduction for a fuller explanation of these rhetorical concepts).

Table 1.1 Articles in the Sample

Author and Title	Date Published	Journal
Albrecht, James M., "Saying Yes and Saying No: Individualist Ethics in Ellison, Burke, and Emerson"	January 1999	*PMLA*
Berger, Courtney, "When Bad Things Happen to Bad People: Liability and Individual Consciousness in *Adam Bede* and *Silas Marner*"	Summer 2000	*Novel*
Burton, Stacy, "Rereading Faulkner: Authority, Criticism, and *The Sound and the Fury*"	May 2001	*Modern Philology*
DiPasquale, Theresa M., "Woman's Desire for Man in Lanyer's *Salve Deus Rex Judaeorum*"	July 2000	*Journal of English and Germanic Philology*
Elder, John, "The Poetry of Experience"	Summer 1999	*New Literary History*
Gallagher, Catherine, "A History of the Precedent: Rhetorics of Legitimation in Women's Writing"	Winter 2000	*Critical Inquiry*
Gamer, Michael, "Authors in Effect: Lewis, Scott, and the Gothic Drama"	Winter 1999	*ELH*
Geyh, Paula E., "Triptych Time: The Experiential Historiography of Meridel Le Sueur's *The Dread Road*"	Winter 2001	*Criticism*
Gigante, Denise, "Forming Desire: On the Eponymous *In Memoriam* Stanza"	March 1999	*Nineteenth-Century Literature*
Gigante, Denise, "Milton's Aesthetics of Eating"	Summer 2000	*diacritics*
Gilbert, Sandra M., "'Rats' Alley': The Great War, Modernism, and the (Anti)Pastoral Elegy"	Winter 1999	*New Literary History*

Author and Title	Date Published	Journal
Gilbert, Sandra M., "Widow"	Summer 2001	*Critical Inquiry*
Hayton, Heather Richardson, "'Many privy thinges wimpled and folde': Governance and Mutual Obligation in Usk's *Testament of Love*"	Winter 1999	*Studies in Philology*
Lynch, Jack, "'The ground-work of stile': Johnson on the History of the Language"	Fall 2000	*Studies in Philology*
Matz, Robert, "Slander, Renaissance Discourses of Sodomy, and *Othello*"	Summer 1999	*ELH*
May, Brian, "Memorials to Modernity: Postcolonial Pilgrimage in Naipul and Rushdie"	Spring 2001	*ELH*
Mazzola, Elizabeth, "Brothers' Keepers and Philip's Siblings: The Poetics of the Sidney Family"	Fall 1999	*Criticism*
McCann, Sean, "The Imperiled Republic: Norman Mailer and the Poetics of Anti-Liberalism"	Spring 2000	*ELH*
McHugh, Susan, "Marrying My Bitch: J. R. Ackerley's Pack Sexualities"	Autumn 2000	*Critical Inquiry*
Nagy, Andrea R., "Defining English: Authenticity and Standardization in Seventeenth-Century Dictionaries"	Fall 1999	*Studies in Philology*
Perloff, Marjorie, "Language Poetry and the Lyric Subject: Ron Silliman's Albany, Susan Howe's Buffalo"	Spring 1999	*Critical Inquiry*
Richardson, Angelique, "The Eugenization of Love: Sarah Grand and the Morality of Genealogy"	Winter 1999/2000	*Victorian Studies*
Schaub, Melissa, "Queen of the Air or Constitutional Monarch? Idealism, Irony, and Narrative Power in *Miss Marjoribanks*"	September 2000	*Nineteenth-Century Literature*
Shoulson, Jeffrey S., "The Embrace of the Fig Tree: Sexuality and Creativity in Midrash and in Milton"	Winter 2000	*ELH*
Staten, Henry, "Is *Middlemarch* Ahistorical?"	October 2000	*PMLA*
Theisen, Bianca, "The Four Sides of Reading: Paradox, Play, and Autobiographical Fiction in Iser and Rilke"	Winter 2000	*New Literary History*

Author and Title	Date Published	Journal
White, Paul A., "The Latin Men: The Norman Sources of the Scandinavian Kings' Sagas"	April 1999	*Journal of English and Germanic Philology*
Zamir, Tzachi, "Upon One Bank and Shoal of Time: Literature, Nihilism, and Moral Philosophy"	Summer 2000	*New Literary History*

Stasis Issues Addressed

As they did in Fahnestock and Secor's sample, definitional propositions predominated; twenty-four (86 percent) of the articles contain definitional claims. The five (18 percent) articles that address the existence stasis are all from long-established and thus perhaps less "cutting edge" journals (*Studies in Philology, English Literary History, Criticism*, and *Journal of English and Germanic Philology*). Twenty-one (75 percent) make evaluative claims, and five (18 percent) address the causal stasis. However, a respectable portion, four articles (14 percent), not only suggest the proposal stasis but also argue explicit proposal claims.

Existence

Such claims include the existence of historical contact among peoples, textual coherence, textual parallels, a thematic commonality, and human effort. Only two focus primarily on the stasis of existence. For instance, the focus of White's "The Latin Men: The Norman Sources of the Scandinavian Kings' Sagas" is the establishment of evidence of "the likelihood of continued contact between Scandinavian travelers to the Continent and the inhabitants of Normandy in the eleventh and twelfth centuries" (p. 169). Three articles that deal with issues of existence progress from there to "higher" stases.

Definition

Categorizing and characterizing are central tasks in this sample. The location of controversy at this stasis appears in articles that vary widely in argumentative styles. Gilbert's "Widow," for instance, begins with over five pages of autobiographical narrative, a rhetorical strategy of confessionalism that J. Williams (1999) saw as a growing literary critical trend during the 1990s; however, her article is ultimately a definitional argument exploring what it means, culturally, to be a widow. On the other end of the stylistic spectrum, an article positioned much more firmly in the philological tradition, Nagy's

"Defining English: Authenticity and Standardization in Seventeenth-Century Dictionaries" also primarily investigates a definitional question, whether seventeenth-century dictionaries are prescriptive or descriptive.

Evaluation

Encomiums to authors and their texts that seek to fix them more firmly in the literary canon are rare in this sample; when they do occur, like existence arguments they appear in long-established journals (*Publications of the Modern Language Association*, *English Literary History*, and *Criticism*). Such commendations of authors and their works appeared to be more prevalent in Fahnestock and Secor's earlier sample. Instead, I found much more frequently (in half of the articles) evaluative claims regarding the state of scholarly discourse upon the article's literary topic used to establish argumentative exigency. Repeatedly, the critics who worked on the topics before the writers in this sample were said to have overlooked and oversimplified, and their criticism needed amendment, extension, or correction. For instance, Richardson's "The Eugenization of Love: Sarah Grand and the Morality of Genealogy" calls attention to a critically neglected author (Richardson notes there had been only one preceding scholarly study of Grand's work) as well as argues that the recent and developing critical thought on New Woman novels portrays these authors as overly politically radical.

Cause

Though causal claims were made in this sample, the evidence and reasoning offered more often supported arguments made at other stases, particularly definition. Gigante's "Forming Desire: On the Eponymous *In Memoriam* Stanza," for instance, seeks "to understand how the *In Memoriam* stanza first emerged from poetic syntax available during the Renaissance" (p. 483) by asking, "What is it about this particular poem that demands a different word pattern?" (p. 484). This search for the "parent" (p. 491) forms from which this stanza form emerged, though, more often operates at the stasis of definition by actually answering, "What is this stanza form?" with characterizations such as "'legless' Petrarchan quatrains" (p. 494).

Proposal

The four articles making explicit proposal claims all urge their audience to read the texts that are their subjects in a new way, an invitation that would seem to be the foundation for all literary criticism. Burton's "Rereading Faulkner: Authority, Criticism, and *The Sound and the Fury*" thoroughly criticizes Faulkner scholarship for its lack of theoretical sophistication, a negative evaluation that leads her to forward a proposal: "Bakhtin's understanding of novelistic discourse suggests that critical discussion of *The Sound and the Fury* must approach Faulkner's later narratives about this narrative much more skeptically than in the past" (p. 613). Burton then specifically points to the "complicated relationship" (p. 625) Faulkner's appendix to *The Sound and the Fury* has with the novel itself as the needed future site of study.

Elder's "Poetry of Experience" stands out for its uniquely pedagogical proposal. The central point of Elder's piece is his claim that "to be alert and receptive readers of [Robert Frost's] poetry, we too need to venture out under the sky, into rain and sun" (p. 658). Though this claim rings of eighteenth-century Scottish belletrism, Elder grounds it in a current disciplinary exigence by claiming that such field trips can offer a corrective to the field of ecocriticism's overreliance on "jargon, self-referentially, and a narrow professionalism" (p. 650). That only one article in this sample makes overt pedagogical proposals indicates the custom of relegating such discussions to other forums that I observed being established in the first issue of the *PMLA* in 1886 (Wilder, 2006) is largely maintained over a century later.

Whereas Fahnestock and Secor saw implicit pushes towards the proposal stasis in each article's unstated intention to more firmly establish a literary work's place in the literary canon and on syllabi, I observed implicit weight placed less on *what* is read and taught and much more on *how*. It is now common knowledge among literary scholars that the boundaries of what has been demarcated "literature," much less "great literature," have fluctuated from the moment they were drawn (see Eagleton, 1983; Graff, 1987; Ross, 1996; Scholes, 1985, 1998; Shumway, 1994; Tompkins, 1985; Warner, 1990; R. Williams, 1977). The ascendancy of a cultural studies approach to the discipline's object of study only underscores that what is at stake in current literary criticism is much less what works are on syllabi and much more the way they are read and taught. It is in these ways of interpretation, the focus of literary pedagogy, where lively controversies exist at the definitional and evaluative stases. Additionally, the explicit arguments concerning methods of interpretation in articles like Burton's highlight the difficulty of demarcating boundaries between literary criticism and literary theory in recent discourse of this field. My examination of special topoi characterizes the methodologies of interpretation these widely diverse approaches to literature share.

The Persistence of Fahnestock and Secor's Special Topoi

An analysis of special topoi searches for what methods the sample tacitly shares, what specific assumptions about effective argumentation these diverse pieces of literary criticism hold in common. All five of the special topoi Fahnestock and Secor first categorized were present in the more recent sample as well. And with the exception of the contemptus mundi topos, their use was widespread. Twenty (71 percent) of the articles in the sample applied the appearance/reality topos, twenty (71 percent) the ubiquity topos, nineteen (68 percent) the paradigm topos, fifteen (54 percent) the paradox topos, and six (21 percent) the contemptus mundi topos. In some ways, the application of these special topoi remains consistent with Fahnestock and Secor's earlier analysis, suggesting they can serve a disciplinarily conservative function. But simultaneously these topoi have evolved with the discipline and prompted new topoi: the mistaken-critic topos, the context topos, and a topos that subverts contemptus mundi, the social justice topos.

Appearance/Reality

My analysis lends support to Fahnestock and Secor's (1991) claim that "the appearance/reality topos is the fundamental assumption of criticism, since without it there would be no impetus to analyze or interpret literature" (p. 85). For instance:

- for McCann, a coherent political vision lies beneath Mailer's "ramblings and ravings" (p. 307)
- for Albrecht, a subway setting in the *Invisible Man* "symbolizes the narrator's underground self-awareness and Norton's blindness" (p. 58)
- in Berger's reading of *Silas Marner,* "Nancy's wholesale rejection of adoption and her coextensive inability to recognize the benefits of cultivating new beliefs represent a broader repudiation of society" (p. 324)
- in McHugh's reading of J. R. Ackerley's work, a "mongrel is not simply a metaphor [. . .] but more importantly a secret sharer of familiar illegitimacy" (p. 27)

Verbs such as "symbolize," "decode," "seems," "masks," "represents," and "underlies" were frequent clear indicators of the application of this topos.

However, I occasionally observed a tension between the application of the appearance/reality topos and a desire to move beyond the seemingly simple polarization its deliberate use seems to suggest. For instance, Perloff declares, "Postmodernism no longer recognizes such 'depth models' as inside/outside, essence/appearance, latent/manifest, authenticity/inauthenticity, signifier/signified, or depth/surface" (p. 408). But she asserts this in the same article in which she uncovers buried meaning in the title of Silliman's poem that "is called *Under Albany—under*, no doubt, because the poet now tries to get inside, behind, and under his earlier statements so as to make some sense of the psychological and social trajectory" (p. 421). The tension such critics express seems to suggest that this topos has evolved over time and that its use in the critical enterprise requires some defense. Deconstructionism has drawn attention to the facility of finding poles of appearance/reality embedded in any text, and New Historicism has encouraged the positing of reality in still other texts, in context and not, as Fahnestock and Secor observed in their sample, in the construction of the critic's imagination. However, at its most basic definition as a perception of two entities, one on the surface and one deep, the appearance/reality topos continues to be a highly prevalent topos.

Ubiquity

Like appearance/reality, the ubiquity topos as Fahnestock and Secor observed it is ubiquitous in this sample as well. And as Fahnestock and Secor noted in the example they presented of this topos, the ubiquity topos is frequently invoked to support the use of another topos with a catalogue of compelling examples. Claims are supported with "ample" and "additional evidence" (White, 1999, p. 162) found "often" (Mazzola, 1999, p. 529), "again and again" (Mazzola, 1999, p. 530), and "at several instances" (Berger, 2000, p. 317). And as with appearance/reality, critics apply this strategy to a diverse range of texts for diverse ends: Zamir tracks a "psychophilosophical pattern" (p. 541) in *Macbeth*, McCann traces the politics that "runs all through Mailer's fiction" (p. 319) and "haunts all his work" (p. 312), and Burton finds unquestioned reliance on Faulkner's supplementary materials to *The Sound and the Fury* in "virtually all critical analyses of the novel" (p. 607). The ubiquitous nature of a textual feature can be presented as sufficient cause for investigation; Gigante introduces her piece by noting that the word *taste* appears "thirty times in Book IX of *Paradise Lost* alone" (p. 88).

Though it may seem self-evident that literary critics should shore up as much textual evidence as they can to support their claims, a tension exists between this topos and warrants favoring uniqueness (see the discussion of loci of quantity and quality in Perelman & Olbrechts-Tyteca, 1969; Secor, 1984). Evidence of this tension occasionally appears in this sample. In two articles, critics assumed uniqueness as a foundational warrant for their arguments. DiPasquale values the subject of her argument because of Aemilia Lanyer's unique and unprecedented views. DiPasquale has "discovered only one other author who elaborates upon" similar ideas (p. 367). And although she finds exigency in ubiquity in "Milton's Aesthetics of Eating," Gigante finds exigency in the unique in "Forming Desire: On the Eponymous *In Memoriam* Stanza": "The striking absence of the form ever *since* Tennyson is marked by a notable exception, a 'brief lay' by Oscar Wilde" (p. 503). Even Gilbert, whose two articles in this sample rely heavily on the ubiquity topos as a way to synthesize diverse texts (and autobiographical experiences), pauses to point out the uniqueness of a small number of male poets who have taken on "certain qualities of the female-authored lament as opposed to the male-crafted elegy" (p. 571). This tension manifests also in Perloff's call for critics to use the term *signature* to discuss the unique qualities attributed to individual Language poets and her use of the ubiquity topos to characterize Susan Howe's signature: "Consider the leitmotif of framing and being framed that runs through both prose and visual poems, crisscrossing, in myriad ways, the related motifs of war and colonization" (p. 426). Similarly, Staten employs the ubiquity topos throughout his discussion of "the breathless undertone of political instability that runs through" *Middlemarch* while in his conclusion celebrating the novel's unique capacity to contain so much ubiquitous material:

> History has many dimensions, which move at different speeds, and few novels represent as many of them, in as much detail, as does *Middlemarch*: rise of the professions, scientization of medicine, development of modern party politics, increasing influence of the press, modernization of estate agriculture, aristocratization of the bourgeoisie, increasing interpenetration of town and country, and more. (p. 1003)

The above examples are the only explicit invocations of the value of uniqueness in this sample, and thus it does not seem appropriate to designate another special topos. Though it may be a value antithetical to ubiquity, its invocation by Staten and Perloff demonstrates that it is possible to search for the ubiquitous within a unique text. In fact, this may be an assumption so embedded within literary critical practice that there is little need to remind readers that a text under examination is in some way unique.[1] In her survey of citation conventions across disciplines, Dowdey (1992) noted that the humanities privileges the uniqueness of texts by "accentuating the importance of exact words" (p. 333) through numerous quotations, an observation that helps explain this synthesis of these two opposing values. On the other hand, because of the effect of the rise of cultural studies on perceptions of the object of study, perhaps the location of uniqueness is in the process of being displaced from the literary text to the critic's observations.

Paradigm

The strategy of elucidating a literary text by applying a conceptual template that Fahnestock and Secor noted as recurrent in their sample appears in 68 percent of this sample as well. To be sure, some authors more than others fully explicated the macroparadigmatic lenses through which they viewed a text. In "The Four Sides of Reading: Paradox, Play, and Autobiographical Fiction in Iser and Rilke," Theisen takes an uncharacteristic (for this sample) amount of space, sixteen pages, to explicate Wolfgang Iser's theory of reading and compare it to other theories. After this setup, Theisen examines, in six pages, Rilke's *Notebooks of Malte Laurids Brigge* in light of Iser's theory. Clearly, the emphasis in Theisen's article is placed more on the theoretical, macrostructural frame than its application to a merely "exemplify[ing]" text (p. 121). Much more frequent in the sample are instances of macroparadigmatic "name-dropping" in which theorists or theories are alluded to, with an assumption of familiarity with them on the part of the audience. In "Authors in Effect: Lewis, Scott, and the Gothic Drama," Gamer states his macroparadigmatic intentions early on; departing from the macroparadigms applied by previous scholars, Gamer "aims to complicate this notion of the Romantic author by viewing it through the lenses of Gothic drama and fiction rather than that of poetry and copyright" (p. 833). Likewise, Staten acknowledges his use of macroparadigm by stating that "all the major characters can be mapped onto a system of social relations that manifests the continued dominance and stifling effect of the class ideology derived from the aristocracy" (p. 992), as does Gallagher when she states that Max Weber's scheme of legitimate authority "is the skeleton of this essay" (p. 311).

Less frequently, instead of providing a mere reference suggesting theoretical underpinnings, a critic would challenge the validity of the chosen macroparadigm by testing its full applicability to the chosen literary text. May exemplifies this strategy in his claim that *The Satanic Verses* and *Area of Darkness* conflict with certain aspects of current postcolonial theory: "neither of these two postcolonial novels bears out in precise detail the patterns blueprinted by the large body of established postcolonial theorists, at least where questions of modern individuality are involved" (pp. 260–61). However, May ultimately concludes that Bhabha's recent works of theory make an excellent fit with Salman Rushdie's and V. S. Naipaul's texts. Geyh, too, points to incongruities between a macroparadigm she applies and the literary text she examines while maintaining the usefulness of the macroparadigm: "Although Le Sueur's protagonists move through the space of the Southwest on a bus with a predetermined route, and so their travels apparently lack the choice and volition present in de Certeau's conceptual framework, it still seems to provide a productive way in which to conceptualize the actions of the two women on their journey" (p. 89). As with Burton's proposal argument on theory, this work of testing and refining conceptual frameworks in May's and Geyh's arguments indicates that the objectives of literary criticism can be to contribute to the discourse on theory as well as on textual interpretation.

Five articles applied the paradigm topos microstructurally by finding and extending "a small structural unit in the text, which becomes the center of ever-larger concentric applications" (Fahnestock & Secor, 1991, p. 89). Because Fahnestock and Secor did not indicate the prevalence of this form of the topos in their sample, it is impossible to compare findings with certainty, though this small number may indicate a decrease in the prevalence of the microparadigm version of this topos. If indeed a shift away from locating the origins of patterns in literary texts has occurred, perhaps it can be explained by the decreasing validity of New Critical approaches that treat texts and a critic's response to them in isolation and an increasing perception of the discipline as a community of researchers interested in explaining texts with previously constructed theories and in testing social theories with texts.

Paradox

That 54 percent of the articles in this sample invoked the paradox topos came as a surprise since, influenced by comments made in overviews of the history of literary studies concerning the now-outmoded New Critics' penchant for paradox (see Ohmann, 1996, p. 75), I had hypothesized that this topos would be the most likely to have gone out of fashion. And yet, the critics in

this sample seemed to point to dualisms of apparently irreconcilable opposites when they could. Within this sample, the paradox topos plays the
most central role, as its title indicates, in Theisen's "Four Sides of Reading:
Paradox, Play, and Autobiographical Fiction in Iser and Rilke." Repeatedly
Theisen asks readers to see "a simultaneity of presence and absence" (p. 123),
"the simultaneous inclusion in ourselves and exclusion from ourselves" (p.
123), and a "duplicity between meaning and saying" that "explores the paradoxical simultaneity of both their difference and their unity" (p. 113). For
Theisen, her object of study is paradoxical in nature: "Unfolding paradoxes
of observation, modern art intends to be observed as observer itself" (p. 120).
And with such a macroparadigm established, her reading of Rilke's *Notebooks
of Malte Laurids Brigge* naturally points to paradox: Rilke's actress Eleonora
Duse "seen by all [. . .] became invisible" (p. 126).

Much more typical than such primary applications of the paradox topos
are instances of apparent paradoxes pointed to in passing on the way towards
making other more central argumentative points, and within those articles
the location of paradox was more frequently in the historical context surrounding the literary text or in the reception of the text as opposed to the text
itself. Gigante, for instance, notes of Tennyson's *In Memoriam* that "indeed,
the fundamental paradox of the poem is that it has long been embraced by
an audience that recoils from some of its most powerful erotic energies"
(p. 481), and Perloff claims that "indeed, the paradox is that, like the earlier
avant-garde movements of the century, Language poetics may well become
most widely known when it starts to manifest notable exceptions" (p. 433).
This location of paradox differs from its location in the literary text found in
the examples of the paradox topos Fahnestock and Secor provide and would
seem to indicate a significant shift in the use of this topos that relates to the
development of new topoi discussed below.

Contemptus Mundi

Though the paradox topos continues to thrive, the thematic topos Fahnestock
and Secor playfully named contemptus mundi appears to have receded in
prominence. Only six articles in the current sample clearly exhibited "an
assumption of despair over the condition and course of modern society"
(Fahnestock & Secor, 1991, p. 88). Although some critics such as Gilbert are
working with genuinely "dark" topics such as widowhood and the effects of
World War I on elegy and thus may be said to value "works which directly

express such despair" (Fahnestock & Secor, 1991, p. 88), I noted little in this sample of what Fahnestock and Secor (1991) claim is "even more indicative of the appeal of this topos [. . .] the search for unresolvable tensions and shadows in literature that at face value seems optimistic" (p. 88). I rarely noted the expectation of "a woeful nod of tacit agreement whenever they mention the alienation, seediness, anxiety, decay, declining values, and difficulty of living and loving in modern times" (Fahnestock & Secor, 1991, p. 88) because these qualities were rarely dwelled upon. To be sure, Staten celebrates the greatness of *Middlemarch* by shelving it among the dire and bleak: "And, like the work of the great French realists as described by Lukacs and Auerbach, *Middlemarch* documents the choking of authentic human possibility by the banality and venality of ascendant bourgeois culture" (p. 991). But only a handful of other articles in the sample contain similar gestures. Elder's plea for direct experience of nature to inform not just readings of Robert Frost but all ecocriticism, for instance, bemoans at one point that "such an experience must be rare for most of Frost's readers today. Our own work out of doors so often involves the noise of engines" (p. 653). However, in addition to sharing the contemptus mundi topos, the articles by Staten and Elder also endorse a related assumption shared by a considerably larger number of articles in this sample, a new topos that favors action over despair.

New Special Topoi

Social Justice

It appears the contemptus mundi topos, present in only 21 percent of the current sample, has receded in prominence to be replaced by a topos I named the social justice topos, which I observed in nineteen (68 percent) of the articles. The assumption in this topos is that literature and life are connected—that literature, regardless of when it was written, speaks to our present condition. But more precisely, the articles that invoked this topos sought in that assumed connection avenues towards social justice through advocating social change. I observed a wide range in intensity of adherence to this topos. Five of the articles in this sample boldly bring this assumption to the surface of their arguments. Geyh draws the connection between literary text and pursuit of a just society in her article's conclusion. According to Geyh, Meridel Le Sueur's

> *The Dread Road* instructs its readers in an activist reading practice that is not just applicable to the text, but also to the world, in fulfillment of Le Sueur's lifelong vision of art as action.

How viable Le Sueur's populist/Marxist/feminist historiography might be for our historical moment is another matter. [. . .] [E]ven if the answers she had in mind are not quite the ones we might ultimately want, her writings expand the conceptual, historical and political space of this questioning and might help us to find some answers. (p. 98)

Likewise, for Burton, Faulkner's Compsons exemplify failed readers as well as failed lives from whose "experience" we can profitably learn: "For in a heteroglot world difference and uncertainty are the inevitable, often difficult, yet always potentially productive state of things" (p. 627). In a related vein, Schaub's critique of Margaret Oliphant's shortcomings as a writer includes Oliphant's lack of a clear program of feminist action: "The narrator's irony allows us to see this 'truth' about the world, but not to do anything about it" (p. 225). Yet, even this shortcoming yields a significant lesson for politically engaged writers today: "Her novel stands as an example of the difficulty of using comedy in a novel for political purposes" (p. 225).

The usual placement of these overt claims in the arguments' concluding remarks means that the leap from literary text to life is a largely sugges-tive gesture. In fact, a general lack of backing in support of this warrant is common among these articles (when invoked for an audience who shares their disciplinary values, a special topos does not require the backing a more diverse audience would likely request). On becoming aware of this topos, I began to see it in less-overt gestures throughout the sample. DiPasquale, for instance, values the overlooked Aemilia Lanyer for her feminism and because she "addresses the problematic situation of the female heterosexual in a sexist society" (p. 378), leaving unsaid that this problematic situation is one femi-nists continue to address today. And though what DiPasquale leaves unsaid borders closely on the contemptus mundi topos, I categorize it as applying the social justice topos because of its hope for social change and resonance with existing social movements for women's rights.

In fact, a sense that the world has always been problematical, as opposed to the fallen condition that the contemptus mundi topos assumes, can be gleaned from several articles and seems to only fuel a desire for social change. In his Foucauldian analysis of *Othello*, for instance, Matz does not suggest that early modern English society is any better or worse than society before or after this period, but he does critically examine political and social relationships for contradictions and inequalities of race and gender. When Matz mentions that early modern England did not distinguish between heterosexual and homosexual (p. 264), he implies that we can gather from reading *Othello* a sense of the possibility of alternatives to current social structures. Similarly, Mazzola, in a parenthetical comment after describing some emotional benefits of the weak familial bonds predominant in early modern England, suggests that we should see in early modern English family structure the possibility for alternatives to a structure that is currently causing us problems: "The internalization of family ties that encourages deeper, more intimate affections and desires may partly explain the problems tearing at the fabric of modern nuclear families" (p. 515).

The rise of the social justice topos may have tipped the balance upon which literary critics' views of history rest: what was once nostalgically portrayed as modernity fallen from a glorious past is now portrayed as a past and a present riddled with problems but reaching towards an improved future. Or, in Popper's (1966) terms, the field has shifted from a view of history as retrogression to a view of history as progression, points of view historically tied to conservative and radical political agendas. That most of the few articles invoking the contemptus mundi topos also appeal, however weakly, to the social justice topos speaks to how far this balance has been overturned. Elder, for instance, takes care to include in his brief overview of the development of ecocriticism some praise for the subfield's inclusion of works by "authors of color" (p. 650) among its objects of study.[2]

Mistaken Critic

In twenty-four of the articles (86 percent), I observed a permutation of the appearance/reality topos that ultimately called for its own category, the mistaken-critic topos. The distinctive features of this topos are its location of the dualism not in the literary text but in the critical discourse surrounding the text and its affinity with the evaluative stasis.

Like all applications of the appearance/reality topos, the mistaken-critic topos is grounded in the spatial metaphor of surface and depth; however, its most frequent manifestation is as a metaphor of perception, particularly sight: Previous critics who treated the literary work under discussion did not see some aspect of the text correctly. Richardson's reading of Sarah Grand's promotion of race perpetuation through women's traditional domestic roles is offered because so many other critics have presented Grand as a radical feminist: "Grand's views, superficially resembling those of radical feminists, were in fact quite different" (p. 238). Though a "perceived contradiction" between

Grand's portrayal of unhappy marriages and her insistence on indissoluble marriage vows "has led to a recent concentration by critics on the more radical aspects of her fiction" (p. 248), Richardson argues against current critical perception to locate Grand's views as distinctly ultraconservative.

Like many of the other critics in this sample who employed this topos, Richardson then names and corrects the previous mistaken critics. For instance, one of Grand's character's assertions that she is "going to write for women, not for men" that is "usually taken as a radical feminist statement (Mitchell, v; Showalter, *Sexual Anarchy* 66), may be seen to signal this intention to educate women eugenically through the novel" (p. 241). Similarly, the "light" Richardson's argument sheds should encourage readers to return to and refine the work of previous critics: "[I]n this light, Elaine Showalter's argument that New Woman novels are characterized by the rejection of self-sacrifice (*Literature* 31, 181) requires amendment. Women were not to sacrifice themselves to unsuitable men, but to the community at large" (p. 230). Frequently, the perception metaphor employed in the service of the mistaken-critic topos indicated not a faulty perception but an entire lack of perception of some key aspect of the literary text. Hayton, for instance, attributes "part of past critical neglect endured" by Usk's *Testament of Love* "to the text's perceived lack of structure" (p. 23).

Clearly, one of the functions the mistaken-critic topos serves is to provide exigency for a critic's new work on a previously thoroughly discussed, dismissed, or unknown text. Frequently, this topos is invoked in the early paragraphs of an article where it likely serves the "establishing a niche" function of the second "move" in the "create a research space" model Swales (1990) constructed from his study of research article introductions. However, corrections of cited critics were also likely to appear throughout these articles, suggesting they served as much an ongoing dialogic function with the disciplinary discourse community as a counterclaim or gap function.[3] The use of this topos suggests a new tendency for members of this discipline to build new knowledge by constructing an inventory of consensual knowledge and then staking strategic claims against it, as Kaufer and Geisler (1989) observed in the discipline of philosophy. In contrast, Bazerman (1981) noted of an article published in 1978 on a sonnet by Wordsworth that though the writer "criticizes a normalized reading—i.e., conventional criticism—as inadequate to the poem [. . .]. In the text of the essay no explicit mention of Wordsworth criticism is made, and in the notes the only reference to any critics are to

Longinus and Kenneth Burke, both of whom discussed concepts analogous"
to the critic's (p. 375). Likewise, MacDonald (1992, 1994) observed that other
critics were rarely named in the sentence-subject positions in her sample of
Renaissance New Historicist scholarship published in the 1980s. The prevalence of the mistaken-critic topos in the current sample may suggest a recent
shift towards the epistemic and socially negotiated practices among literary
scholars like those MacDonald observes among social scientists.

Highlighting the subjectively constructed nature of this dialogic style,
however, are those moments when, instead of citing other critics as the mistaken critics, a critic will name a hypothetical critic or even him- or herself
as the mistaken one. Perloff, for instance, puts words in the mouth of an
imagined critic she can then debunk: "Here, Howe's detractors would say, is
a cryptic Language poem that denies the very possibilities of the expressivity
one wants from lyric. Or does it?" (p. 426). Such a strategy was also observed
by Geisler (1991) in an academic philosopher's practice of abstracting what
another philosopher *might* have said. May includes himself as one of the
previously mistaken critics: "Indeed, we have been so ready to see Rushdie
celebrate melange and mixed-ness that we have usually failed to note Rushdie's own mixed feelings in the fiction" (p. 259). And Gallagher's opening
account of her own early disappointment as a feminist academic with early
modern women writers not only places her work in the growing trend of
confessionalism noted by Williams (1999) but also encourages her audience
to identify as likewise mistaken and open to discovery. Though there is a
range of possible identities for the mistaken critic, from well-documented
citations of other scholar's statements to hypothetical critics to the self, this
strategy's recurrence through the sample warranted its own classification.

Context

Theorists whose names were dropped in macroparadigm invocations were
more frequently advocates of bringing contextual historical details to bear
on the interpretation of literary texts, and appearance/reality distinctions
were more likely to be unlocked and paradoxes located through elucidation
of historical and cultural context. Sixteen of the articles (57 percent) invoked
what I came to call the context topos by presuming, frequently without stated
justification, that historically contextual details should be brought to bear
upon textual interpretation. In contrast, Fahnestock and Secor (1991) mentioned only one example in their sample of this specific type of appearance/

reality maneuver (p. 86) while observing that more often the critics in their sample point out allusions without arguing the authors were familiar with the allusions' source texts and do not "distinguish between finding and constructing a reality, or worry over the possible difference" (p. 85).

Yet, in the more recent sample, I observed several applications of the mistaken-critic topos in which previous critics are faulted for their anachronisms. Recall that Richardson's reappraisal of Sarah Grand as less a radical feminist than other critics have recently claimed likewise faults these critics for their anachronism. Richardson claims critics perceive a contradiction in Grand's portrayal of marriage as "the result of ideas imported from our own fin-de-siècle to that of the nineteenth century [. . .]. It is only by historicizing Grand's novels that we can guard against interpretations which would have baffled and alarmed their maker" (p. 248). Indeed, great care is frequently taken to document connections between the allusions critics claimed they saw in literary texts and the authors of the literary texts. For instance, Albrecht justifies his paradigmatic application of Kenneth Burke's work to Ralph Ellison's by stating that these two writers knew each other and admired each other's work. And though Hayton is less sure of Usk's familiarity with Aristotle's *Ethics*, she does take care to point to the likelihood of this familiarity when she spots an allusion to *Ethics* in Usk's *Testament of Love*: "Although we can't be certain of Usk's primary encounter with Aristotle's *Ethics*, he does cite Aristotle by name" (p. 33). Clearly, the critics in this more recent sample are worrying over the difference between finding and constructing a reality.

But beyond greater attention to historical probability, the primary aim of several articles in this sample is to elucidate a literary text by placing it in its appropriate historical context. This application of the context topos works in concert with the appearance/reality topos to clarify textual elements opaque to contemporary readers who lack the necessary knowledge of historical, contextual detail. "To fully engage the various levels of meaning found in the *Testament*," Hayton informs us, "it is essential that we acknowledge the highly politicized nature of certain metaphors Usk employs" (p. 24). Thus, reading Usk's *Testament of Love* against the political events of Usk's London, we are better able to read the text as Usk's original audience might have, and the text's obscure elements become clearer. For example, "Usk's audience could easily draw from the analogy a political statement about London's factional politics" (p. 6).

Repeatedly, these critics invoke "knowledge of context" (Mazzola, 1999, p. 526) and work to reattach a publication "so often detached from its original context"

(Gilbert, 1999, p. 180). Even Elder, for all his privileging of direct experience of the natural world, ultimately turns to *Newcomb's Wildflower Guide* to understand the New England landscape as Frost would have seen it. Only Burton makes a case against using contextual materials in her objection to critics' reliance upon Faulkner's appendix to *The Sound and the Fury*. Unlike so many of the other critics in this sample who draw from authors' correspondence, journals, and other publications to support their arguments, Burton disapproves of similar use of Faulkner's appendix in part because it, written seventeen years after the original publication of *The Sound and the Fury*, is anachronistic. Thus her disapproval, which at first seems to thoroughly contradict Richardson's concern that "we can guard against interpretations which would have baffled and alarmed their maker" (p. 248), does not stray too far afield from the current shared assumptions of this discourse community.

Overall Value of Complexity

Fahnestock and Secor (1991) concluded their analysis with the observation that the five special topoi they observed "reduce to one fundamental assumption behind critical inquiry: that literature is complex and that to understand it requires patient unraveling, translating, decoding, interpretation, and analyzing. Meaning is never obvious or simple" (p. 89). As every article in this sample is steeped in the same assumption, my analysis reaffirms their point. A "reality" beneath surface appearances still requires rigorous insight to reveal; paradigms, despite the unifying simplicity they suggest, are still far from obvious and must be applied with special skill and knowledge; ubiquitous textual elements are still somehow not identifiable as ubiquitous until deftly illuminated; and paradoxes still confound as much as clarify. The newer topoi also reiterate textual complexities:

- the social justice topos links texts to views of social and political realities in which issues of identity are complicated by so many factors—race, gender, class, sexuality, family dynamics, nationality, and historical moment
- the mistaken-critic topos reminds readers how many other well-equipped readers have misread
- the context topos reminds readers of the seemingly infinite reinterpretations unearthed contextual connections invite

And yet, because complexity as a value is so frequently appealed to in this sample, I would like to briefly explore how these articles portray complexity, and in so doing trace some tensions they set up between it and textual "ease," "clarity," and "coherence."

First, forms of the term *complexity* as terms of praise are ubiquitous among these articles. Geyh echoes many of the critics in this sample by valuing her subject, Meridel Le Sueur, for "the complexity of her aesthetic and political vision" (p. 82). For Geyh, Le Sueur fills a gap left by Karl Marx and Friedrich Engels because they "did not ultimately address the issue of women's particular oppression with the attention its complexity deserves" (p. 83). To lack complexity, according to this sample, is to be simple, easy, clear, resolved, reduced, and/or unambiguous. The frequent linking of "merely" to one of these adjectives only amplifies the devaluing of simplicity and ease. Many times, this disciplinary preference is invoked in applications of the appearance/reality and mistaken-critic topoi that seek to establish the exigency for the critic's current undertaking, as Secor (1984) observed, "the exigence for argument is often established by calling attention to *apparent* simplicity which masks *real* complexity" (p. 108).

But because simple, straightforward explanations of a text are always considered suspect, an interesting tension emerges concerning just how much resolution a critic can provide to a reading of a text. Zamir appears to anticipate his audience's concern that the philosophical treatment of literature he is advocating could appear to reduce complexity by portraying the act of such criticism as a tightrope walk with "the ideal of nonreducible ethical insight" (p. 530) balanced over a tempting but avoidable sea of simplicity. Zamir repeatedly reassures his readers that in his reading of *Macbeth*, "things are somewhat more complicated than a simple story of loss" (p. 529), "nihilism is not merely an experience in which things are seen as valueless" (p. 532), and "things are more complicated then confirming or refuting" (p. 545). Thus when Zamir chides, "Let us avoid the temptation to reduce all this to a philosophical position" (p. 532), his audience should know this is a temptation he works diligently to avoid.

An entire lack of resolution is celebrated in several of the articles. Gilbert enacts this celebration in "Widow" with an unconventional argumentative structure, mixing autobiography, extensive references, and phrasing of claims as questions. She also celebrates the "unresolved—*never* resolved—struggles to get beyond the grave" in Thomas Hardy's poems that come closer in this way to Gilbert's favored "female-authored lament as opposed to the male-crafted elegy" (p. 571). In "Forming Desire: On the Eponymous *In Memoriam*

Stanza," Gigante also lauds not just the difficult to resolve but also the un-resolvable aspects of Tennyson's poem: "Despite various gestures towards resolution [. . .] the message that Tennyson formally builds into the structure of the poem is that there can be no satisfactory 'answer' to the problem of his 'lost desire'" (p. 497).

However, despite a general valorization of the unresolvable and irreducible, each critic does seek to resolve some issue or delineate a reading. Schaub brings this tension to the fore when she reprimands those critics who avoid resolution while chastising those critics who simplify matters: "Such an open-ended formulation retreats from final interpretation, a move that is too easy and too common in our post-deconstructionist critical environment. The ambiguity and constructedness of queenliness in *Miss Marjoribanks* certainly can be explained, but not simply by seeing Oliphant as either feminist or antifeminist" (pp. 197–98).

The tensions surrounding resolution in this sample are mirrored in the tensions surrounding coherence. Mazzola elevates Philip Sidney's poetry by comparing it to his siblings' less-complex—and mundanely coherent—work. In Mary and Robert Sidney's poetry, Mazzola argues, is an effort to "comprehend their brother's doubts through the unveiling of more stable and coherent worlds" (p. 534), while in Philip's poetry she finds "elaborate dissembling," "secrecy," and "suggestiveness" (p. 518). Yet, McCann reveals coherence beneath the apparent chaos of his subject's work: "Beneath Mailer's various literary experiments, his ramblings and ravings, in other words, lies a coherent political vision" (p. 307). And Hayton responds to the critical neglect Usk's *Testament of Love* received due to its "perceived lack of structure" (p. 23) by locating "coherent meaning and structure in the text" (p. 24). Because the object of such searches would likely be valued, the status of coherence, whether a sought for ideal or a mark of simplicity, does not appear to be fixed in this disciplinary discourse community.

A noteworthy aspect of this overarching value of complexity is the vast array of theoretical and ideological differences it unites. On one hand, Burton's endorsement of poststructuralist theories is in like company with the majority of critical views expressed in this sample. She notes that "few critics since the 1970s" have shared the presumption that *The Sound and the Fury* "is inherently unified; indeed, most have focused on its contradictions and the ways it complicates attempts at resolution and undermines attempts at closure" (p. 610). This observation, however, prompts her to chastise critics for their overreliance on the trustworthiness of a simplifying text, Faulkner's appendix, the impetus behind which "was to transform a very complicated dialogic text into a strictly monologic account" (p. 614). On the other hand, a critic such as Richardson whose argument that New Woman author Sarah Grand was not nearly as radically feminist as critics have recently described her would seem to argue against the spirit of the social justice topos widespread throughout this disciplinary discourse community. And yet, despite this tarnishing of a potential feminist hero, Richardson takes care to defend the implications of her project in terms of its avoidance of reduction: "However, this reading does not reduce but rather broadens the cultural significance of the New Woman, shedding light on an emergent concept of moral biology and civic motherhood, and revealing the social significance of the late nineteenth-century romance plot" (p. 248).

Perhaps the clearest example of a critic arguing against the grain of the current climate of literary theory while still appealing to complexity is Elder in his "Poetry of Experience." His sharp critique of the "jargon, self-referentially, and a narrow professionalism" of "contemporary theory" (p. 650) is furthered by his use of personal narrative to describe and inspire a return to appreciation of the natural world. This goal is consonant with those of the belletrists of over a century ago.[4] And yet, Elder's appeals to the value of complexity speak directly to his contemporary audience, claiming to complicate readings of Frost even further than applications of contemporary literary theories do:

> My purpose in the present reading is certainly not to reduce the poetry to its germinating instance. Rather, it is to suggest the value of cultivating, in our own physical experience, an appreciation of the soil from which the art has sprung [. . .]. This is a helpful way of formulating the never resolved yet intimate relationship between a finished poem, with its tempered complexity, and the surges of impulse and experience that inspired it and that are perpetuated within it [. . .]. Any reading of Frost's poetry that reduces the physicality of the landscape or the labor of farmers to nothing more than intellectual argument or abstract music is itself a fantasy in this sense—an escape from the texture and solidity of fact. Both work and nature are more than tropes for this poet. (p. 654)

Whether or not Elder's strategy is successful, his vehement appeals to complexity, irreducibility, and lack of resolution may allow him to be heard by a potentially hostile audience.

One last observation on the overarching value of complexity concerns its association with pleasure. Fahnestock and Secor concluded "The Rhetoric of Literary Criticism" (1991) by noting that "the pleasure principle is not absent in criticism" but is instead "transferred from the literature to the criticism" (p. 94). With the possible exception of the pleasure Elder seems to take in recounting his day's experience operating a scythe and subsequent return to Frost's "Mowing," pleasure was not an explicit principle for criticism among the articles in this sample. However, a lack of pleasure was occasionally associated with the much-maligned state of simplicity. Hayton, for instance, includes in her list of erroneous reasons for the critical neglect of Usk's *Testament of Love* the perception that this text is "dull" (p. 22). Likewise, Gallagher depicts her early, mistaken reactions to Margaret Tyler's work as filled with disappointment because Tyler "not only failed to be a heroine but also failed for boring and obvious reasons" (p. 310). Both Hayton and Gallagher go on to argue that Usk's and Tyler's works are far more complex than these previous critical responses to them have understood. Thus, as Fahnestock and Secor speculated, there does appear to be a link between the value of pleasure and the value of complexity, that central, highly flexible value of this disciplinary discourse community.

Conclusion

This analysis demonstrates both the disciplinarily conservative and progressive functions of the stases and the special topoi. Amidst so many opposing points of view (so many other "mistaken critics") and tumultuous paradigm shifts accompanying the advance of new literary theories, some common approaches to the conduct of literary criticism have survived. They may be what allow such an apparently disciplinarily conservative, even belletristic, critic as Elder to discourse with, or at least appear in the same journal as, Theisen, a poststructuralist determined to suspend meaning in deconstructivist play. The appearance of these commonalties spread across articles appearing in long-established journals with roots in philological studies, journals established during New Criticism's heyday, and more recently established journals that have had enough time in circulation to develop a reputation for their nourishment of contemporary theoretical approaches.

And yet, there have been important developments to the special topoi since Fahnestock and Secor's analysis. The rise of the mistaken-critic and context topoi signals a dramatic shift away from the practices of isolated meditation on textual particulars observed by Fahnestock and Secor (1988, 1991), Secor (1984), Bazerman (1981), and MacDonald (1987, 1989, 1992, 1994) and towards a program of knowledge building that shares some features in common with the rhetorical practices of the sciences. Though these fields continue to differ in obvious as well as subtle ways (recognition of their opposing value preferences in the complexity/simplicity binary gets to the heart of a key difference), they are analogous in their portrayal of their projects as continuing conversations, to which the individual contributions advance larger projects beyond the scope of any one contribution. In this sample, Richardson's attention to an author who upheld far from praise-worthy eugenic beliefs helps clarify this shift. Richardson calls for greater attention to authors such as Grand not because they are literary exemplars but because they help critics achieve a more accurate, if less-glorious, picture of history and feminism.

In this way, recent literary criticism can be seen as returning to the practices modeled on science of the philologists who in the late nineteenth century established many of the field's disciplinary organizations and apparatuses, including several of the journals in this sample.[5] It is important to note this apparent resurgence of disciplinary "rigor" and its conventions in light of the critiques of disciplinarity made by literary scholars (see Downing, Harkin, Shumway, & Sosnoski, 1987; Downing & Sosnoski, 1995; Ohmann, 1996; Sosnoski, 1994, 1995; Spanos, 1993). In fact, because all of the articles in this sample repeatedly invoked long-standing stasis and special topoi conventions of this discipline, this analysis may be read as suggesting that an entirely clean break from disciplinarity, which some of these scholars advocate, may not be possible, whether as a result of profound disciplinary enculturation or a conscious desire to communicate effectively within the disciplinary discourse community.

Yet, while Ohmann (1996) may have accurately described the conservative nature of disciplinarity having a slowing effect on progressive change within his field, change has not altogether been thwarted, and his arguments can be seen as influencing this change and leading to the development of a new convention, the social justice topos. The supplanting of the contemptus mundi topos with the social justice topos suggests the powerfully persuasive possibilities of working within some conventions to defy others. What was once antithetical to this discourse is now so conventional as to sometimes be invoked mantra-like in even the most disciplinarily conservative arguments.

The shift in topological conventions documented in this analysis supports Hyland's (2000) depiction of genre "manipulation" within disciplinary discourse communities as "generally subtle and realized within the boundaries of what is conventionally recognized as typical practices" (pp. 173–74). Hyland posited three possible sources of change in the genres central to a disciplinary discourse community: "from users inside the discipline manipulating conventions; from peripheral members seeking to assert new practices; and from macro-level developments within the discipline or wider culture" (p. 173). The disciplinary histories of literary studies suggest that to some degree all three of these sources may have contributed to the changes in literary analysis described here. Most notable, the opening of the profession—and the larger academy—to women and minorities may have had an impact on disciplinary discourse practices. Hyland accounted for such influences this way:

> [I]ndividual writers are [. . .] members of multiple communities and experience a range of discourses as a result of their age, gender, race, professional subculture, political orientation, and so on. As a result, they have the potential to read situations differently and to employ these other discourses in constructing their own, moving outside the standardised communicative behavior of the genre-at-hand to introduce new elements which subtly transform it. (p. 173)

In Ohmann's new introduction and afterthoughts to *English in America: A Radical View of the Profession* (1996), he acknowledged that literary studies has changed a great deal since his 1976 depiction of the MLA as a staunchly conservative organization antagonistic to younger members' political projects for social justice. Ohmann celebrated the development of feminism, postcolonial studies, poststructuralism, cultural studies, and queer studies as projects encouraged by the MLA (p. 337) and conjectured that now "many students choosing graduate work do so in part because in English they have found an ethos hospitable to the ideal of social justice" (p. xxxv).

However, some articles in this sample in their portrayal of a hypothetical interlocutor are not unlike the 1978 article Bazerman (1981) analyzed, which positioned itself in opposition to conventionalized criticism. Though this practice may be a residual feature of an earlier phase of this discourse community, it raises the question: Is knowledge building a necessary aspect of a disciplinary discourse community's work? Or put another way, how can we measure this aspect of a discipline's work? Without the luxury of hindsight, how can rhetorical posturing to argue for exigency be distinguished from presentations of knowledge new to the arguer and the audience? As Swales

(1990) and Berkenkotter and Huckin (1995) have demonstrated, the conversation scientists contribute to and build upon is selectively, subjectively structured in the writing of a research article's opening literature review, what the scientist Berkenkotter and Huckin studied described as a "phony story" (p. 55). The many articles in this sample with meticulously documented citations of critics and theorists whose work is being corrected or amended may be said to constitute knowledge building in a similar way. Recency of secondary citations has been discussed as evidence of knowledge building in the natural and social sciences, and the predominance of citations of theorists and literary scholars much more recent than Longinus in this sample may further indicate a shift towards a knowledge-building program since Bazerman's (1981) analysis and Dowdey's (1992), whose examination of the October 1989 *Publications of the Modern Language Association* reveals that the majority of citations of secondary works were of sources older than ten years (p. 335). However, the dates of citations were not investigated in the current study, and recency of secondary citations itself as a criterion to determine knowledge building deserves further exploration. Perhaps works within a discipline may be understood along a spectrum of knowledge building, with those texts that primarily reiterate a mantra to the discipline's values on one end and those that rigorously supersede this epideictic function to produce new communal knowledge on the other.

The tensions surrounding resolution in literary critical argument further suggests some of the difficulty this study poses for conceptions of knowledge building. Growing a stable body of accepted truths in this discipline will seemingly be undermined by its current rhetorical practices, and yet its theoretical knowledge about irreducibility may grow. As in the sciences, the bigger payoffs for the discipline, and greater prestige for the scholar, may be at the level of theory rather than in fine-grained understanding of the discipline's objects.

A limitation of the rhetorical analysis method I employ here is its lack of consideration for the intended audience's reaction to these articles. Paul, Charney, and Kendall (2001) rightly remind us of the limitations of assuming that publication equates to rhetorical success. Studies that examine members of the disciplinary discourse community in the act of reading and interacting with these texts are needed to refine the role the special topoi play in an argument's effectiveness. Do these readers distinguish texts that function as epideictic value reiterations from texts that extend the field's knowledge?

Additionally, research is needed to explore how strongly certain values and special topoi become tied to specific disciplines. In this analysis I sought to map the strength of adherence to several special topoi among a broadly defined disciplinary discourse community. I do not, however, map the boundaries of this discourse community by determining which topoi may be exclusive to it. Other disciplinary discourse communities may also use special topoi characterized here, especially disciplines that rely on textual analysis. For instance, Toulmin, Rieke, and Janik (1979) described a warrant common to "aesthetics and psychology" that resembles the ubiquity topos—they explained that in these (broad) fields, it is understood that exemplification, rather than reliance on formula or calculation, is a solid source of grounds for a claim (p. 52). Certainly, rhetorical analyses such as this one employ ubiquity, appearance/reality, and paradigm topoi. However, WID research points to some important differences in discursive practices among disciplines in the humanities that rely on textual evidence. For instance, as Beaufort (2007) pointed out, prominent genres in the discipline of history focus their investigations at the causal stasis, indicating that these scholars use textual evidence for a distinctly different end than is conventionally found in literary analysis. And though my analysis of the first volume of *PMLA* (Wilder, 2006) indicated that the brand of historical linguistics practiced by its contributors helped to define the stases conventional to current literary analysis, their special topoi conventions differ markedly from this later literary analysis.

Ultimately, this study shows some of the ways in which disciplinary discourse communities maintain themselves (a conservative impulse) while admitting new members and changing in response to external and internal social pressures (progressive impulses). Beyond the object of study—the definition of which has changed significantly so that, for instance, to include *Gone with the Wind* on a syllabus would no longer be an act requiring defense as Secor (1984) once portrayed it (p. 107)—special topoi may well serve as the almost imperceptible and generally taken-for-granted fibers that hold together this disparate and diverse discourse community.

2

"You Wouldn't Want to Introduce That to Undergraduate Students": Literature Professors' Views of Disciplinarity and Student Discourse

Though their use of shared special topoi may link them, literary scholars hold wildly varying views on the place of their professional discourse practices in undergraduate classrooms. On one end of the spectrum are advocates for consciously sharing professional disciplinary practices, methodologies, and debates with students, and on the other are advocates of "postdisciplinary" pedagogies. In practice all parties in the debate may share a blind spot towards a deeply seated preference for the kinds of disciplinary discourse practices discussed in the previous chapter. This chapter contrasts the published debates surrounding literary pedagogy with the expressed goals and methods of instructors and charts the ambiguous role of professional rhetorical practices in the range of approaches to required undergraduate literary study.

One viewpoint holds that literary scholars need to bridge a gap they perceive between current scholarly practices and undergraduate classrooms. Graff's (1992) influential proposal to "teach the conflicts" encouraged professors to share and address the issues debated in their professional discourse community with students, and his refinements of his proposal (Graff, 1995) indicated that he considers the discourse conventions and vocabularies of literary scholars to be inextricably linked to the content of their debates and thus important to introduce to students. Similarly, Scholes's (1985) influential *Textual Power* urged professors to not only demystify literary theory for undergraduates but also to impart procedural knowledge, claiming "our job is not to produce 'readings' for our students but to give them the tools for producing their own" (p. 24). And more recently, Showalter (2003) has argued that "rather than emphasize content" in their undergraduate courses, literary scholars should "stress the process by which critical work or literary production is carried out" by sharing "how literary scholars think, read, analyze, annotate, evaluate, and interpret texts" (p. B7).

The textbook market also provides evidence for a developing interest in imparting disciplinary practices to undergraduates beginning in the late 1980s and early 1990s. Anthologies such as *Bridging the Gap: Literary Theory in the Classroom* (Davies, 1994) and *Practicing Theory in Introductory College Literature Courses* (Cahalan & Downing, 1991) encourage professors to lessen the perceived gap between cutting-edge scholarship and introductory literature courses. Anthologies of essays on literary theory intended for use in undergraduate courses further support viewing undergraduate literature instruction as an introduction to the professional discourse community of literary scholars. Such anthologies include *Critical Terms for Literary Study* (Lentricchia & McLaughlin, 1995) and *Falling into Theory: Conflicting Views on Reading Literature* (Richter, 1994), an anthology that specifically seeks to facilitate Graff's proposal. Editions of texts published with criticism, such as the Norton editions and the editions of *Adventures of Huckleberry Finn* (1995) and *The Tempest* (2000) edited by Graff and James Phelan, serve a similar function. Many textbooks designed for introductory literature coursework likewise published or updated in the 1990s also encourage this view by presenting an overview of different theoretical approaches to literary study (Barnet, Berman, Burto, Cain, & Stubbs, 2000; Barnet & Cain, 2000; Callaghan & Dobyns, 1996; Guerin, Labor, Morgan, Reesman, & Willingham, 2005; Jacobus, 1996; Kirszner & Mandell, 2001; Meyer, 2001; Roberts, 1999; Roberts & Jacobs, 1998; Tyson, 1999).

While supporting the infusion of current theory into pedagogical practice, some professors oppose the implication that all theoretical approaches are equal and advocate instead for a pedagogy rooted in one theoretical approach, such as the Marxist-influenced transformative pedagogy as described by Giroux (1983) and Watkins (1989). Literary scholars following Michel Foucault's analysis of discipline and disciplinarity, and who consequently regard any socialization of students into the disciplines as perpetuating power structures that ought to be challenged, advocate for a "postdisciplinary" pedagogy. C. Freedman (1994) criticized the disciplinary enculturation project of Graff's "teach the conflicts" proposal because Freedman claims it overlooks how "the academy in general and the literary academy in particular currently help to reproduce—but also potentially to resist—the relations of oppression that govern the society at large" (p. 60). Sosnoski (1994, 1995), Downing and Sosnoski (1995), Spanos (1993), and Harkin (1987) objected to the culture of argument, competition, and refutation of the disciplines because these practices are, they claim, antifeminist. The "postdisciplinary" pedagogy Downing and Sosnoski (1995) prescribed asks students (or rather "collaborators") to write personal narratives, counters "the academic ethos that splits intellect from emotion" (p. 277), does not assign grades, discourages competition, while it also, and without examining the potential contradictions, encourages research and publication as well as the discussion and application of theories collaborators have learned in their other classes (p. 280).[1]

Seeking similar outcomes as the "postdisciplinary" pedagogues but for different reasons, some literature scholars advocate for treating undergraduate literature instruction, especially at the introductory level, as "predisciplinary." Ohmann (1996), Hedley and Parker (1991), Trimbur (1995), and Fleming (2000) would rather, particularly in introductory coursework, professors not see students as novices to a professional discipline and instead work with them on developing more generalizable critical thinking and reading skills, which they see the humanities uniquely fostering. Attempts at collaborative, WID-focused pedagogy in such introductory courses have led WID advocates such as Diller and Oates (2002) to caution that rhetorical WID pedagogical approaches may be misplaced when professors adhere to such "predisciplinary" expectations for student writing.

Just as there are "writing about literature" textbooks facilitating Graff's "teach the conflicts" model of introducing disciplinary discourse, there are also a number of recent "writing about literature" textbooks claiming to facilitate improvement of students' general critical thinking and writing skills (Manlove, 1989; McMahan, Day, & Funk, 1996; Roberts, 1999). Moreover, many of the textbooks that cover professional critical approaches do so in appendixes or chapters added to largely unchanged previous editions (see Barnet, 1971; Barnet & Cain, 2000; Roberts, 1983, 1999). Thus, often these textbooks offer conflicting advice to students, presenting themselves as rhetorics with insights for improving writing in general and in the context of the specific discourse community of literary studies. Roberts (1999), for instance, prefaces his textbook on writing critical analyses of short stories, poems, plays, and films with a declaration that students' development of the skills needed to succeed at these writing tasks will also improve their writing in their other coursework in academic disciplines as diverse as the natural and social sciences (pp. xiv and 16). And well beyond coursework, according to Roberts, the study of literature can improve multiple facets of students' lives, helping them develop compassion, maturity, appreciation, and shape their goals and values. Literature, claims Roberts, "makes us human" (p. 3), and in these bold assertions he may well articulate many of the beliefs that support the placement of literary study in the center of "predisciplinary" general education curricula.

Though the views represented in the published debates and textbooks on the place of disciplinary discourse in undergraduate literature classrooms are diverse, they are unlikely to fully represent the range of approaches to this widely required "gen. ed." core course. As is the case with most disciplines rooted historically in the American appropriation of the German university model, scholarship on pedagogy is usually not considered highly prestigious in literary studies, and thus the views of the disciplines' high-status researchers may be underrepresented in this debate as much as the views of its lower-ranked and less-published instructors. In an attempt to include voices of those "in the trenches" and not necessarily represented in the published debates on literary pedagogy, this chapter presents findings from my interviews and observations of literature faculty regularly charged with teaching "intro. to lit."

Interview Procedures

I interviewed literature professors at two universities. At a large, public research university in the South, I interviewed eight professors who teach a "Masterworks of Literature" survey course in one of its three variations (world, American, or British), a course that fulfills a general education requirement for many majors. When I interviewed them, five of these professors had achieved the rank of full professor, two were associate professors, and one was a lecturer. These interviews were conducted in November 2000 and April 2001 in the professors' offices and were tape-recorded and transcribed.[2] I also collected syllabi, sample assignments, and exams for this course from these professors and from an additional twelve professors who had taught this course between 1998 and 2001, and my interview findings are informed by my analysis of these materials and my ethnographic study of one professor's classroom, a study discussed fully in Wilder (2002).

In November 2005 and January 2007, I similarly interviewed five literature professors at a smaller, private, metropolitan university in the Midwest. These professors routinely teach a writing about literature (WAL) course that is a required "gateway" course for their English majors, though a number of nonmajors take the course to fulfill a writing-intensive general education requirement. These professors served as instructors of the "control" sections in the study described in chapter 4 by teaching WAL as they normally do. When interviewed, two were at the rank of visiting assistant professor (Caldwell and Evans), one at assistant professor (Cooke), one at associate (Carter), and one at full professor rank (Clark).[3] These professors also allowed me to examine their syllabi, assignments, and textbooks.

In all interviews I asked the professors to describe their goals and objectives for their introductory course. I asked about how they see the course fitting into their department's curriculum and into students' courses of study. I asked what effect, if any, their students' status as English majors or as students majoring in other fields has on their course preparations, plans, and evaluation techniques. Survey instructors were asked if they required any writing assignments and if so for what purposes. WAL instructors were asked about the methods they use for teaching writing and which methods they find particularly successful or dissatisfying. Lastly, I asked all instructors to compare the writing they ask students to do with their own writing.

The Survey Course for Nonmajors

It is possible to see the history of the discipline in the current survey course for nonmajors. Its survey structure organized by nationality and sequenced chronologically harkens back to structures meaningful to and established by the philologists who so consciously set in motion the modern discipline of literary study in the late nineteenth century. And resonating with the belletristic study of literature that historically preceded the philologists' rage for scientific order, six of the eight professors indicated that cultivating their students' appreciation of literature was a primary pedagogical goal. The lone lecturer described his approach to the course as New Critical, conceding that his approach may be "a little bit old-fashioned." One of the associate professors described her course as presenting an introduction to an array of critical approaches in keeping with Graff's call to introduce these approaches in lively conversation with each other. The other associate professor teaches within the framework of one critical approach, a branch of cultural studies that she uses in her own scholarship.

However, despite these clear ties to disciplinary legacies, only one of the eight professors I spoke with described her course as presenting an introduction to the discipline. This tendency is embodied in the assertion two professors made when they said they have no intention "to make English majors" of their students. Acutely aware that their students in this course were primarily there to fulfill a requirement en route to becoming business, science, or engineering majors, these professors strove to make the course relevant—or at least not boring—to this group, and associations with disciplinary enculturation appear to be seen as conflicting with this goal.

The intentions of the professor whose approach to the course is congruent with Graff's proposal to teach disciplinary discourse through disciplinary conflicts stand in sharp contrast, then, to those of her colleagues. As she put it, "I want to give them a glimpse of what looking at literature for a major might seem like." However, she also appears to intentionally downplay this goal in the classroom by not explicitly naming the disciplinary sources of some concepts she presents. For instance, in this anecdote she indicates that she uses ideas she has drawn from Stephen Greenblatt without explicitly naming the theoretical approach to literary study with which he is associated:

> I mentioned to a colleague that I really have to beef up my background because it has been a long time since I looked at this material and some of the material I hadn't worked with at all, and so I mentioned in passing that I was reading this New Historicist collection that was going to help me with some of the early literature, and the professor remarked, "Oh well you wouldn't want to introduce that to undergraduate students." And I didn't introduce it explicitly, but I certainly used Stephen Greenblatt kind of ideas. [. . .] So I think you don't have to say this is New Historicism.

Thus even for the one professor intending to provide some introduction to the discipline, disciplinary discourse practices appear to function largely implicitly in the course's background.

Where the real fault lines emerged between their different practices was in their vision of the discipline worth imparting where a tension exists between older, more traditional visions of the discipline and newer, more cutting-edge visions of the discipline. Some of the professors I spoke with made a point to challenge the "Masterworks" title of the course while others sought to uphold traditional understandings of national and Western literary canons that solidified in the nineteenth century. For instance, the associate professor who specializes in cultural studies explained to me that this "vantage point" encourages her to go "outside the category of literature" and work to challenge the notion of a literary canon. Meanwhile, a full professor who teaches the "world literature" variant of this course very consciously defended his approach towards teaching a traditional canon of texts, or what he called an "intellectual heritage" that is "universal." The conflict over the course's goals captured in these two professors approaches poses a struggle over definition of the discipline's object of study: one more narrowly defined by nearly a century of precedent in the discipline as canonical, the other so expansive as to make the issue of object of study irrelevant and emphasize instead disciplinary "ways of seeing" or "critical thinking" tools.

Another version of the same conflict between older and newer visions of the discipline promoted by the course emerges in the professors' level of adherence to the social justice topos. For instance, the associate professor who works in cultural studies stated that "a bottom line on this course is a sort of anti-racist pedagogy." Meanwhile, a full professor sought to assure me that his course was in no way "political." Since my analysis in chapter 1 suggests that the social justice topos only recently emerged as a shared value in the field, professors' decisions to employ it in the classroom may be reflective of the "generational version" of the discipline they present to students as dominant.

What both camps in this generational divide have in common, interestingly, is their tendency to identify the opposing camp's approach to "intro. to lit." with disciplinarity. One camp resists working with students at a current cutting edge of the discipline's scholarship because they see this as inappropriately disciplining nonmajors. The other camp associates disciplinarity with older permutations of the discipline that more rigidly defined itself by its object of study, and thus they resist perpetuating traditional, New Critical approaches to literary pedagogy. This may help explain the label *postdisciplinarity*. Proponents of postdisciplinarity appear to see this pedagogy—and scholarship—as a revolutionary break from disciplinarity and thus the next phase of history. In contrast predisciplinary advocates merely wish for some gen. ed. courses unaffected by the transmission of disciplinary knowledge and practices at more advanced levels of study.

Students enrolled in an introductory course taught by a professor on either side of this divide likely experience some exposure to disciplinary ways of thinking, reading, talking, and writing, though in ways associated with different moments in the discipline's shifting history of rhetorical practices. However, because it appears these professors shy away from naming theoretical trends and camps in the introductory class, it seems unlikely that they help students become aware of the place in disciplinary debates and trends that their courses assume as foundational.

The place of writing in the course poses a further roadblock to clarifying the rhetorical and disciplinary context of the discourse for students. Almost half of the eighteen professors from whom I collected course materials do not assign papers to be written outside of class, including the lone professor whose stated goal was to provide a taste of what being an English major is like. Understandably, the institutionally imposed logistical challenges of assigning writing are daunting: most sections of the course enroll over two hundred students. However, by treating the introductory course as solely an opportunity for the transmission of the discipline's "domain knowledge"—whether this be defined as its canonical texts, its questions, its terminology, its understandings of historical context, or even a particular professor's interpretations of literary texts—this liberal arts core gen. ed. literature requirement enacts the same deep divide between domain content and rhetorical process knowledge for which the large lectures for introductory courses in the sciences have been critiqued. Geisler (1994) described the long history of maintaining this divide as one of the most powerful means of denying the possibility of acquiring expertise to the vast majority of people:

> [T]he separation of expertise into the distinct problem spaces of domain content and rhetorical process is an important mechanism by which our society delivers expertise to some but withholds it from others. Expertise, which was restricted in the late 19th-century to the indigenous culture of the upper-class eastern elites, appears to have been taken over by the middle-class professionalization movement and divided into two distinct components: a formally explicit knowledge of domain content that became the mainstay of a universal education aimed at producing laypersons, and the more informal and tacit knowledge of rhetorical process that remained the more or less hidden component of advanced training aimed at producing a new class of professional experts.
>
> As a result, our current educational sequence provides all students with a naïve understanding of the more formal component of expertise but withholds an understanding of this tacit rhetorical dimension. (p. 89)

Even the professors who do require writing appear to do so in ways that undercut the potential experience of disciplinary rhetorical expertise that

Geisler described. All four of the professors who assign writing described these assignments as having elements in common with the kinds of writing they do professionally, such as close analysis. Yet, in the ways these professors describe these assignments to students and to me, they mask the disciplinary context for work in this genre and thus obscure what could be helpful rhetorical information about audience and purpose. In short, as Russell (1995, 2002) and Thaiss and Zawacki (2006) have noted of experts in other disciplines, the professors in this study tend to universalize the rhetorical context of the writing they assign and produce. For example, the lecturer stated, "I tell them [students] from the beginning that the object of any writing course in English for nonmajors is that you are learn to read critically to write critically, logically to prove your points with evidence, and this applies to any kind of reading and writing, and so our subject just happens to be literature, but what I expect you to do is to use techniques that lawyers or sociologists or historians use." Similarly, the associate professor told me, "Oddly enough the same things I would recommend for prospective English majors [about their writing] are also the things I think are valuable for anybody in any field." Thus, though their descriptions of their expectations for student writing strongly suggest the disciplinary genre of literary analysis, they do little to clarify the specific rhetorical purposes and strategies of this genre by insisting to students that the "good writing" they seek defies genre and disciplinary contexts.

I observed this unacknowledged preference for disciplinary discourse practices and its effects during a semester-long study of one professor's section of the course, Professor Gregg's (see Wilder, 2002). Here, genre conventions of literary analysis such as the special topoi were transformed into oral, instructional discourse. For instance, Professor Gregg implicitly guided students to use the ubiquity topos with questions such as "What's important there? In other words, what word gets repeated?" Similarly, teaching assistants would encourage students to use the paradigm topos with their counsel to read a work of literature through the "frame" of a work of literary theory on the syllabus. And Professor Gregg spent a great deal of time and energy clarifying how to use the appearance/reality topos in a manner that corresponds to the discipline's overarching value of complexity. He "outlawed" simplistic "symbol hunting" in favor of more nuanced investigations of "resonances," "representations," and "associations" informed by careful consideration of context. A teaching assistant attempted to mollify students' anxieties over the stress placed upon complexity by urging them to "get comfortable with uncertainty."

However, the guidance students received on their writing in this course more often stressed issues of mechanics and coherence and seldom explicitly instructed students in how to manipulate the disciplinary rhetorical tools implicitly modeled in the professor and teaching assistants' discourse. Professor Gregg, like his colleagues whom I interviewed, espoused a desire to support students' development of "general purpose" writing skills. Though I observed the professor and teaching assistants regularly employ disciplinary special topoi in lectures and discussions, their use as warrants was not made explicit. As warrants are effectively used with an audience that shares their assumed value, the special topoi of literary criticism were used by the experts in the class to make claims about texts without the backing needed to support their use with a more diverse audience. However, in this introductory course that serves as a general education requirement for majors other than English, no such relationship between rhetor and audience who share membership in a disciplinary discourse community can be presumed. In fact, on several occasions I observed students reject the values embodied in the special topoi in their claims that the professor was making too much out of an actually "simple" or straightforward work of literature.

Perhaps as a consequence, students varied widely in their abilities or inclinations to intuit what I saw as the implicit rhetorical curriculum of the course. My qualitative analysis of a sample of student papers, traced through the process of drafting, revision, and instructor feedback, revealed that some students persisted in arguing that the simple meaning of a literary text is "perfectly clear" in papers that tended to receive low evaluations. Other students appeared to either enter the course already practiced in manipulating the discipline's conventions or remarkably adept at intuiting the implicit rhetorical instruction of the course. Such students used sophisticated applications of topoi such as paradigm to sometimes directly challenge the professor's readings of texts in papers that greatly impressed him. But I also saw some indications that explicit instruction in such disciplinary rhetorical practices had the potential to support less-familiar or less-adept students in acquiring this procedural knowledge. Occasionally a teaching assistant's well-timed intervention during revision helped students use special topoi in their papers to more effectively persuade their audience of their interpretations. Surveys I administered similarly indicated that students more inclined to see their purpose in writing as persuasive and more adept at distinguishing disciplinarily appropriate arguments that use special topoi were significantly more likely to receive higher grades in the course.

Understanding the role disciplinary rhetorical practices and values played in this course usefully complicates understandings of gen. ed. coursework as "predisciplinary." Other WID research indicates that an implicit relationship between professional and pedagogical discourse is by no means unique to literary studies but rather frequently occurs in introductory courses across the curriculum (Beaufort, 2007; Herrington, 1985, 1992; McCarthy, 1987; Russell, 2002; Thaiss & Zawacki, 2006). However, a profound hesitancy among literary scholars to introduce their discipline to introductory students seems to stand in sharp contrast to the practices of professors in other disciplines, perhaps most notably the sciences. Kaufer and Young (1993), for instance, describe a biology department in which the professors have no compunctions about seeing their large, introductory lecture course as training students to become researchers in this discipline, despite the fact that they know that only a small percentage of students in the course will actually go on to become such researchers (p. 75). Within literary studies, poststructuralist critique of disciplinarity appears to fuel a desire to transcend it with postdisciplinary pedagogical practices, while predisciplinary advocates would prefer to see introductory courses preserve a space for "direct" engagement with domain knowledge unfettered by disciplinary rhetorical practices and methods. The prominent role of disciplinary rhetorical practices and values in the classroom I observed suggests that pre- and postdisciplinarity advocates may be unaware of the extent to which disciplinary rhetorical practices and values have come to tacitly permeate their discourse and expectations.

The Writing Course for Majors

A writing course situated in a department's curriculum as "the gateway" course to its major would seem to be a much less contentious site for conscious disciplinary enculturation and for cultivating the rhetorical process knowledge possessed by disciplinary experts. For instance, one of the full professors I spoke with at the large public university suggested that he would be much more likely to impart disciplinary rhetorical process knowledge in courses intended for English majors when he said he "might have more writing and more intensive literary criticism" if the students in his introductory survey "were people who would be continuing in English." Yet, similar tendencies to universalize disciplinary rhetorical strategies and genre features emerged during my interviews with faculty who teach a writing intensive gateway course at a midsized private university. While on the whole they are less troubled by the prospect of imparting disciplinary domain knowledge to these students in the form or disciplinary terms and theories, their approaches to conveying disciplinary rhetorical process knowledge are similarly veiled behind claims of universality.

As one might expect, these professors spoke less ambivalently about seeking to prepare students in their writing about literature (WAL) course for more advanced study in English. Professor Clark described his first objective for the course as "learning how to walk the walk and talk the talk of an English major." All five professors listed research skills and familiarity with formatting papers and citing sources in the MLA style as key elements of this enculturation. However, beyond these two goals, these professors approached the course with different emphases that the camps of the published debate do not do justice in characterizing. I came to categorize these emphases as "the terms," "theory overview," "civic discourse," and "expressivist" approaches to the course. The approaches may—and do—overlap in practice, but most instructors appear to emphasize one approach above others. Further, tensions may exist among different approaches, which appear to contribute to tensions within these professors' department on a common vision for the gateway course and which sometimes emerge as contradictions within one professor's own course.

The Terms

"The terms" approach places emphasis on students gaining understanding of a vocabulary used by literary scholars to describe features of fiction, drama, and poetry. Some examples of terms emphasized in course units on fiction are "plot," "setting," and designations of characters as either "round" or "flat," while examples of terms used in units on poetry include the names for particular genres such as "sonnet" and their defining features and the names for kinds of rhyme schemes and meters. The number of such terms emphasized can apparently be quite expansive: Professor Caldwell requires her students to purchase and consult regularly Abrams and Harpham's *Glossary of Literary Terms* (2005), whose most recent ninth edition runs 393 pages. Most other professors, however, require one of the many available "writing about literature" textbooks that cover fewer terms but that are organized around them, with separate chapters devoted to the concepts such as character, plot, setting, metaphor, and prosody. In this department, Roberts's (1999) *Writing about Literature* is widely used. The syllabi of the professors who emphasize this approach further stress "the terms" with their organization in units that correspond to terms associated with various broad genres (fiction, poetry, drama) and the related chapters in a writing about literature textbook. This approach to WAL appeared to be dominant in this department, with all professors remarking on some ties to this approach in their comments to me. However, Professor Clark, whose dominant approach emphasized theory, does not require a particular "terms" textbook but instead merely suggests student purchase a "handbook to literature"; he spoke to me of "certain conventional things . . . we're *supposed* to go through" that he illustrated with "we *have to* go through conventions of how you read place and what the elements of drama . . . what are the conventions in you know, reading fiction." These comments and others indicate that while this approach to the course is endorsed by the department's dominant culture, some instructors of the course may discreetly resist it is as the primary emphasis.

Theory Overview

Professors who emphasize understanding theory tended to require one of the available textbooks that distill and present an overview of various "schools" of literary theory, with a chapter devoted to each, such as feminist, cultural studies, psychoanalytical, deconstruction, and reader response. These textbooks also tend to illustrate and distinguish the application of each approach by presenting brief analyses of one or more literary works through the lens of each theoretical paradigm. Professors Clark and Cooke assign such texts, specifically Tyson's (1999) *Critical Theory Today* and Guerin et al.'s (2005) *Handbook of Critical Approaches to Literature*. They also assign one or more of the literary texts that these textbooks use to illustrate the various theoretical applications so that they can use essays in their textbook as models in their teaching.

Civic Discourse

Professor Cooke is the clearest advocate of the civic-discourse approach to the course due to her final paper assignment on *The Adventures of Huckleberry Finn*. This assignment asks students to answer the question, "Should *The Adventures of Huckleberry Finn* be censored?" As such, it requires students to follow the conventions of public discourse by engaging the evaluative and proposal stases, whereas academic discourse in literary studies, with its interpretive purpose, conventionally focuses on the definitional stasis (as described in chapter 1). Though inspired by Graff's proposal to "teach the conflicts," the emphasis on justifying action or establishing public policy distinguish this particular conflict as extending far beyond the confines of a specialist academic discourse community. Both Graff and Professor Cooke acknowledge this in a passage from Graff and Phelan's (1995) introduction to an edition of *The Adventures of Huckleberry Finn*, which she quotes on her assignment sheet: the "aim of literary education . . . is to help you excel in the kind of analysis and reasoned argument that will make you an effective citizen as well as a good student" (p. 11). While no other professor I spoke with went so far as to require students to compose in a genre more typically associated with public policy debates than scholarly literary analysis, the values embedded in this approach may be detected in other professors' claims, like those of the professor whose course I observed, that literary study is useful citizenship training.

Expressivist

The expressivist approach is so labeled for its resonances with the goals of a branch of composition instruction that Berlin (1988) labeled expressivism. Only Professor Caldwell approached WAL with predominately expressivist goals, though she appears to follow "the terms" approach almost equally strongly (she requires use of Abram and Harpham's *Glossary*), and other professors may hold as secondary values expressivist objectives. While her declaration that for all writing "the most important thing is developing your own creative ideas" may be shared by other WAL instructors, the freedom Professor Caldwell offers her WAL students to pursue writing in forms beyond the academic, thesis-driven essay separates her pedagogy from the majority of her colleagues. She herself is aware of this:

> I see other people have this theory that it [student writing] should look a certain way. And mine don't always, my students don't. I have had students hand in papers that have been in rhymed heroic couplets . . . the whole paper . . . because that is what they were doing. And then they have footnotes in the couplets. And I accept it. [. . .] The thing I worry about in my teaching is maybe I'm not form driven enough, because when they leave my classes, I'm a little worried that someone else doesn't want rhymed couplets, and they want a thesis statement in the first paragraph. [. . .] But I can't. If I had to do that, I would just quit right now. I want [the students] to find their own voice, do their own creative thing, have insights, get excited. That's what I want to see happening.

Students' self-discovery and enjoyment, goals shared by many of the instructors of the nonmajor survey course, appear to be her primary pedagogical goals, though she also expects students to master "the terms" vocabulary in equal measure. To achieve these goals, she allows students to compose in what has recently been termed "alternative discourse" (Schroeder, Fox, & Bizzell, 2002; Thaiss & Zawacki, 2002, 2006).

It should be noted that *all* five of these professors employ a wide variety of writing instructional practices in WAL backed by decades of composition research and theory. They each use some combination of portfolio assessment, commentary on multiple drafts, conferences, peer review, and informal prewriting. Some point students to models of the type of papers they wish students to write, and Professor Clark even shares his own drafting process with the class. Professor Clark and Carter discussed with me the efforts they take to teach issues of style and argumentation through lessons drawn from students' drafts and through specially devised handouts. It cannot be said that these professors are irresponsible in their attention devoted to student writing in this writing-intensive course.

However, while support for developing students' writing processes is undoubtedly strong in this course, I see a potential schism between the course's focus on mastery of writing processes and "expert" domain knowledge. The writing processes the course espouses are "general" or "all-purpose" processes while the domain knowledge, chiefly "the terms," is disciplinary. In other words, exposure to rhetorical process knowledge useful to experts that a writing about literature as a WID course would presumably introduce is notably absent or obscured in many professors' approaches to the course. The course's main focus on acquiring domain knowledge via memorization of "the terms" follows the pattern Geisler (1994) described, where disciplines have historically used general education classes to make expertise appear universally available but in fact reserve the rhetorical process knowledge of expertise for a much-smaller minority who succeed at advanced undergraduate and graduate study (p. 89). One implication of this is that "the great divide" Geisler described between disciplinary experts and laypeople is maintained even in a course that purports to be a "gateway" to the major, presumably deferring instruction in disciplinary rhetorical process knowledge until advanced undergraduate study or even graduate school but perhaps more likely never offering this instruction explicitly (see Sullivan, 1991). These professors—as well as their colleagues in other disciplines across campus—are unlikely to be *consciously* withholding rhetorical process knowledge from their students and instead are more likely to be unaware of the extent to which they themselves have slowly, tacitly acquired rhetorical process knowledge shared by other members of their discipline.

Perhaps the clearest illustration of this is the course's near-universal emphasis on "the terms." This emphasis privileges developing students' domain knowledge over their rhetorical process knowledge. All but one of the professors I spoke with began their description of the course's objectives by prioritizing reading over writing; they first list the importance of students' exposure to the three "genres" (fiction, poetry, drama) and then their mastery of literary terminology. When asked how she teaches students to write about literature, Professor Carter's response is typical in this regard:

> We spend a lot of time in the classroom talking about literature, we move through a lot of different genres. We start with short stories and move into poetry, we include a class on drama, and as we are moving through each one of those categories, I introduce different sets of terminology which I often refer to as a toolbox, [. . .] ways of thinking about literature that one gets familiarized with within the discipline.

Professors repeatedly referred to "the terms" as "tools" and as "conventions." However, it quickly becomes clear that these are tools and conventions at the disposal of literary authors, not students. Rather than inventional tools for students, they are literary devices for which students should be on the lookout while reading. This became clearer as Professor Carter elaborated this aspect of her course objectives:

> For example, "theme" is something that I start with almost immediately because it's so central to the course in general, whether you talk to me about short stories or poetry or drama. From there in short stories we move into plot and structure. We look at point of view, whether it's first person, whether it's third-person omniscient, and of course these kinds of distinctions make a real difference in terms of how you're talking about a text. The writers are constantly employing different kinds of distinctions. Also, moving on to things like setting, moving on to things like character, whether the character is round or flat, different characters, protagonists, antagonists, et cetera. Writers are consciously deploying these different elements of the toolbox to achieve different effects in their writing and this is something that we look at while we're trying to conceptualize or [. . .] talk about a text in general.

When speaking of "writers," Professor Carter refers to the authors on her syllabus. Students are primarily portrayed as "readers" who talk about these writers' texts by identifying and labeling stylistic, rhetorical, and aesthetic choices these writers made. The emphasis of the course's pedagogy is on learning to make these identifications and apply appropriate labels. But what to do with this domain knowledge in their own writing—what rhetorical process choices students can or should make in *their* texts—is not so clearly available for discussion as a course objective.

The "expressivist" professor, Professor Caldwell, describes this prioritization of domain knowledge over rhetorical process knowledge this way:

> Well, my goal is to help them be able to use the sort of the conventions of how to read. I think I perhaps focus more on the reading and understanding of literature than the writing about. But then they show their reading and understanding by the writing, and so I try to help them do for themselves and to do collaboratively, break open texts and make them exciting and interesting and see underlying meanings and then write about that.

Again, the emphasis of instructional time and resources is on reading over writing, but as she notes, the evidence of students' successful acquisition of domain knowledge is assessed primarily through students' writing. The demonstration of this knowledge in writing is presented as a transparent transition: discover an understanding of literature and then "show" that understanding in writing with little explicit instruction in rhetorical strategies for making this demonstration—or argument—persuasive. As Russell (2002) described, disciplinary rhetoric is understood by the established disciplinary discourse community member as transparent.

Professor Carter uses quizzes to encourage and assess students' mastery of "the terms," but while this sidesteps the problem of assessing domain knowledge by means of relatively "untaught" rhetorical skills, it deepens the divide Geisler (1994) described between expert and layperson by perpetuating the tendency to focus on domain knowledge at the introductory level and keeping rhetorical process knowledge reserved for experts. Professor Carter's intention, however, is to prepare students for more advanced work in the discipline, primarily by helping students to be able to recognize "the terms" when they encounter them again rather than actually use the terms themselves in their own texts. When asked if she requires students to use in their writing the terminology her syllabus, textbook choice, and quizzes emphasize, Professor Carter replied:

> I don't require that they do, that they use it at all or if they use it a certain number of times. I tried to recollect my own college experience in the terminology that I was learning then. I remember it, being afraid to use it. I remember often attempting to use it and using it incorrectly and getting pretty solid marks on the paper, you know, saying, "Haven't you learned by now, etc.?" So I figure [. . .] if they have an introductory segment in each chapter telling them about each one of these terms, and if they've been quizzed on these terms, [. . .] then at least you'll have some familiarity so that the purpose of the course being a gateway course will serve them when they move into [. . .] the upper division. And a professor throws out a term [. . .] the student will at least have that in their passive vocabulary, if not in fact in their active vocabulary. [. . .] So I acknowledge that one may not find a lot of these terms in the essays themselves.

Her intent then is to prepare students to understand their professors' discourse in light of these experts' deep domain knowledge that they may not always stop to explain, something she was sensitive to in her desire to enable students "to understand terminology that someone who has a graduate degree in literature is throwing around." Surely, this is a WID goal aimed to help and empower students. But as her "active" and "passive" distinction makes clear, it is a limited empowerment in its emphasis on reception and understanding over use, invention, production, and response.

Likewise, students' use of "the terms" in WAL appears to be expected more during class discussions than in their written work. For instance, Professor Caldwell, open to students writing in alternative discourses, expects for students' participation during class discussions to be informed by disciplinary vocabulary:

> I don't even have to say bring the glossary [Abrams and Harpham's *Glossary of Literary Terms*] every day because they know I get them in their groups and they're looking in that glossary. They're looking things up because I just expect the vocabulary to be the professional vocabulary when we discuss about everything.

Of course, disciplinary experts use "the terms" in their professional writing. As in other disciplines, jargon functions as a specialized lexis useful in facilitating communication among a group of disciplinary insiders by drawing on shared knowledge. And like other distinguishing features of disciplinary discourse, they also contribute to ethos and pathos appeals by marking a rhetor as one who shares knowledge and values with his or her disciplinary audience. Further, they have an affinity with several of the special topoi of literary analysis. Often, using a "term" helps a critic explain layers of meaning in a text in applications of the appearance/reality topos (proper use of terms such as *metaphor* would seem to necessitate the appearance/reality topos). *Paradox* functions both as a "term" and as a special topos when a feature of a literary text is identified and labeled as such *and* its significance for understanding the meaning of the text is explored in the critic's written analysis. A critic's search for multiple applications of a literary device the terms name could facilitate the critic's use of the ubiquity topos in his or her written analysis. And finally, an understanding of literary conventions within which an author worked that some terms clarify would facilitate applications of the context topos. A pedagogical approach to WAL that emphasizes "the terms," then, has the potential to be compatible with a WID pedagogy that seeks to impart rhetorical process knowledge. However, as I have suggested here, mere acquisition of the domain knowledge embodied in "the terms" and assessed by quizzes does not necessarily mean that students have acquired rhetorical process knowledge for effectively using these terms in disciplinary genres in equal measure.

But "the terms" approach is not alone in its failure to confront the expert/lay divide through explicit instruction in rhetorical process knowledge. The civic discourse approach as enacted by Professor Cooke asks students to compose in a rhetorical context, with implied audience, purpose, and genre different from all their other required papers in her course, different from the models in their textbooks, and different from the expectations of most other papers they will be asked to write in this discipline. However, the assignment sheet she uses and her discussion of this assignment with me suggest that these differing rhetorical constraints are not explicitly addressed with students. Practice in the rhetorical work of public policy debates certainly ought to be relevant to students, especially when undergraduate education is seen as preparing citizens. However, if work in these genres is presented as typical of writing in literary studies, students who detect some differences in conventions or who detect differences in their professors' unannounced expectations may attribute these differences to the professors' idiosyncratic, unpredictable, or even unfair standards (see chapter 5). Even if this does not happen, an opportunity is missed to teach rhetorical process knowledge in either civic discourse or in disciplinary discourse.

The "expressivist" professor also misses this opportunity, but since Professor Caldwell's main writing instruction goal is to promote students' enjoyment of and excitement about reading through informal writing, this opportunity may not figure into her version of WID aims. Accordingly, she repeatedly described her methods of writing instruction as "nondirective," saying, "I don't give them a lot of guidance for what the paper's supposed to look like." However, other aspects of her approach to WAL indicate some contradictions to this expressivist goal and suggest that elements of disciplinary rhetoric infuse this professor's expectations for student writing. Most obvious is her advice to students on the audience for their writing:

> We talk a lot about audience. [. . .] The discipline of literary criticism
> is your audience, and who is that, and how are we part of that, and so
> how can you respond to them and all that.

By specifying this discourse community as the audience for student writing, Caldwell further indicates that students should tap into knowledge of this discipline's preferred genres, conventions, and shared values and knowledge to produce successful discourse. But she resists guiding students in tapping (and developing) this rhetorical process knowledge to make appropriate choices out of a belief that this guidance would overly constrain their creativity.

Further, Professor Caldwell actively presents the genre work of literary scholars as no different from the writing of scholars in other disciplines, thus likely contradicting the usefulness of specifying a discipline-specific audience. Her tendency to see the genre features of literary analysis as rhetorical conventions common to all disciplines emerged in her discussion of the occasional presence of students from other majors in her sections of WAL. When explaining that an aim of WAL is to prepare students for further work in the English major, she indicated that this training is relevant for students from other majors by appealing to the universal qualities she perceives in all academic writing:

> I mean, what's so different really about writing about literature? And we
> even [discussed] that in class one time, and the students were talking
> about how this was just exactly the way it is in justice administration
> or in psychology, biology, all these other majors that they have.

Yet, just moments before making this claim on the universal applicability of writing about literature skills, she had been speaking with me about the benefits of the different perspectives students from other majors bring when then enroll in WAL:

> I like the mixed group because I think some of the majors really bring an interesting side. And well, I have a justice administration person right now. [. . .] I don't know what our class would be without her because she has such an interesting way of categorizing. I don't know if that's required for justice administration, but she thinks in categories, and it's just a way English majors don't think. And so it's been really helpful.

Here Caldwell distinguishes students in different majors by the culturally inflected ways of thinking experience in their major has developed in them. So while she acknowledges that different majors have different cultures (or perhaps that students with previously established inclinations or ways of thinking are attracted to the distinct cultures of different majors),[4] she resists seeing writing as one of the cultural practices in which these disciplinary differences may manifest.

Of these approaches to WAL, the "theory approach" has the potential to be the most rhetorically savvy. It seems clearly designed to support students in using the paradigm topos, and as Professor Cark indicated, it also resonates with the context topos "because quite clearly modern critical theory implies context." The professors who follow this approach often provide students with examples of texts in the target genre of theory-informed analysis they seek to help students write, and such models may help students better infer the appropriate conventions to follow (Charney & Carlson, 1995). Given that the overview of literary theory illustrates how individual thinkers develop their ideas in opposition to or alliance with previous theoretical knowledge, this approach would seem to resonate with Graff's proposal to encourage students to enter professional debates. In this vein, Professor Clark also strongly encourages his WAL students to become further involved and socialized in the discipline by attending a regional conference and encouraging them to see their final paper as a text that could be published in the kind of journals in which they have previously located secondary sources.

The "theory overview" approach to WAL appears to be somewhat controversial in this department because, as one professor explained to me, there exists a senior-level course devoted exclusively to literary theory. Covering an overview of theories in WAL is thus seen by some as covering material that is more appropriate for a more advanced class and detracting from time that should be spent either on "the terms" or other aspects of writing instruction. From a concern for supporting instruction in WID and rhetorical process knowledge, drawbacks to the "theory overview" approach might include its emphasis on coverage of nearly all viable theoretical paradigms in this discipline since the mid-twentieth century at the expense of supporting students as they navigate the complexities of actually using the paradigm topos in their writing. Another issue that may obstruct rhetorical instruction is the tendency for the textbooks that support this approach to condense theoretical arguments and, most important, present them all in the same voice of textbook authority rather than as contending *different* voices in scholarly "conversation." This is, of course, a tricky issue as finding model professional texts pedagogically suitable for an introductory course can be challenging. As Professor Clark explained to me, the textbook he uses is one that "a lot of people complain" is "reductionist" and thus contrary to the discipline's widely shared value of complexity.

The one aspect of disciplinary discourse that all five professors explicitly teach, the MLA style for citing sources and formatting manuscripts, is the kind of surface feature of disciplinary rhetoric that MacDonald (1987) argued students are more likely to notice and successfully emulate on their own. With these professors' tendencies to require this disciplinary convention while also insisting on the broad, universal applicability of the genre of literary analysis, one might expect students to struggle to infer the more tacit disciplinary conventions of this genre.

Indeed, the ways in which these four approaches to WAL correspond to camps in the published debate highlight how in practice professors' stated objectives may be undercut or clouded by adherence to traditional views of disciplinary rhetoric as transparent. The "theory overview" and "terms" approaches echo proposals like Graff's to involve students in disciplinary ways of thinking and discoursing, but these approaches can stress that students learn to understand disciplinary experts rather than converse with them. The objectives of the civic discourse and expressivist approaches may most closely match "predisciplinary" pedagogical goals. However, the practice of the professors who employed both these approaches certainly presents challenges to making this a clean match. Both stressed the importance of acquiring disciplinary vocabulary, of writing for a scholarly audience, and of learning to locate, use, and cite professional literary criticism.

The next chapter goes beyond stated course objectives to explore literature professors' reactions to actual student papers, amassing further evidence of the ways in which disciplinary enculturation influences their shared understanding of "good" student writing. Such tacitly shared expectations, then, could be what such a WID course aims to clarify, and chapter 4 discusses a pedagogical experiment that sought to do just that. However, because such an approach has the potential to require a great shift in professors' established approaches, even requiring professors to rethink what has previously seemed "natural" about their own ways of thinking, teaching, and writing, it is an approach that will face resistance, an issue I take up in chapter 6.

3

"This Is How We Do Things": Professors' Expectations for Student Writing

Although literary scholars have written extensively about their goals for teaching literature to undergraduates, there have been few explorations of literary scholars' expectations for and evaluations of student writing. McCarthy's (1987) case study of a student writing across the curriculum revealed that the student's poetry professor graded written work on the basis of whether or not students agreed with his interpretations. Herrington's (1988) ethnographic analysis of an introductory literature course found that the student papers deemed successful by the professor could be distinguished by their tendencies to engage scholarly concerns related to meaning, literary technique, and dissonance. Weaker papers largely summarized the literary work, restated "points made in class discussion" (p. 162), and attempted to "tie up" interpretations "too neatly" (p. 163). Schmersahl and Stay's (1992) interviews of faculty at one liberal arts college found that English professors consistently expected students to imitate the professional genres of their discipline, yet without "a high degree of self-consciousness" (p. 143) about the disciplinary context of such genres. However, Thaiss and Zawacki (2006) placed the English professor they interviewed among the group of professors "aware that what they want students to do is discipline-based rather than generally academic" (p. 62).

WID studies by Herrington (1988), Russell and Yañez (2003), and Thaiss and Zawacki (2006) and my own observational study of an introductory literature course discussed in chapter 2 suggest that professors often fail to make their expectations for student writing explicit to students and, indeed, that professors themselves may be unaware that their evaluation standards may be related to discipline-specific rhetorical practices. Because tacit disciplinary values may be unlikely to emerge in scholars' discussions of teaching in the abstract, in this chapter I delve beyond what literary scholars publicly claim about their pedagogical goals and examine their actual evaluation practices. After asking five literature professors to evaluate a set of the same student papers, all final papers written for sixteen different sections of the writing about literature course described in the previous chapter, I interviewed four of these professors to discuss their rationales behind their evaluations and explore possible reasons for their apparent divergences of opinion on some papers.

Interview Procedures

The faculty I interviewed served as the raters Wolfe and I employed in our study of the efficacy of explicit instruction in the special topoi of literary analysis, a study described in the next chapter and in Wilder and Wolfe (2009). These interviews were my opportunity to learn what the raters felt they valued in the 145 students' literary analyses we asked them to evaluate. Their ratings of these papers favored student papers that used more of special topoi in ways consistent with the discipline's overall value of complexity. They also indicated a preference for papers written by students who had experienced explicit instruction in the special topoi. However, these faculty raters were unaware of the study conditions when they first rated these essays and during our follow-up interviews. Only at the end of our interview did I describe the quasi-experimental study's purposes and share these findings.

I interviewed four of the five faculty members who served as raters (due to logistical difficulties I was unable to interview the fifth). I spoke with them individually in September 2007 for approximately an hour each. When they first rated the student papers, they were all members of the faculty at the same Midwestern metropolitan university but at different stages of their careers: one a seasoned full professor (Ryan), two visiting assistant professors (Reese and Rogers), and two tenure-track assistant professors (Ross and Revel).[1] All have PhDs in literature or a related field (Ross has a degree in women's studies), and all had taught lower- and upper-level literature classes at this university and at other institutions during other phases of their careers. When I interviewed them, the two former visiting assistant professors were teaching at other institutions.

To prepare for our interview, they each re-read six student papers they had previously evaluated for the purposes of our study. They were provided with the ratings on a 5-point scale they had previously given these papers. I selected the papers for us to discuss in order to direct our attention to some on which raters were in strong agreement on their quality (both low and high) and some on which raters evaluations diverged.[2] Logistically it was necessary for me to prepare two separate packets of six papers so that each professor would review papers she had rated previously.[3] As a result, I analyze here discussions of twelve different papers, each evaluated and discussed by two professors. The faculty raters were aware these papers came from their department's writing about literature (WAL) course, though they did not know they were all final papers or that some were written by students who had participated in an experimental curriculum.

The procedures I followed during the interviews were similar to the procedures several WAC administrators and consultants recommend in order to encourage faculty to have contextually grounded and realistic discussions during departmental assessments of student writing (Carter, 2007; Thaiss & Zawacki, 2006; Waldo, 2004). However, I spoke with faculty individually because for research purposes I was uninterested in their working towards consensus and instead wanted to learn the degree to which their views on the same papers converged or diverged. I asked each professor to explain the rating she originally gave each paper. I allowed the professors to determine the order in which we discussed the essays, and as a result we frequently discussed them in either ascending or descending order of the professor's original ratings. This sequencing facilitated making comparisons between papers, and I asked questions to elicit comparisons between papers if the professors did not otherwise bring up such comparisons on their own. I also asked if on re-reading and further reflection there were any papers for which they wished to change their original ratings and their reasons for wishing to do so. Regarding papers they had given low ratings, I asked what advice they would give the writer for improving the paper. Additionally, I asked them to compare their ratings of these papers with their usual grading practices. I concluded each interview by revealing the ratings each essay had been given by two other anonymous raters and asking each professor to speculate about why some of the ratings diverged and others did not. Throughout, we each had before us copies of the six essays that contained no identifying information or instructor comments, as they had appeared when they were originally rated. We consulted and quoted from the essays frequently.

Notable Consistency in Evaluative Criteria

Though we sometimes discussed papers for which raters had originally given divergent ratings,[4] there was remarkable consistency in the reasons all four professors said guided their ranking decisions. Common values they mentioned included abstractions one often hears in discussions of student writing: originality, clarity, coherence, organization, and style. Their sense that student writers should make a central "thesis" claim and that this claim be supported with "evidence" and "sophisticated" reasoning also emerged as shared concerns. Very few evaluative criteria emerged as distinctive of only one professor. "Emotional sincerity" emerged as such a potentially divergent criterion. Only Professor Reese indicated that her evaluation was influenced by her sense that a student had emotionally engaged with a literary text. Of one paper, she noticed that when "the writer seems to become more emotionally involved in the story, that's when I thought the writing really picked up steam." And when discussing another paper she found otherwise weak, she appreciated those sections, signaled by the student writer's use of "I," where it appeared to her that the student "seemed to get involved and wasn't trying to stick to whatever he or she sees as the rules of responding to literature. It seemed to come more naturally and come from the heart."

It is perhaps not surprising that there should be such consistent agreement across different professors' discussions of what they value in student writing at such an abstract level. As Thaiss and Zawacki (2006) demonstrated through a comparison of different departments' grading rubrics, it seems rather unproblematic for members of the same discipline, and even different disciplines, to agree under the rather large semantic umbrellas of values such as "clarity," "evidence," "originality," and "sophistication." The reasons the literature professors gave for favoring these values and the specific passages in the student papers they pointed to as either possessing or lacking these values shed greater light on the ways the professors' disciplinary training may inflect the meaning of these otherwise common values. In these moments, the special topoi emerged as disciplinary values—signals that indicated to the professors that students' not only correctly understood the tasks of literary analysis but also approximated the discourse patterns of professional colleagues.

Appearance/Reality

Not surprisingly given its overall centrality in the interpretive work of this discipline and the significant correlation we found between this topos and professors' ratings,[5] the appearance/reality topos emerged as valuable to all four professors. When invoked to describe what a paper has done well, this topos would often appear in the professors' use of verbs such "deepens," "exposes," and "complicates" to indicate that a student writer explored beyond a "surface" reading of a text. However, this topos was even more likely to emerge in professors' explanations of how a paper fell below their expectations. For instance, of a paper that had received the lowest-possible ratings from all three raters, Professor Ross said, "It's just this totally surface reading of the text. There's no nuance to it." Ross objected to another student's apparent attempt to use the mistaken-critic topos by entirely rejecting other previous critics' interpretations of Christina Rossetti's poem "The Goblin Market." She disliked that a published interpretation was treated "like it's an illegitimate reading." I understood her discomfort to stem from a strong preference for uses of the appearance/reality topos that seek to uncover multiple layers of meaning rather than seek to wholly "shut down" other readings and legitimize only one. Professor Ryan echoes this concern in her distaste for another paper's use of the appearance/reality topos to discuss what she called "those heavy-handed symbols" that never "moved" beyond the obvious. This preference for uses of the appearance/reality topos that acknowledge several complex layers of meaning may possibly extend into Professor Rogers's discussion of style. Praising a paper's "moments of quality language," Rogers read aloud an excerpt that would appear to highlight this nuanced application of the appearance/reality topos: "'the poem's apparent moral . . . may refer,' and I thought that was good sentence construction." The student's qualifiers "apparent" and "may" suggest this savvy application of the appearance/reality topos by maintaining other possible interpretations, thus indicating that even professors' discussions of stylistic virtues or flaws may be infused with discipline-specific rhetorical conventions.

Paradigm

In each subsample of papers that we discussed, at least two papers evidenced engagement with literary theory, so it should also be no surprise that all the professors invoked the paradigm topos in their descriptions of strengths and weaknesses in these papers. In one subsample, two students cited Sandra Gilbert and Susan Gubar's *Madwoman in the Attic* in papers on two different literary texts, allowing us to compare how these students used this work of scholarship. Only one of the papers used the paradigm topos by using key concepts of Gilbert and Gubar's feminist literary theory to make sense of events in Toni Morrison's *Bluest Eye*. Both professors pointed to this paper as using Gilbert and Gubar's text in a more sophisticated and successful manner than the other paper, which cited Gilbert and Gubar in an attempt at the mistaken-critic topos, dismissing their claim that a relationship depicted in Christina Rossetti's "Goblin Market" may be covertly and ambivalently lesbian. Professor Rogers pointed to how the *Bluest Eye* paper uses "Gilbert and Gubar more effectively" in the student's "introductory paragraph" where "at least it is clear why she's using them, even if she doesn't use them necessarily brilliantly well." Professor Ross similarly linked issues of arrangement to a successful implementation of the paradigm topos, noting that the weaker paper brought in Gilbert and Gubar "oddly, just kind of abruptly into the third, fourth paragraph, and it has nothing to do with anything. So there's kind of extraneous stuff that doesn't speak to the thesis." Meanwhile, she praises the other paper's use of "a model provided by Gilbert and Gubar to do this analysis, so there's an attempt to put a theoretical lens onto it." This "model" appears in the paper's first paragraph where the student summarizes Gilbert and Gubar's argument that the literary depiction of women historically falls "into two categories: angels and monsters." However, this professor did not "find it convincing, in terms of the evidence that is brought in," and it seems she found the use of this particular lens to be somewhat forced and inaccurately applied. Thus, audience expectations about arrangement issues for the use of this topos—clearly describing the paradigmatic lens early in an analysis and convincingly matching the specific points of the lens text to points of the literary text throughout the subsequent analysis—appear significant. Moreover, following this structural arrangement even if the argument is not followed through in a persuasive manner is likely to be noticed by a professor as an approximation of successful, appropriate discourse.

Ubiquity

The ubiquity topos, while not a predominate topic in our conversations, did emerge as an important value for three professors, and again the comparisons between more and less successful implementations of this topos help explain how the use of general abstractions such as "evidence" or "use of quotations" may be inflected with disciplinary and genre-specific significance. One of the papers in the sample contained two very long block quotations of dialogue from Henrik Ibsen's *Doll's House*, each a full page or more long. The professors faulted this paper for such extended quotations. Rogers explained that papers such as this one had inspired her to specify an evaluative criterion she called "use of quotations" because it allowed her to describe what she felt was not working in this paper:

While the writer does use substantial quotations, it's clear that they don't know how to use . . . according to sort of the basic MLA guidelines for why and how we should use quotations. She or he wants to show that they're doing some close reading, but it's not clear why they've chosen these particularly long quotations.

She found another paper on *A Doll's House* to more successfully perform appropriate "close reading" practices: "when he's using outside sources, he's quoting sparingly, as needed, and even when he's quoting from the play, [. . .] he gives the line, and then he glosses the lines, so very effective use. . . . This is how we do things."

Professor Ross echoed her complaint about the weaker *A Doll's House* paper; she complained that "the attempts to use evidence from the text are not convincing because they're pages long. So there's no highlighting of specific sections to really support a clear thesis," and this led her to declare it a "totally surface reading of the text." This stood in marked contrast for her to a paper on Margaret Atwood's *Handmaid's Tale* that she had given the highest possible rating to and that she described as containing "really close readings of the text itself." When I pressed her to clarify what she meant by "close reading," she explained that not only are "there are a lot of examples" but they also referred to apparently minor characters and incidents in the novel and connected these elements to the paper's central argument. As she put it:

This student . . . is able to reach to those specific points, grab them out, and put them together so that it's like this block of knowledge that they're giving to me, the reader. . . . It's clearly directed, right. You get this sense that "I'm going to direct your view now to this."

For both these professors the disciplinary concept of "close reading"—a phrase that may misleadingly seem to an outsider to this discipline to wholly signify a *reading* rather than a *writing* practice—appears to be tied to the use of the ubiquity topos. One demonstrates (or perhaps *performs*) a close reading through use of multiple, specific, and potentially obscure textual examples pointed to through use of select quotations that are explained in a way that highly directs the reader's attention to the significance of textual details for the writer's overall interpretive argument.

Social Justice

While frequently a student's use of this topos went unremarked upon (for instance, the professors did not comment on the feminist bent of an analysis), two professors indicated that students' use of this topos positively influenced their evaluation. Both noted how this strategy tends to appear in the conclusion of literary analyses, and they appear to appreciate having this expectation for placement met. Professor Rogers explained her high evaluation of the paper on *The Handmaid's Tale* by pointing to the student's use of the social justice topos in its final sentence: "They're just sort of brave, bold, clever moves that she makes in this paper that even with the ending with the question, 'If the same idea that led to the foundation of Gilead remained in the language of the future, could it all happen again?' She takes risks, and they work in this case." The student's question clearly invites readers to connect the novel's totalitarian state to their social context, and it appears the professor appreciated the cautionary lesson for contemporary audiences that the student gleaned from the book.

Again, comparing a paper that illustrated a less-successful implementation of the topos with one that used it more effectively allowed Professor Ryan to clarify her expectations for this topos. She appreciated the "attempt at the end" (though actually this appears in the fifth to last paragraph) of a paper on Jane Smiley's *Thousand Acres* "to try to make that argument significant beyond the novel itself" by suggesting a feminist interpretation of the novel's images of animals. Ultimately, however, she found the paper too narrowly focused on the literary text without much consideration for the larger social implications of the interpretation. As she put it, the paper "didn't make any kind of statement other than 'these things get used in the text.'" However, in another paper on *The Handmaid's Tale* that she rated more highly, she found these expectations fulfilled:

Whereas with the Atwood, I thought that there was this argument to say, "Well, language (and I guess this is one that "English people" like) but that language matters and that language is a source of power. And it's not just in this text . . . that there's this kind of way in which it matters generally," you know. [. . .] And I think this person tried to make that move, even in her ending, which might have been a little hokey, but, you know, "It is of greater consequence that we understand the tools, specifically language, we already possess that can lead to substantial changes." So there's this movement that the novel matters, not just as an artifact but as something that helps us grow and change and recognize our powers. So that's what made it more interesting to me.

In both *The Handmaid's Tale* analyses' concluding passages, the students employed the social justice topos in a manner very much like the scholars who used this strategy in the sample of journal articles I rhetorically analyzed: The writer claims the analysis of the text holds implications for social life outside the text, though generally speaking this argument is more gestural than fully fleshed out. This lack of development of the analogy to contemporary life does not appear to be seen as a flaw by the professors I spoke with, nor, presumably, the editors of the journals that published articles making similar concluding gestures. It is, instead, an illustration of the ways special topoi work as what Toulmin called warrants—assumptions shared between audience and rhetor and thus not in need of defense.

Context

The same two professors who drew attention to the social justice topos as a rhetorical strategy they value also invoked the context topos. They appreciated the effort students took to "situate" a literary work in the historical, cultural environment in which it was originally produced or that it depicts. This, of course, requires constructing an analysis that does not solely focus on the literary text and brings in knowledge obtained elsewhere, often cited from other texts. Professor Ryan found these references noteworthy because they suggest "that you [the student writer] didn't just come to this as a reader without any knowledge of anything and as a writer without any knowledge of things." While she found problems with the paper that I will describe further, she valued a student's attempt to see the events depicted in Michelle Cliff's *Abeng* in larger historical contexts such as colonization and class struggle:

> They [the student writer] use a couple of sources in this that attempt to situate their reading. . . . At least they were trying to engage an argument that was bigger than their own, private reading, acknowledging that something outside of the text helped them understand the text.

"Originality" and the Mistaken-Critic Topos

The topos that drew the most attention from all four professors was another topos frequently related to student writers' use of citations, the mistaken-critic topos. All four professors highly valued the ability to craft an "original," "new," or "unique" argument in the context of previous interpretations. Faculty detected this "originality" in a variety of ways: they "sensed" it on the basis of what they know about typical classroom lecture and discussion dynamics, they noted the rhetorical positioning of citations that signaled novelty, or they intuited an argument's relative originality on the basis of their familiarity with published criticism on the literary text analyzed. However perceived, "originality" appears to be a highly sought-after ideal, though not all professors expect every student to attain it.

Three of the professors repeatedly used the metaphor of conversation to describe how students should ideally rhetorically position their analyses. Professor Ross even obliquely referred to Kenneth Burke's (1973) parlor metaphor when explaining how a paper erred in its application of the mistaken-critic topos:

> There's a friend of mine here on campus who also describes that introduction in academic work as being like a cocktail-party conversation, right? You just don't jump into the conversation when you arrive late at the party. You wait to see what other people said, and then you reflect upon what they've said. And if you're going to do that reflection, it better be accurate.

They were greatly impressed when student writers "situated" or "located" their argument about a text in the previous "scholarly conversation" or "dialogue" or "discourse" about a text. Thus, a student writer's "originality" seems to be valued less in the sense that the student acquired knowledge new only to her or him and more in the sense that the student attempts to contribute new knowledge to a disciplinary discourse community. These professors thus exhibit a rhetorical and social constructivist understanding of "originality," which Shamoon and Burns (1999) described as happening "when both writer *and* reader (i.e., student *and* instructor) recognize a piece of writing as fitting into the conversational field" of their discipline (p. 191).

For Professors Ross and Ryan, this conversation could have a literal meaning when they described a paper's relative novelty in comparison to the classroom discussions that likely preceded the student's writing. They described their sense, on the basis of what they know about typical classroom lecture and discussion dynamics, that a student's paper may have not moved far enough beyond what had likely been said in class to qualify as breaking new ground. As Ross put it, "It sounds like the student is kind of hazily trying to regurgitate something that the teacher said in class about this being a feminist piece." Ryan said of a different paper, "Sometimes I felt like they were just repeating what had been said in class. I could tell." In contrast, she praised a paper for likely extending class discussion into "original" territory by developing what may have been a passing comment in class.[6]

Most often, "originality" was deliberately signaled to the professors by the student writers through permutations of the mistaken-critic topos consistent with the variations of this topos I saw in professional discourse in literary studies (see chapter 1). Thus, sometimes student writers crafted an image of a hypothetical "conventional" interpretation that they set out to argue against or supplement with a more complex interpretation. At other times, student writers cited specific critics with whom they claimed to disagree or depart from in some way. Either way, students staked explicit claims for the originality of their arguments, and the professors appear to have greatly relied on these cues as they determined whether a student argument approached their ideal of originality. For instance, a paper on Keats's poetry appealed to Ross and Rogers because of the apparent "newness" of its interpretation. In the opening paragraph, the student used the "hypothetical" version of the mistaken-critic topos by positing that his or her argument would depart from what "many people" think about Keats:

> Many people read Keats' poetry as a man who was obsessed with death. The word or idea, death, appears in many of Keats' work and it is easy to read his poems and letters and put a generic stereotype on him as someone who longed for death in ways and also viewed death as a fear and a solution to his problems. What is wrong with this stereotype is that it paints a morbid idea of what Keats was writing about and his true message is lost in our readings' stereotype. I intend to show how although Keats wrote about death it wasn't in the context as we generally view it. Keats wasn't writing about death, he was writing about life. Keats' view of death isn't about longing for the grave; it is about longing for life. I intend to show this through two of Keats' poems, *Ode to a Nightingale* and *When I have fears*.

Rogers specifically pointed to this passage in her explanation of her highest possible rating of this paper's "sophistication of argument":

> I gave the writer credit for having something new to say about Keats's view of death. So right there, "Keats' view of death isn't about longing for the grave; it is about the longing for life." It's an ambitious claim to

make because after a couple of centuries, it's a different way of looking at that. And I think it's pretty sophisticated, too.

Ross had originally given this paper the lowest-possible score due to its repetitiveness and "clunky" language, but she explained that on reevaluating it, she would now considerably raise the score because she "got a sense that this person actually felt that they were discovering this text, like this actually wasn't just a recycled, 'I'm going to grab this person's opinion and this person's opinion.'" She now links this student's claims for originality with what she sees as the student's praiseworthy use of the paradox topos—the only time this topos was invoked during these interviews: "I think that's kind of a distinction now that I think a lot of students wouldn't be able to make, that, yes, there's a focus on death, but it's through focusing on death that you focus on life."

Perhaps further influencing these professors' perceptions that this student writer was venturing an "original" argument was the student writer's use of citations to distinguish his or her argument from published criticism, a frequent permutation of the mistaken-critic topos in the professional discourse I examined. At two points in the body of this paper on Keats, the student quoted published critics who had stated that Keats poetry indicates he was "obsessed with death" or sought "escape from mental labor that death brings." The student represented these quotations as "a common train of thought with critics and scholars" of Keats and then rebutted these passages with reiterations of his or her claim that Keats's primary theme was in fact life. At these points, the student applies the mistaken-critic topos through the use of named critics and citations and follows the conventions of first introducing the other critics and their books or articles, representing their views with an apt quotation, and then responding. Ryan had pointed to the lack of these tactics in a paper written by another student:

> They do try to engage some criticism, I think. [. . .] They're trying to do something, but they haven't learned how to do it in a way that we would say is the right way, I guess. So it's not introduced, you know, as "In an article, this scholar says," or whatever. It's just thrown in there.

The significance these professors attributed to citations as markers of "originality" supports Shamoon and Burns's (1999) speculation that students' "fitting" citation of sources signals to instructors that originality within the context of a disciplinary conversation has been achieved (p. 191).

These conversation and citation cues appear to be highly important to these professors; they pointed to passages that used them repeatedly to explain what impressed them about highly rated papers. For example, a paper that "locates itself from the beginning within the context of discussion on Henrik Ibsen's *Doll's House*" was held up for praise while a paper that "wasn't locating itself within the discourse on Henrik Ibsen's *Doll's House*" received a weaker evaluation. Rogers decided to raise the evaluation she had previously given to a paper on "The Goblin Market" because

> it has the idea that it's supposed to take part in a conversation. I'll say that much for it. It's been interpreted in many ways, so many ways that it has been interpreted, but then she says she wants to say it's about sisterhood and togetherness. So that's really well and good, I think, as the idea behind the blueprint for what she should be doing.

Ryan similarly described the basis for her evaluation in terms of the clarity with which a student writer characterized previous "typical" criticism and then staked out a new interpretive claim:

> The reason I liked it was because I thought that it was aware of a kind of typical analysis of *The Handmaid's Tale*, which was that criticism of government and power in a certain kind of way, that it took a slightly different take on that by talking about the way language worked. So I thought that it was slightly more sophisticated than some of the other ones that I had read.

This rhetorical strategy was so important to Rogers that she chose to specify an evaluative criterion that she called "scholarly conversation," which she clarified means:

> a knowledge of the kinds of arguments, not only that literary scholars make about texts in general but also being able to enter the conversations, the analyses that have already been made about a text, so that you're not pretending to do it for the first time yourself. [. . .] To sort of situate the argument within some part of a scholarly community that's already discussed this novel. It's the recognition that we don't come to a text for the first time on our own.

That the positioning required to successfully carry out the mistaken-critic topos can be related to issues of arrangement is revealed by a paper on *A*

Thousand Acres. In the opening paragraph, the student follows convention by introducing and quoting a critic, Steven Kellman, but then does not distinguish her or his own argument until the bottom of page 4 with these words:

> However, what Kellman fails to recognize is the own duality going on in Ginny and even Rose as well. This isn't an issue between only Jess and Larry Cook and the other farmers. We see the same fight taking place in the Cook women, and through it, I think that Smiley tried to argue that neither side is the total paradise.

The delay in the announcement of "originality" with the signals "however," "what Kellman fails to recognize," and "I think" indicate that the first four pages of this seven-page paper summarize Kellman's argument (though the student draws textual evidence to support Kellman's thesis directly from the novel). Both professors who read it commented on this phenomenon; both praised the student's attempt to use the mistaken-critic topos (or to "situate in a scholarly conversation"), though both felt that the difficulty the paper presents them in distinguishing Kellman's views from the students' prevented them from giving this paper the highest rating (one had added the note "takes awhile to discover what's new" to the rating form). This arrangement appears to frustrate the evaluators' expectations for the placement of an "original thesis statement." Reese described this difficulty as one that alarmed her:

> The one problem, and it's a fairly big one, is that the thesis in the opening paragraph is not her own. It's a quotation from someone else, so again, there's the understanding that you can build off other people's ideas, but to me, this read as the presentation of someone else's thesis. However, I did see what I thought was an original thesis on page 4 . . . maybe not until page 4. As I read it, I thought that focusing on the women, now that expands upon that article that is quoted.

Ryan, expecting a writer to somehow depart from a critic that is quoted so early in an essay, found herself confused by the abrupt announcement of disagreement on page 4; she had been reading the student's text after the introduction as the student's original contribution that builds upon Kellman's argument:

> This person clearly is engaging an article, this Kellman article, and trying to use it as a springboard for their own argument. And I think that's what many of us do who are writing, as we're writing, so I saw it

as a more sophisticated attempt to understand how scholarly articles get made. . . . We don't just come up with these analyses and publish them without looking at what else has been done . . . because I thought this was this sort of attempt to engage. . . . There are times when it's sort of a little clunky, like right here on page 4, where it seemed to me, at least in this reading, that even though Kellman is up there in the first paragraph and discussed as the source that we're engaging with and using as a springboard, here it seems like this was this writer's own analysis. And then there's this "However, what Kellman fails to recognize." I couldn't figure out what it was that Kellman . . . what this person's arguing against, given that it was his or her own argument up here.

The professors' reactions to this paper reveal a number of things about the intricate steps necessary to effectively implement the mistaken-critic topos. First, the professors do tend to see these student papers as approximating the professional genre of the journal article. Three of the professors stressed this sentiment by using the plural first-person pronoun in phrases such as "this is how we do things" to describe discourse community practices that they expect WAL students to take on. The mistaken-critic topos for at least one professor seems to more strongly signal this successful approximation than any other topos. In fact, though all the papers Ryan rated were final papers from WAL sections, she indicated to me that she assumed those papers that did not engage with secondary criticism must be papers from earlier in the semester, papers that "no one would publish" but from which students are to learn other components of literary criticism. By the end of the semester in WAL, she expects students to "be taking on the role of a critic" through engagement with the "scholarly conversation."

Second, like the procedures Swales (1990) and Kaufer and Geisler (1989) described as conventional in the sciences for establishing exigency, successful implementation of the mistaken-critic topos requires several intricate, interconnected steps. The rhetorical moves that enable scholars to "create a research space" (Swales, 1990) or stake claims against a persuasive distillation of a discourse community's consensual knowledge (Kaufer & Geisler, 1989) do not necessarily reflect the path of discovery the writer took to come to the "original" idea. Instead, they are just as likely a rhetorical construction aimed at leading readers to see the argument at hand as exigent. Reese acknowledged her awareness of this possibility when discussing the *Thousand Acres* paper with its "problematic thesis up front, which seems to be a reiteration of what somebody else has said." As she put it, "it could be that the student picked up on this and found the topic of meat and food very interesting, and then went and did the research, and then plopped somebody else's. . . . So who knows how it all came to pass."

Indeed, because the special topoi function as both inventional strategies and as rhetorical appeals to shared values, readers of these texts cannot know a writer's actual sequence of thought; that is, it is impossible to know whether a writer actually decided to intervene in a conversation as a consequence of reading secondary literature in the manner that this topos suggests or whether the secondary literature has been retroactively assembled to make a convincing rhetorical position. Thus, the mistaken-critic topos as an appeal to the shared value of originality can be seen as crafting a sort of fiction; thinking of the topos in this way underscores that appropriate rhetorical posturing may be more important or valued than "actual" originality in the sense inherited from Romanticism (Howard, 1999; LeFevre, 1987), which may be impossible to assess, and when seen from a poststructuralist perspective, entirely elusive (Larochelle, 1999).[7]

Third, the expectation that student literary analyses approximate contemporary scholarship through using the mistaken-critic topos reveals that literature professors appreciate highly professionalized exigencies even in student writing. To create audience interest by arguing that one's work fills an interpretive gap, corrects or amends previous criticism, or significantly builds on previous contributions is to have a scholarly understanding of exigency. To fulfill this expectation requires that a student see her or his audience as valuing these motivations as self-evident goals. To argue for these exigencies persuasively, students must not only situate their arguments in relation to what scholars have previously written but must also situate themselves in relation to their audience and the scholars they cite as fellow scholars who share these goals. Like the theory of originality embedded in the mistaken-critic topos, these relations may feel like fictional constructs to the rhetor. At the same time, they profoundly resonate with their scholarly audience via the pathos appeal perhaps most relevant to scholarly discourse, the feeling of reading the words of a "colleague."

Complicating this image of "originality as crafted fiction," some professors claimed that wide knowledge of criticism on a particular text may enable a reader to ascertain whether an interpretation forwarded as original does in fact add something new to the related body of scholarship. For instance, when confronted with a considerably lower score another professor had given a paper on *A Doll's House*, Ross conceded that this other professor "might be more familiar with criticism about the *Doll's House* to begin with, so they might be saying, 'Well, I've seen this so often that it's really just a silly, redundant thing,' whereas I've read the play, but I'm not familiar with a lot of the criticism." In this acknowledgment, she suggests that for those texts with which she is familiar with the secondary criticism, she would likely hold the student to higher standards of meeting the originality ideal—not just new to the discussions of the classroom but new to the discourse community of scholars who interpret this text. Though she grants that this ambitious ideal is rarely fully met by beginning English majors, she does think that professors likely have this expectation:

> The ideal would be to have somebody who obviously knows what's been done before and makes that clear in their writing, but then is doing something that yeah, I've never seen or heard. And I think that's really, really rare for that to happen, so I don't expect that, but yeah, I mean the hide-and-seek [image from *A Doll's House* that the student refers to] could just be this thing that's like, "Let's go through this again," or they're clearly borrowing from somebody, they're perhaps not attributing anything. . . . I just don't know enough about the criticism of this work to know that.

Thorough familiarity with the secondary criticism on a text allows a professor to detect ideas "borrowed" without attribution. It also enables them to determine originality beyond class discussion without the explicit cues of the mistaken-critic topos. Thus, when students write on texts for which their professors have studied a significant amount of secondary criticism—perhaps themselves even written on—the standards and stakes for originality may greatly increase. Of course, this scenario would not at all be uncommon in courses for which instructors select the texts on their syllabi and especially in advanced courses with narrower topic, period, or genre foci. Thus, a student's use of the mistaken-critic topos may be unmasked as "empty posturing" if its claims for originality can be rebutted by a professor familiar with a range of published scholarship on the text the student has written about. Two professors acknowledged specifically how their areas of specialization within the discipline, women's studies and cultural studies, may affect their evaluations by shaping their expectations for what counts as exigent.[8] It appears likely that as students advance towards their degrees, the stakes of their originality claims become increasingly higher just as these claims become increasingly more important and expected for students to make.

Tempering Expectations for Originality

The challenge of meeting audience expectations for originality is indeed difficult and persists for those who pursue graduate study (Sullivan, 1991) and the profession. However, the professors I spoke with did appear aware of the steepness of this challenge, and they described how to varying degrees they try to modulate their expectations for beginning majors. Two professors described how, precisely because novelty is so difficult to achieve in the context of a scholarly conversation, they value other criteria more highly when evaluating student work, especially stylistic clarity and an organized presentation of evidence. Ross came to this realization about her usual evaluation practices when discussing her decision to raise the score she originally gave the paper on Keats because it declared the newness of its take on his poetry:

> You know, I know that I do this. When I read papers, I really look for a thesis that's going to pop out, and it's actually clear that, "OK, here's what I'm going to be arguing," and I probably value that more than, "is this idea necessarily new or unique, but is it clearly stated, and then is there an attempt to bring in evidence from the text, in addition to support from other sources?"

Reese defended the highest possible score she gave to a paper on *The Handmaid's Tale* by valuing these qualities over originality:

> *The Handmaid's Tale* paper . . . just because I know a lot about that novel . . . the issue of language has been done a lot, so it wasn't the most unique thesis in the world, but the flow of the writing, the deepening of the argument, many examples, great organization, that, to me, kind of compensated.

Repeatedly she stressed that she is aware "that this could be a person's first foray into this kind of writing," and she tries "to keep that in mind" to temper her expectations and differentiate them from those she brings to professional texts.

Being Wrong in Lit. Crit.

An interesting challenge to this leniency was presented by a paper on *Abeng* due to its misrepresentation of Marxism, a theoretical construct its student writer attempted to apply as a paradigmatic lens. One example of this misrepresentation appears in the introduction where the student wrote, "Marxism is the weapon used by the establishment of the colony to protect English values and possession, in effect fighting rebellion." Both professors who rated this essay pointed to this student's distortion or misunderstanding of Marxism as a recurrent problem with this paper. Ryan described the problems with the paper's treatment of Marxism this way:

> That whole Marxist thing is kind of screwy, the way they talk about Marxism in this paper. I mean, this person seems to get that Marxism is not an analysis of class struggle but is the class struggle, and so somehow Marxism becomes the perpetrator of inequity, rather than the thing that reveals it.

Yet, as I discussed previously, Ryan greatly appreciated the contextual, historical stance to the novel this student attempted, and so to a degree she was willing to overlook these infelicities (she gave the paper a midrange rating). Though Ryan represented herself as expecting a great deal from students in terms of situating their work in scholarly conversation, she also repeatedly used the phrase "learning papers" to describe how she modulated her expectations (and to describe how she assumed that some of the papers she rated were not final papers for WAL but assignments from earlier in the semester). Of the *Abeng* paper she said, "You feel a learner, somebody who's been asked to use a tool to help them analyze this, and they're learning it and they haven't quite gotten it right, but that's what [WAL] is." When I shared with her that another professor had given this paper a lower rating than she had, she speculated that the difference may be due to the other professor's greater concern that theory be understood and represented accurately. As she put it:

> It could very well be that the theory person says, "They got this all wrong." And that that's what's most important, whereas I might say, "Well, they got it kind of wrong, but it's an impressive attempt to do something more sophisticated."

Reese, who had originally given this paper the highest-possible rating, on returning to it for our interview said, "When I reread it now, my rating surprised me a little bit." She explained that while she may have initially been impressed by the student's attempt to "contend" with "some deep ideas" and "weighty topics" like Marxism and "cultural dominance," now the student's mischaracterization of Marxism would lead her to lower her rating. Thus, ultimately, it appears all three of the professors who rated this paper may respond to its "incorrectness" by giving it a lower, but not failing, evaluation.

Students being "wrong" in their papers came up as an issue negatively influencing the evaluation of two other papers. Reese explained that at least part of the reason she gave a low score to another paper was because the terms "symbolism" and "irony" were "misused throughout the whole piece." Ross explained that a student's "misreading" and inaccurate representation of Gilbert and Gubar's feminist literary theory led her to lower the rating she gave to a paper that otherwise impressed her with its "attempt" to use the paradigm topos. Thus, despite the allowances these professors grant for novice attempts at approximating their discourse, it is clear that getting some things "wrong" negatively influences their evaluation. Yet, what troubled these professors was students' demonstrations of not fully understanding literary theory or terms of literary analysis. Students' interpretations of literary texts themselves were not faulted for being "wrong," though they certainly were for being "unpersuasive," "unoriginal," or "simplistic."

Of course, as I hope to have demonstrated here, faculty understandings of persuasiveness, originality, and complexity appear to have been so thoroughly shaped by their disciplinary training that student essays are found more persuasive, original, and complex the more they follow the conventions of the professional genre of the literary-analysis journal article. These professors' consistent treatment of student papers as more or less persuasive "turns" in an ongoing conversation on interpretation stands in marked contrast to the few earlier glimpses of more New Critical approaches to literary pedagogy identified in ethnographic studies such as McCarthy's (1987). The poetry professor that McCarthy's undergraduate case-study participant encountered apparently graded student's papers on the basis of whether or not he agreed with their interpretations. He "told students that he was being objective, finding the meaning of the poem in the text," but he told McCarthy "that his responses to student papers were to argue his interpretation of the poem and, thus, to justify his grade" (p. 252). It may prove to be the case that a pedagogical shift away from New Criticism's exclusive focus on the primary text (the poetry professor in McCarthy's study discouraged the use of secondary sources) accompanies a shift towards a social constructivist view of student writing. As a result, students' rhetorical skill at approximating disciplinary discourse practices may receive greater scrutiny than the "correctness" of their interpretations.

Limits to Traditional Approaches to WAL

Included in the subsamples of student papers we discussed were five papers by students from sections of WAL taught by the professors whose pedagogical approaches to WAL characterized in the previous chapter as "the terms," "theory overview," "civic discourse," and "expressivist," approaches that I argue in various ways obscure the rhetorical process knowledge disciplinary experts bring to literary analysis. The four professors' reactions to these papers suggest additional limits to these traditional WAL pedagogical approaches to student writing.

The Terms

A student's opening paragraph from a paper on Thomas Hardy's "On the Western Circuit" gives a sense of its central use of literary terminology, as well as its personal, rather than professional, exigency:

> I have picked two elements we have been studying that are going to further explain the short story of *On the Western Circuit*. The two elements are symbolism and irony. My goal in this paper is to pull these two elements from the story and explain the mystery and richness of them in the story. The reason I chose this short story was because there was a sense of realism in the story that I could relate to. Also there was suspense right from the start that kept me hanging on till the last page.

The paper goes on to define "symbolism" and "irony" with quotations from Abrams and Harpham's *Glossary of Literary Terms* and point to examples of these concepts in the story. Though both professors who gave it a low rating faulted the paper for incorrectly matching these concepts to the events in the story, what seemed to trouble them even more was the lack of argumentative exigency for using these terms. Reese explained that although literary scholars use these terms, they use them for different ends: "We talk about symbolism, and we talk about different characters, and we talk about irony, and we talk about all of those things, but it just seems like the student just sort of took a handful of all of this and sprinkled it down." Ryan explained that she saw it as a problem that "rather than developing an argument, there's repetition.

[. . .] There's a kind of 'maybe if I just keep writing, something will happen,' and I don't think it does."

Ryan readily grouped this with another paper on poems by Elizabeth Bishop and Regina Barreca. She proposed discussing them together

> because it strikes me that those came out of the same kind of assignment or that they came out of the same class. And certainly one part of [WAL], for many faculty, is teaching people to recognize the formal elements of text, whether they're poetry or they're short story elements, and these two seem to me to be the kinds of papers where somebody said, "Take a poem and show what formal elements are being used in it. Or take a short story and da, da, da." So they seemed similar.

The other professors had also given this paper a low rating, but Ryan made an evaluative distinction between them, giving the Bishop and Barreca paper a relatively high score, though she said that on re-reading it, she would lower it a bit (but still not at low as the other professors' ratings). For her, the key difference between the two papers was that the Bishop and Barreca paper tied its formal observations to a discussion of meaning:

> I think this person does a better job of showing that he or she really gets what those formal things do, in terms of content. There's a way in which it's not just, "Oh, look, here's a symbol or oh, look, here's rhyme." It's that the rhyme serves some sort of idea that the poet had, as well as the formal choices. And so I thought that was sort of interesting, you know, particularly in this paragraph on the rhyme and the enjambment and all that. It struck me that there was this consciousness of the poets having these rhetorical tools that they were using consciously for certain effects, and I thought that was more sophisticated.

Interestingly, the student's paragraph that refers to rhyme and enjambment was the section of the paper that Reese pointed to when she speculated why this professor may have given this paper a higher rating. She thought another professor might have been impressed by "maybe page 3, where we get into structure . . . how the form shapes and reflects the content." Though she disagreed and thought meaning and form were not productively brought together by the student, she acknowledged that a professor who found the paper more successful might have been impressed by this attempt. Thus, both professors indicated that in order to meet their expectations, students' use of these terms must be tied to argumentation at the conventional definitional stasis, where interpretation (rather than the kind of belletristic evaluation seen in the use of "the terms" in the Hardy paper) connects with the professional disciplinary discourse community's shared exigencies. As Ryan put it, she expects "students to see how the formal elements of a text serve some sort of purpose that has something to do with the content, whatever you want to call that, the meaning, whatever, that we do."

However, Ryan explained that she gave the Bishop and Barreca paper a higher score assuming that it was one of the first papers the student wrote over the semester: "I mean, this is a learning paper. A paper in which you show you've learned the form and you're demonstrating that you've learned it. By the final paper, I expect them to try to be taking on the role of a critic, which is a little different. No one would publish this." When I shared with her at the end of our interview that all of the papers she rated had been final papers from WAL, she returned to discussing this paper, saying that as a "last paper" she would want "more." Given such consistent faculty evaluative feedback, I believe pedagogical approaches to WAL that heavily stress acquiring "the terms" (as many textbooks for such courses on the market do) overemphasize memorization or application of a list of vocabulary at the expense of providing guidance on rhetorical strategies for using this disciplinary language.

Civic Discourse

Papers on the censorship controversies surrounding *Huckleberry Finn* likewise appear to have distinguished themselves because their student writers had not adequately taken on "the role of a critic." And again, the problem appears to be one of the writers' overall purpose; the stasis issue and exigency patterns for these papers do not follow disciplinary conventions. Instead, the assignment asking students to take a stance on censorship issues surrounding the novel encourages students to focus on the proposal stasis, with an implicit public policy rather than a scholarly exigency. Interestingly, Reese explained that she thought the specific *Huckleberry Finn* paper that appeared in the subsample we discussed "picks up steam" and "the writer seems to become more emotionally involved" on page 3, just where the student writer settles into supporting the stasis issue conventional to literary analysis, definition, with the claim that "Huck Finn is a realist novel." Ryan insisted that on the whole, the *Huckleberry Finn* papers, including the one in the subsample we discussed, "were not the same kind of character as the other papers," so much so that she really "couldn't quite compare it to" the other papers "doing some kind of analysis." "It was," she explained, like comparing "apples and oranges." Indeed, because they do not follow the stasis conventions of literary analysis, these papers would perhaps best be described as participating in a different genre tradition, perhaps public policy or literary journalism. Assignments that encourage participation in these traditions may unwittingly confuse students expecting to use the assignment as preparation for the genres expected of them in their major.

Theory Overview

An additional problem evidenced in one *Huckleberry Finn* paper appears to stem from the writer's treatment of literary theory. (This paper had been written by a student enrolled in a section of WAL that in addition to the civic discourse approach, introduced in digest form various theoretical approaches to literature.) On the paper's fourth page (of five), the student begins a paragraph with this sentence: "There are many different types of methods to critique literature with." Then the student writer organized three paragraphs each devoted to a "different type": the "archetypal method," the "psychological approach," and the "easiest method [. . .] the reader response method." In each of these paragraphs, the student suggests in four to five sentences what each method supposedly reveals about *Huckleberry Finn*: the significance of the river, Huck's search for a mother figure, and the student's own "opinion" of the text, which is "very simple. . . . A racist writer would not bother to show these feelings of a runaway slave." Both professors found flaws in this three-paragraph segment. Reese described this as "superficial" and "trying to do far, far too much." Ryan saw it as a desperate attempt to meet the specified length of the assignment without a purpose, or as she put it:

> So, "Now I'm going to talk about the psychological approach. . . . Now I'm going to talk about the reader-response approach . . . archetype." At that point, I think they just completely lost any engagement with the issue.

Both described this segment as contributing to the paper's lack of focus and development.

While, clearly, the three theory paragraphs represent this student's attempt to apply the paradigm topos (or to apply it distinctly three times), the student's "errors" in using this topos may shed light on how professors expect novices to use this topos. For one, it seems clear that the student did not use the paradigm topos in concert with appeals to textual complexity—in fact, the student would appear to argue against this value with the claim that a reader-response approach is easy and the suggestion that the meaning each paradigmatic lens can reveal may be exhausted in a few simple sentences. But, further, the student writer's lack of commitment to a particular paradigmatic lens may pose a problem that literature scholars would describe in terms of superficiality and lack of focus and development. To use the paradigm topos persuasively in this discourse community, the writer may have to plausibly inhabit the viewpoint of the metaphoric "lens." Thus, as is the case with the scholarly, collegial, relationship between self and audience that persuasive student writers appear to assume, student writers who persuasively use the paradigm topos must assume (though not necessarily uncritically) the scholarly viewpoint of the selected theoretical lens. It may be the case that the approach to introducing literary theory taken by textbooks such as the one assigned in this student's section of WAL—where a single textbook author presents brief overviews of multiple theories in the same stylistic voice—sends students a misleading message about using the paradigm topos. In fact, this student's decision to briefly interpret one novel through several theoretical lenses is an approach taken by several such textbooks.

Conclusion

The Importance of Pathos and Ethos Appeals in Scholarly Discourse

The professors' reactions to students' use of professional disciplinary genre conventions and scholarly approaches to constructing exigency suggest that a novice writer's use of ethos and pathos appeals can profoundly influence these experts' evaluations of their writing. While student's use of the special topoi and appeals to complexity can signal shared values and function as pathos appeals, they can also contribute to crafting an image, or ethos, of the novice writer as a potential colleague and more-than-provisional discourse community member. These interviews make clear the importance of these ethos appeals, something that my textual analysis of student papers and observations of classrooms may have otherwise obscured. Certainly, the numerous assignment descriptions I have collected from literature professors do little to clarify these expectations for the ethos students should seek to project. This expectation would appear to be the kind of rhetorical knowledge that some students are more adept at intuiting from the tacit rhetorical curriculum of the discipline.

Reese's description of what she called "the principles of literary analysis" demonstrates how her expectations for student writing appear to conjoin such ethos and pathos appeals with logos. She used the phrase "principles of literary analysis" during two moments of praise for different papers. Each time she used it, I followed up by asking her to clarify what she meant by this phrase. The first time she explained that a paper she said exhibited "above and beyond a basic control over the basic principles of literary analysis" meant that

> there was a certain confidence displayed. It seemed like the writer had a very good understanding of what a thorough literary analysis entails. [. . .] Some of the others seemed to be trying to do too much or seemed to be using terminology and language and things like that that they didn't seem quite comfortable with. And I didn't really detect any of that in here, that kind of hesitancy.

This clarification emphasizes her sense that a successful student writer projects a "voice" or stance that is confident and unhesitant, in contrast to the student writers who seemed to use disciplinary terminology with some discomfort. It seems as if she appreciates student writers who assume a voice of authority, who relate to their audience as fellow literary scholars. However, when I pressed Reese to clarify what she meant by "the principles of literary analysis" the second time she used the phrase, she explained the student writer "is looking at a particular recurring issue in the novel and delving into how that deepens the plot, advances the plot, exposes what's going on with the different characters, bringing in some interesting outside research to complicate and enrich the argument a little bit." In this clarification, Reese emphasizes strategies of argumentation, specifically invoking several special topoi of literary analysis: the ubiquity and appearance/reality topoi and possibly the context and the mistaken-critic topoi in her reference to research (the paper she praised used all of these topoi). Perhaps a student's effective use of such special topoi helps to produce the voice of authority that she find projects a "good understanding of what a thorough literary analysis entails."

Apparent Intermingling of Expressivist and Disciplinary Values

Reese, who used the phrase "principles of literary analysis" to praise two papers, also indicated that she values students' demonstrations of emotional sincerity and personal connection to literary texts. In this way, she seems similar to Professor Caldwell (see chapter 2), who extolled largely expressivist pedagogical goals for WAL but who also insisted that students study Abram and Harpham's *Glossary of Literary Terms* in order to master a professional disciplinary vocabulary. These professors' pedagogical practice may be similar to Fulwiler's (1992) expressivist approach to teaching American literature, which asks students to compose in both expressivist genres and the disciplinary genre of literary analysis. These overlapping approaches suggest it is possible to explicitly emphasize pre- or postdisciplinary pedagogical goals while implicitly rewarding the acquisition of disciplinary terminology, habits of thought, and conventions of argumentation. Fulwiler (1992) described his students' noticeably increased struggles with writing and responding helpfully to one another's literary analyses in contrast to their relative facility with expressivist genres (pp. 162–63). While to Fulwiler it appeared his students misunderstood "some very basic things: making careful assertions and providing evidence to support them," which he sees as "the kind of reasoning and writing that really goes on in every discipline in this university," he ultimately realizes he needs to "point out how one provides evidence in literary studies" (p. 163). Though he claims to "not want to turn these students into little literary critics," when they write in the discipline's primary genre, he does expect them to follow key conventions that to him signify they have learned "how to read with a critical consciousness" (p. 163). The four professors' expectations brought to light here further suggest the potency of disciplinary rhetorical conventions in shaping such expectations.

Disciplinary Values May Be Stronger Than Personal Idiosyncrasies

When WAC researchers have previously investigated professors' goals and standards for student writing, they have found that although some professors will consciously describe their goals and standards as shaped by their specific discipline, many more are inclined to describe their understanding of "good writing" as universal, or as a set of skills widely applicable across all disciplines and contexts (Russell, 2002; Thaiss & Zawacki, 2006). The close focus on actual student papers working in the disciplinary genre of literary analysis appears to have encouraged an awareness of the role of disciplinary values and goals among the four literature professors I spoke with, one that perhaps may not have emerged so clearly had we been discussing teaching writing in the abstract. It was not uncommon for them to use "we" in describing "how we do things" in a disciplinary genre. Likewise, the faculty frequently expressed a desire that students attempt to join in the "scholarly conversation" of their discipline. I believe that this "we" typically denoted the disciplinary discourse community of literary studies rather than all of academia, though, of course, there were times when this broader sense may have applied.

The "subdisciplinary" (Thaiss & Zawacki 2006, p. 60) emerged in two professors' explanations of their evaluative criteria when they described the possible influence of their specific subfields—women's studies and cultural studies—in shaping their expectations. However, the rationales these two professors provided did not appear to differ from the other professors' as a result of their announced subdisciplinary allegiances. In fact, the two topoi one might expect to be most closely connected with these two subfields, the newly emergent social justice and context topoi, were more evident in the explanations provided by the other two professors. What did emerge as a potentially potent influence of subspecialty on evaluation practices were the increased standards for "originality" when a professor was more familiar with the published scholarship on the texts students analyzed in their papers.

Likewise, the professors would on occasion reference local, institutional influences on their standards (Thaiss & Zawacki, 2006) when they referred to their contextual awareness of the WAL course's place within a departmental curriculum, including departmental discussions about course goals, prior knowledge of colleagues' approaches to the course, and their own expectations for what the course should accomplish. These concerns emerged most clearly in my discussion with Ryan, the full professor, who, as she put it, has "been around a lot longer and [has] taught [WAL] probably a lot more and [has] seen a lot more papers." Indeed, some issues recurrent in this sample of student papers may have emerged due to the unique institutional context. For instance, the stress placed on students' acquisition of "the terms" may be unique to this department, though the larger number of textbooks that cater to this approach would indicate that other programs elsewhere must share a similar emphasis.

However, wholly personal idiosyncrasies (Thaiss & Zawacki, 2006) did not seem to emerge as a plausible explanation for differences among the ratings on the same papers. If anything, the explanations two professors would offer for their evaluations of the same paper were strikingly similar, despite the fact that I interviewed each professor separately and that sometimes their original ratings differed. Though Reese's desire to see evidence of students' emotional involvement with the literary texts stands out as a potentially id-iosyncratic evaluative criterion, what emerges as a more potent explanation for the differences in ratings (which sometimes were reduced when professors decided to change their original ratings) are differing degrees of adherence to disciplinary conventions as ideal standards. For instance, Ross explained that while she values originality, she is aware that usually she ranks clarity of argument and organization as higher priorities, while Ryan expects students to meet (or at least rhetorically signal) her expectation for originality by their final paper in WAL.

Such potential differences in intensity of adherence to disciplinary conventions as evaluative standards may be seen in some subtle differences in preferences among the special topoi of literary analysis. Though I never asked directly about any of these topoi conventions, that they all were invoked during these interviews further affirms the vitality of these topoi as conventions of the discipline. As perhaps should be expected, the appearance/reality topos was clearly favored by all the professors. Similarly, the ubiquity topos was invoked by three professors, though I speculate that they all may have had something like this topos in mind when they spoke of students using evidence effectively. Somewhat surprising, all professors indicated a preference that students use the mistaken-critic and paradigm topoi, two strategies of argument that require juggling multiple, often difficult sources and careful positioning of the relationship between the sources and the writer's argument. But the "newer" topoi—social justice and context—were only invoked by two professors, perhaps indicating that the topoi's newness in the professional disciplinary discourse community makes them less universally dominate in the undergraduate classroom.

These subtle differences do not appear to be like the kinds of widely divergent, idiosyncratic preferences that students sometimes report facing and struggling to navigate as they move from course to course through their major (see W. Anderson et al., 1990; Beaufort, 2007; Herrington & Curtis, 2000). They also do not seem to call into question the usefulness of the concept of disciplines as social constructs that influence and are shaped by scholars' writing and teaching practices in the way Thaiss (2001) called this concept into question as a wholly "arbitrary category" (p. 316). When speaking about student writing in concrete terms, these professors seem more apt to describe their expectations in terms of shared disciplinary norms and conventions. And they all affirmed that the ratings they performed for me were similar to their usual grading practices.[9] A productive outcome to emerge from this study might be a greater, explicit acknowledgment to students of the socially constructed factors, especially disciplinary, that influence the evaluation of their work. Rhetorical theory has long taught that such knowledge of audience values should help rhetors produce more effective discourse. That the professors I spoke with valued students' arguments that attempted to engage them as intellectual and professional colleagues suggests that such insights from rhetorical theory would help students enter, and possibly productively redirect, this disciplinary discourse community.

4

"Some Tools to Take with Them": Making Disciplinary Conventions Explicit

In the preceding chapters, I have argued that a cluster of special topoi are stable enough in the genre of literary analysis to be described even as their application by literary scholars has changed over time. Further, given their "stable enoughness," I go so far as to describe these special topoi as conventions that members of the disciplinary discourse community come to expect other members, even the most recent newcomers, to use to demonstrate their communal understandings of effective argumentation and good writing. My observations and interviews, along with broader WID research of literature instruction from secondary through graduate school (Beck, 2006; Herrington, 1988; Schmersahl & Stay, 1992; Sullivan, 1991), indicate these expectations are seldom stated explicitly in classrooms for a variety of reasons ranging from instructors' lack of conscious awareness of the existence of these conventions to their deliberate intentions to work with students on what are understood to be more widely applicable, generalized rhetorical skill and knowledge. Yet, because they appear to play a significant role in instructors' evaluations of student writing, evaluations that frequently determine students' prospects for continued work in a discipline, and because students appear to vary in their abilities to infer and apply the traditionally tacit rhetorical instruction in their use, the effects of explicit instruction in special topoi warrant investigation.

The Explicit-Instruction Debate

Scholarly opinion varies on whether explicit instruction in genre conventions would help students learn to effectively apply disciplinary conventions. Inspired by theories of situated learning, which stress the social rather than cognitive nature of learning, some genre theorists contend that explicit (or "direct" or "abstract") instruction within the context of school is incongruent with what we know about how individuals routinely acquire genre knowledge necessary for effectively entering into communities of practice. Lave and Wenger (1991) developed the concepts of "communities of practice" and the "situated learning" newcomers' experience within them based on a series of studies of how apprentices gain expertise without any apparent explicit instruction. These concepts highlight the importance of tacit procedural knowledge—a felt sense of "know-how"—and identity formation that can take place within meaningful social interaction. In order to clarify how situated learning differs from learning encouraged by traditional educational institutions, Lave and Wenger (1991) stressed that "in a community of practice, there are no special forms of discourse aimed at apprentices or crucial to their centripetal movement toward full participation that correspond to the marked genres of the question-answer-evaluation format of classroom teaching [or] of the lecturing of college professors" (p. 108). Use of such classroom genres promotes students' enculturation into "the community of schooled adults" rather than into a specific discipline, such as physics:

> The actual reproducing community of practice, within which school-children learn about physics, is not the community of physicists but the community of schooled adults. Children are introduced into the latter community (and its humble relation with the former community) during their school years. The reproduction cycles of the physicists' community start much later, possibly only in graduate school. (pp. 99–100)

Building on this distinction between the community of school and the communities of the disciplines, professions, and workplaces, genre theorists have heightened writing instructors' awareness of important differences between genres of workplace and classroom writing, stressing the limits of classroom "simulations" of workplace writing and questioning the usefulness of explicit instruction in genre features (A. Freedman, Adam, & Smart, 1994). Unlike feminist and cultural studies critics of WID who question the project of disciplinary enculturation on the grounds that it supports the perpetuation of unequal power relations, genre theorists who take a hard stance against explicit instruction tend not to question the larger project of disciplinary enculturation. On the contrary, inspired by theories of situated learning, they wish to support students' transitions from a school community into disciplinary and professional communities; their concerns about explicit genre instruction relate to its effectiveness at achieving this goal. In an exchange on this topic in *Research in the Teaching of English*, A. Freedman (1993a) contended that explicit instruction in these conventions is unnecessary, may not be possible, and may even be harmful or "dangerous" (p. 245). She argued such instruction is unnecessary because students have been observed to gain sufficient genre knowledge without it. She questioned its feasibility on the grounds that the fluid, dynamic, complex, and tacit nature of most genres may make pinning down and articulating their features adequately and accurately an impossibility. If attempted, the instruction drawing from such analyses could encourage students to ignore their tacitly acquired and more accurate genre knowledge and instead misapply or "overgeneralize" the explicit genre "rules" and produce rhetorically ineffective discourse (p. 245). Rather than explicit instruction informed by the results of recent WID research of disciplinary genres, A. Freedman suggested that the genre knowledge needed to participate in a disciplinary discourse community can best be acquired tacitly and through immersion, as children acquire language. Similarly, based on research that indicates more-advanced graduate students, without any explicit instruction, were better able to compose in a scholarly genre in their field than less-advanced graduate students and undergraduates, Hare and Fitzsimmons (1991) concluded that "time alone seems to be sufficient to inculcate would-be members of a community with knowledge of basic discourse conventions" (p. 375).

Undoubtedly, genre knowledge can be and is regularly acquired tacitly through immersion in a discourse community—in fact, the history of disciplinary socialization practices indicates that tacit immersion is typically the only form of rhetorical genre instruction the disciplines offer. However, many WID scholars question the efficacy and ethics of calls to maintain this tacitness in the light of what research has uncovered about novices' attempts to gain expert genre knowledge. For instance, in her study of collaboration among a professor of physics, a postdoctoral fellow, and a graduate student, Blakeslee (1997) identified the implicit nature of situated modeling and mentoring practices as an impediment to learning genre and recommends making such instruction more explicit. Lingard and Haber's (2002) observations of medical students' acquisition of genre knowledge necessary to deliver oral case reports indicated that it is possible for students to infer inaccurate rhetorical "rules" from the complex social interaction of their immersion experience. As a result, especially given the potential consequences that "having inferred a rule, students may then proceed to apply it acontextually [. . .] and unknowingly adopt an erroneous orientation towards the patient, his condition, and the medical response to that condition" (p. 167), Lingard and Haber argued "that there *is* a role for rhetorically explicit genre instruction in the context of situated practice" (p. 168, emphasis in the original). Disrupting the traditional tacit route to discourse community participation with explicit genre instruction may increase the efficiency of this process while decreasing misunderstandings and psychological distress.

Recurrently, WID ethnographies have found that the tacit acquisition of disciplinary genre knowledge can be so stressful and frustrating that some otherwise-motivated students turn away from—or are turned away from— further disciplinary participation (see for instance Casanave, 1992). A. Freedman's (1993a) and Hare and Fitzsimmons's (1991) studies of genre knowledge acquisition appear to overlook students who fall between the cracks because of their failure to adequately *and quickly* infer the tacit rhetorical instruction a discipline provides. A. Freedman acknowledged that her focus on competence within a genre, for which "no distinction was made between A papers and C papers," left open "the issue of expertise, in the sense of outstanding proficiency" (p. 246). Because the writer of C papers, although technically passing, may never be admitted up further rungs of a disciplinary hierarchy, student writers whom A. Freedman classified as sufficiently acquiring genre knowledge through tacit means may nonetheless be barred from further disciplinary participation. Similarly, because the highest-performing group Hare and Fitzsimmons examined was already "culled" by graduate-admissions committees, their findings may have been influenced by more than simply time spent within a disciplinary context. The doctoral students who performed best on their genre knowledge task may not only have had further experience within a discipline but also may have previously been among those undergraduates who seemed to possess a greater "knack" for intuiting implicit rhetorical instruction.

The sense that complex social circumstances likely support the development of some students' apparent special "knacks" for intuiting the implicit rhetorical instruction of the disciplines motivates many arguments in favor of explicit rhetorical instruction on the grounds of social equity. Recognition that the discourse practices of the community of school more closely match, indeed stem from, the discourse practices of the white middle class leads many to claim that students from other backgrounds are placed in distinct disadvantages in this context, especially when instruction makes no attempt to acknowledge and bridge different discourse community practices. This recognition motivated a group of Australian systemic-functional linguists to develop curricula for explicitly teaching genre features to culturally diverse school children. As they put it, problems

> arise when teachers and students do not share knowledge about language and genre. Guidance becomes at best indirect, and may well be absent completely. Only bright motivated middle class children are sure to read between the lines and learn to write, apparently effortlessly, without being taught. (Martin, Christie, & Rothery, 1987, p. 73)

In the United States, Delpit (1995) and Purcell-Gates (1995) sharply called into question literacy "process" (or "expressivist") pedagogies, which tacitly favor as seemingly "natural" white, middle-class discourse practices, and argued that there is a place for explicit instruction in these cultural literacy practices. Indeed, those who first called on WID researchers and teachers to make explicit the conventions of academic discourse, such as Shaughnessy (1977), Bizzell (1982), and Bartholomae (1985), were motivated by their sense that those beginning college students routinely labeled as "basic writers" in need of remediation were in fact socially rather than cognitively disadvantaged. Tacit rhetorical instruction, such scholars argued, effectively excludes from further participation in the disciplines students who arrive at college not already immersed in privileged discourse practices (Comfort, 2002; Kaufer & Young, 1993; Sternglass, 1997) or with less experience in learning new genres (Russell, 1995). Sternglass argued that beyond being implicated in perpetuating social injustice, disciplinary discourse communities (and the larger society their work aims to affect) are diminished by their lack of exposure to the diverse perspectives and experiences these students could bring. Moreover, promoting the status quo of tacit disciplinary enculturation practices would seem to only further maintain the deep divide between expert and lay rhetorical knowledge that Geisler (1994) critiqued.

For these reasons, some rhetoric and composition scholars advocate for an approach to writing instruction in the disciplines that is both informed by situated learning and enhanced by explicit instruction in genre features. Like Delpit, Flower (1994) is concerned that the immersion experience provided by traditional apprenticeship approaches to writing instruction may not be sufficient for some students:

> Supportive environments (that avoid direct instruction and ignore cognition) can achieve remarkable results, especially with a portion of the

class. But *opportunities* to perform or to learn always offer the great-
est benefit to the most prepared. Situations that *support* performance
(only) depend on students' prior knowledge and their ability to read
the situation accurately, to seize the opportunity, and to perceive the
indirect cues to the thinking this situation allows (and tacitly calls for).
The critical problem is that supportive situations support insiders most.
(p. 124, emphases in original)

Thus, to reduce the likelihood of "traumatic immersion, in which students
learn to sink or swim" (p. 122), Flower drew on the concept of "cognitive
apprenticeship" from situated learning advocates such as Brown, Collins,
and Duguid (1989). Flower stressed that cognitive apprenticeships in writing
should differ from traditional apprenticeships in their need to "externalize"
(p. 119) and make explicit rhetorical procedural knowledge that is difficult or
impossible for students to observe in use, such as "thinking processes associated with planning, invention, self-monitoring, diagnosis, self-correction, and
other key moves" (p. 119). Similarly, Russell (1995) speculated that

if neophytes have some skillful help from adepts in the activity system,
through conscious—even systematic and explicit—teaching, they may
learn to perform an action more quickly and more easily than if they
simply "picked it up." Students might do better at learning to use the
genres of writing in some activity system if they had specific, conscious
coaching, mentoring, or formal instruction in those genres of writing.
Activity theory research suggests that by consciously creating more
effective zones of proximal development, activity systems may be able
to improve a novice's acquisition of the systems' genres. (p. 70)

Studies of the Effects of Explicit Instruction

A few studies suggest some potential benefits of explicit instruction in procedural knowledge traditionally imparted tacitly. Motivated by findings that
demonstrate differences in the tacit knowledge possessed by experts and
novices in a variety of professions that "were consequential for career performance" (Wagner & Sternberg, 1985, p. 452), some cognitive psychologists have
sought ways to determine if direct instruction can reduce tacit knowledge
gaps among individuals. For instance, Sternberg, Okagaki, and Jackson (1990)
found that seventh graders who experienced explicit instruction in the kinds
of tacit knowledge generally expected and rewarded in school settings (such

as how to allocate time for tasks, how to prepare papers, how to study, and how to talk to teachers) significantly improved their scores on several tests of study skills and practical intelligence in comparison to a control group. Thus, Sternberg and his colleagues, although acknowledging that the "disorganized, informal, and relatively inaccessible" nature of tacit knowledge makes it "potentially ill-suited for direct instruction" (Wagner & Sternberg, 1985, p. 439), hold out hope for the possibility of articulating and imparting tacit knowledge from experts to novices, even in school settings.

Some studies indicate that elements of rhetorical procedural knowledge needed to effectively compose disciplinary genres can be imparted explicitly. Geisler (1994) observed several promising indicators of success as a result of an experimental attempt to impart the rhetorical procedural knowledge possessed by expert academic philosophers. Her interviews with undergraduates at the end of a semester of such instruction indicated that all of the students "understood that they were expected to build a connection between the academic scholarship and their own personal positions," and many could describe the conventional structure of philosophic discourse and "aimed to incorporate it into their final papers" (p. 227). De La Paz (2005) found that direct strategy instruction in argumentative writing and in the reasoning practices of disciplinary experts in history led middle-school students to write essays that were significantly longer, contained more arguments, and were deemed more persuasive and more historically accurate than those written by a control group who received no such instruction. Most interesting, students in her study who were assigned to special-educational services due to learning disabilities appear to have significantly extended their rhetorical and disciplinary skills as a result of the direct strategy instruction, on some measures to levels equivalent to their peers deemed most talented as writers. Though at first these students had greater difficulties understanding the primary-source documents that were part of the curriculum for both experimental and control conditions, "after instruction, both the length and the persuasive quality of papers written by students with disabilities were comparable to the pretest papers written by talented writers" (p. 152).

Some studies suggest that explicit instruction in interpretation strategies may produce similar gains for weaker literature students. Finding the instruction in "the terms" of literary analysis offered in most textbooks to do "little to prepare students to cope with the complexities involved in understanding literary texts" (Smith, 1992, p. 341), Smith drew from Booth's (1974, 1983) descriptions of expert interpretation processes to develop curricula that explicate interpretive strategies for assessing the reliability of narrators (Smith, 1992) and detecting irony (Smith, 1989). Think-aloud protocols indicated that the "reliability" curriculum reduced high-school students' "submission" to literary texts, meaning that the students exerted more authority in their interpretations by rejecting "the interpretation of events that the narrator offers" (Smith, 1992, p. 343) and devising their own "point-driven" interpretations (p. 345). Hamel and Smith (1998) found that applying this curriculum in two "lower-track" remedial high-school English classes encouraged students to take a more questioning stance towards literary texts, make more personal connections to the texts, and disagree with their instructor's interpretations more often. Ultimately, and perhaps surprising given the expectation that direct instruction would lead to an instructor's increased dominance over classroom discourse, Hamel and Smith perceived these changes as contributing to reducing the amount of "teacher talk" and redistributing authority in the classroom. Although Smith's (1989) larger and more controlled study generally found no differences between direct and tacit approaches to instruction in irony on high-school students' performance on a posttest that sought to assess their understanding of irony within poems, he did find that ninth-grade students' performance improved in response to direct instruction more dramatically than did tenth- or twelfth-grade students, leading him to speculate that students with less experience or who face particularly difficult tasks may benefit more from direct strategy instruction.

MacDonald and Cooper (1992) found that explicit instruction in the type of "'claim-and-evidence' writing" (p. 139) valued by a literature professor followed by repeated practice of it in an "academic journal" led to marked gains in performance on college students' final literature essay exams over students who received no such instruction and kept reflective "dialogic" journals or no journal at all. Students who kept the academic journals were less likely to "rely on plot summary" and "simple dichotomies" and were more likely to "discuss complexities and ironies" (p. 150). And though they found that, predictably, students' verbal SAT scores were correlated with their final exam scores in the literature course, they were considerably less strongly correlated for those students who experienced explicit instruction and practice in academic argumentation practices related to literary texts. This means that students with lower verbal SAT scores who experienced explicit instruction performed "better than expected" (p. 149), suggesting that potentially weaker students experienced significant learning and skill development as a result of direct instruction and practice.

Although these findings point to possible benefits for explicit instruction in genre features, especially for underprepared students, they do not conclusively dispel some of the important concerns A. Freedman (1993a) raised, such as whether such instruction carries the "risk of overlearning or misapplication" (p. 226). Indeed, Smith (1989) cautioned that in comparison to tacit methods of instruction, the explicit instruction in irony detection he studied "appears to carry additional risk" (p. 267) because some students after experiencing it actually performed more poorly on the posttest. Likewise, because we learn very little from them about students' reactions to these experimental pedagogies, these studies do not address the concerns of critics who see the WID project as stressing disciplinary homogeneity and stifling students' opportunities to engage in viable "alternative discourses" (Herndl, 1993; LeCourt, 1996; Mahala, 1991; Schroeder, Fox, & Bizzell, 2002). For instance, Spellmeyer (1989) pointedly criticized what he calls the "pedagogy of community conventions" (p. 266) because he fears it inhibits creativity and encourages the mimicry of the seemingly objective, neutral, and infallible voices of disciplinary authority. For these reasons, my research collaborator, Joanna Wolfe, and I undertook an investigation of the effects of explicit instruction in the special topoi of literary analysis. Focus on topological invention strategies may not sidestep these concerns according to Pullman (1994), who, while ultimately supporting explicit topical instruction in literary analysis, notes that "excessively codified" special topoi have the potential to yield "too much rigidity" and "could reduce interpretation to a plodding application of rules that would produce formulaic and uninteresting interpretations" (pp. 384–85).

Effects of Teaching Special Topoi of Literary Analysis

For our study, further details of which can be found in Wilder and Wolfe (2009), we prepared four English professors to explicitly introduce students to the special topoi of literary analysis that emerged as a result of my rhetorical analysis of professional discourse in literary studies (see chapter 1). These professors then worked with beginning English majors in the writing about literature (WAL) course at a midsized state university to recognize and apply these topoi over a full semester. We compared the final essays written by sixty-eight students from these experimental sections of the course to final essays written by seventy-seven students who experienced traditional approaches to the course ("the terms," "theory overview," "expressivist," and "civic discourse" approaches described in chapter 2). We also used questionnaires to solicit students' impressions of the degree to which the WAL pedagogy they experienced encouraged their expression and promoted the exploration of thought and feeling. Additionally, I sought to assess longitudinal impacts of the different approaches to WAL through follow-up interviews with a subset of study participants in the two years following their completion of WAL (see chapter 5).

We found that a semester of explicit instruction and guided practice in using the special topoi of literary analysis to invent arguments and persuade readers led to noticeable gains when compared to students who experienced traditional pedagogies that keep these topoi tacit. First, the essays of those students explicitly taught were deemed to be of significantly higher quality by a group of five experienced literature professors. These professors (who were unaware of the study's purpose or conditions and had been encouraged to apply their usual grading standards) rated the papers written by students in the experimental sections as significantly higher than papers written by students in the control sections in overall quality (on average 3.24 versus 2.77 on a 5-point scale), sophistication of argument (3.2 versus 2.68), and even organization and coherence (3.18 versus 2.74). The professors' explanations of their evaluative criteria, described fully in chapter 3, indicate that they did not find these papers to be "formulaic and uninteresting" (Pullman, 1994, p. 385). On the contrary, given the professors' collective preference for "originality," formulaic qualities were more likely to earn a paper a lower rating.

Second, though students from all sections of this course, experimental and control, used the special topoi in their writing, students who experienced the experimental curriculum employed significantly more of the special topoi in their final papers than did students from control sections, using on average almost four topoi per paper while those in the control sections used closer to three topoi per paper.[1] Not only did students in the experimental sections use more topoi but they also made more effective use of the topoi than students in the control sections. Students in the experimental sections used the appearance/reality, ubiquity, paradigm, and social justice topoi in ways significantly more in keeping with professional practice in literary studies, such as using the topoi to elucidate rather than reduce complexities in the literary text analyzed. To illustrate some of the extreme differences in quality of application of a topos, table 4.1 presents passages from student papers that exemplify weak and strong instances of students' use of the appearance/reality topos.

Table 4.1

Weak and strong examples of students' use of the appearance/reality topos

Weak Examples of Appearance/Reality	Strong Examples of Appearance/Reality
After reading the first line, it was obvious that this poem was about the memories of his wife that had died. Most people would probably think that when first reading this poem it was about the memories of his wife when they were married. Although, after reading his biography and learning of his bad marriage, it was obvious that this poem was not in remembrance of his wife and their life together. I believe Hardy had written this poem in order to escape the guilt and unhappiness that he felt for his marriage being such a failure.	Through public ritual, Atwood again employs language as a device to sustain the structure of Gilead. Language assumes a powerful role at public executions, called "Salvagings," because the Aunts' speeches are used to emotionally rile up the Handmaids. Aunt Lydia's speech clearly illustrates how language has taught her to govern herself properly and police other women. Aunt Lydia says, "We are all aware of the unfortunate circumstances that bring us all here together on this beautiful morning. . . . I am certain we would all rather be doing something else, at least I speak for myself, but duty is a hard taskmaster, or I may say on this occasion taskmistress, and it is in the name of duty that we are here today" (274). This shows that Aunt Lydia very cleverly chooses her words and cunningly makes the women think they have a choice in matters. Lydia even alters the gender implications of her speech by changing "taskmaster" to "taskmistress." She really believes she's in control—Gilead survives and thrives because of this exact manipulation of thought and speech.
While this book is seen as a valuable piece of literature by many, it is also seen as having an openly racist theme and main character, Huck Finn.	Of course, the naked white girl does not entice them, but rather the freedom she represents. She is what the white gentry have that the young blacks do not; she is theirs to do with as they please; to indulge, to enjoy, to flaunt. "All the while the blonde continued dancing, smiling faintly at the big shots who watched her with fascination, and faintly smiling at [the blacks'] fear" (20). Freedom is but a commodity for the whites and an unbearable tease for the blacks.

NOTE: The weak examples are from papers that received the lowest possible scores for use of the appearance/reality topos and that faculty raters gave overall low ratings; the strong examples are from papers that received the highest possible scores for use of the appearance/reality topos and that faculty raters gave overall high ratings. In the case of these sample passages, the weak examples are from final papers written by students who experienced traditional WAL pedagogies, and the strong examples are from papers written by students who experienced explicit instruction in the special topoi. While weak and strong examples of this topos appear in papers written by students from both experimental and control sections of the course, strong examples appeared more frequently in papers written by students from experimental sections.

The difference between the two group's uses of the paradigm topos is particularly revealing. Although several of the control sections based their pedagogies heavily in the "theory overview" approach, assigning critical-theory anthologies that modeled application of various theoretical frameworks, only one student from a control section used the paradigm topos—and this student's use of the strategy was perceived as very poor. By contrast, 35 percent of the experimental papers used the paradigm topos. This dramatic difference would seem to throw into question the stress A. Freedman (1993a) and others placed on mere exposure to genre models and lend further support to Charney and Carlson's (1995) finding that effective writing strategies are better supported when explicit guidance accompanies the use of models.

Like Mathison (1996), who found that four sociology professors preferred students' critiques that more closely followed the conventions of their discipline, our five literature professor raters preferred the essays by students whose use of the special topoi marked their arguments as belonging in this field. They generally preferred papers that evidenced the special topoi, whether written by students who experienced explicit instruction in their use or not. The professors gave significantly higher ratings to those papers by writers who used four or more of the special topoi than by those who used between zero and three topoi. That the explicit special topoi instruction appears to have prompted more student writers to effectively use more topoi in their analyses would seem to provide strong support, then, for offering explicit instruction in disciplinary topoi to help students compose the disciplinary genres expected of them.

However, we uncovered some evidence to support A. Freedman (1993a) and others' concerns that instruction in conventions can lead to ineffective rhetoric. For instance, one student made glaringly inappropriate use of these conventions by writing "when taking into consideration all of the other topoi that exists in Margaret Atwood's *The Handmaid's Tale*" and "deconstruction of the [. . .] appearance reality in Atwood's novel, shows the negative aspects and ineffectiveness of the feminist movement prior to the 1980s." By explicitly *naming* the topoi and claiming that they exist in the novel (rather than *using* them to analyze the novel), she produced phrasings that would never appear in the kind of professional discourse that was the target for this course. While these passages could be seen as unsurprising missteps in the process of mastering a difficult level of professional discourse, it also shows how explicit instruction in conventions may lead to flawed application and new forms of error. It is possible that this student was confused because the terms traditionally explicitly imparted in introductory literature courses—such as "plot" and "setting"—describe literary effects rather than name strategies that critics employ. Such glaring missteps, however, were rare in the student papers we collected. And as Lingard and Haber (2002) demonstrated, it is possible for students to intuit equally faulty understandings of genre from traditional, tacit instruction (p. 167).

Though admittedly a blunt instrument for assessing their perceptions, our questionnaire indicated that students in experimental and control sections felt about equally strongly that their experience in WAL allowed them to freely express themselves and explore their intellectual and emotional reactions to the literature they read—few statistically significant distinctions could be made between the two groups' responses. Students in the experimental sections indicated levels of enjoyment, personal engagement, and interest with the literature they were reading similar to the students in the control sections. Whenever significant differences between the responses of the two groups were found, students in the experimental sections reported higher levels of emotional and intellectual engagement with the texts. Overall, these findings suggest that instruction in disciplinary conventions did not sap students' enjoyment of literature or inhibit their expression of their responses to it any more or less than traditional literary pedagogies. I probe further into their perceptions of these pedagogies during the interviews I discuss in chapter 5.

A Nonreductive Look at Explicit Genre Instruction

My experience implementing and supporting other instructors' implementation of pedagogical practices that seek to support students' conscious acquisition of genre knowledge has led me to question the reductive descriptions of explicit genre instruction that critics appear to use as a straw man. In our experimental curriculum, *discourse conventions* did not refer to a rigid set of templates for writing but to inventional strategies for locating disciplinarily appropriate arguments that are "flexible, not static" (Herrington & Curtis, 2000, p. 389). Similarly, *explicit instruction* did not simply mean listing a set of conventional "rules" but included a range of pedagogical strategies to help students abstract and apply the special topoi of literary analysis. Instructors treated the topoi less as limitations on what could be argued and more as heuristics for opening a text up and considering different interpretive possibilities. "To learn genre" in the classical sense that we sought to revive "was to learn its options; it was not to learn a fixed algorithm" (Fahnestock, 1993, p. 268).

Instructors involved in teaching the experimental sections in our study integrated the special topoi into their courses in many ways. Drawing on the conclusions of Russell's (2001) synthesis of WID research, we sought to use the special topoi to clarify the motivations, identities, tools, and processes of writing in literary studies. Instructors wove explicit references to the special topoi into peer-review guidelines and grading criteria. They asked students to read examples of student writing and published criticism and analyze them for their use of the topoi. They assigned critical theory and modeled for students how to use this theory in service of the paradigm topos. They referred explicitly to the topoi in their written comments on student work and in student conferences. Perhaps most important of all, they demonstrated how to use the special topoi as tools for invention in class brainstorming sessions and in nearly all discussions of literary texts. For instance, an instructor frequently began class discussion of a text by asking students to use the ubiquity topos to note patterns in a text, having students share these patterns with one another, and then brainstorming together as a class ways to use the appearance/reality topos to move from these observations to interpretations. This instruction might be continued in the revision stage of writing by suggesting that the appearance/reality topos used in the last paragraph of a draft be made more central, that the writer make better use of the ubiquity topos to find unexpected examples of a pattern, or that the writer locate additional sources to support use of the context topos.

The explicitness of the topoi also facilitated instructors' efforts to push students to take what often appeared to students to be risks and apply topoi in ways consistent with the disciplinary discourse community's value of complexity and irreducibility. For instance, instructors would ask students to locate evidence to contradict their interpretive claims previously developed using the ubiquity topos and take this counterevidence into account in their interpretations, and they encouraged students to reflect critically on the limitations of theoretical texts otherwise used productively in applications of the paradigm topos and to craft arguments that develop the theory as well as their interpretation. While these comments might seem like advice that any literature instructor might give, the special topoi provided a rationale—a warrant—for why these changes would result in a more persuasive literary analysis, an aspect of explicit instruction in discourse conventions that Herrington and Curtis's (2000) longitudinal research found to be illuminating for college students yet rarely provided by instructors. Instructors first introduced the special topoi as conventions literary scholars share as members of a discourse community, a concept introduced early in the course when instructors invited students to reflect on the practices of discourse communities to which they already belong, and explored and developed further throughout the semester. A further key distinction is that the experimental curriculum gave consistent labels to this kind of advice, which students heard and used repeatedly throughout the semester as they worked on different writing assignments and read model texts.[2]

While many of our experimental pedagogical practices incorporated explicit use of special topoi into widely used elements of writing pedagogy, one innovative way we sought to make explicit and available for instruction disciplinary inventional strategies was through the pedagogical use of think-aloud protocols. Wolfe (2003) described how she used tape recordings of her own process of analyzing literary texts while "thinking aloud" or verbalizing all she could of her thought process in real time, rather than retrospectively (which tends to lead to omissions and a narrative that generally "tidies up" the process). We have since collected and transcribed think-aloud protocols of other literary scholars reading and beginning to write, and Warren's (2006) study of literary scholars using the special topoi provides still more think-aloud excerpts that can be used for this pedagogical purpose. We have asked students to identify the special topoi they see these experts using, which we believe further helps to cement their understanding of them, just as it also illustrates how the topoi can be flexibly used in different ways. But furthermore, observing established experts stumble in their understanding of a text, revise their initial impressions, and use the special topoi to test out and possibly abandon multiple interpretations appears to help lessen students' anxiety and support a classroom environment that values process and experimentation over masterly displays of expertise. For many, it appears to productively challenge their preconceived notion of "expertise."[3]

Pedagogical techniques such as think-aloud protocols may, however, blur distinctions between "explicit teaching" classrooms and "situated learning" classrooms, a consequence that I believe provides a more realistic image of what advocates of explicit instruction in genre have in mind. Think-aloud protocols of experts reading and writing may bring to the writing classroom the kinds of observation of expert practice that situated learning advocates say is crucial for an apprentice to gain entry into a community of practice. But even without such a technique, conferencing, extensive written feedback on drafts, workshops, and collaborative brainstorming may provide occasions "in the company of a competent practitioner" (p. 200) for the kinds of "judgments-in-context" that Macbeth (2006) claims are necessary for explicit instruction in academic writing to be effective.

In fact, while in our shared concern for students' acquisition of useful genre knowledge we may place opposing emphases on either "explicit teaching" or "situated learning," I suspect that there exists more common ground than first meets the eye in the actual classroom practices endorsed by opponents in the explicit-instruction debates. For instance, A. Freedman (1993a) granted a role for explicit teaching in serving to heighten the genre awareness of those who have already tacitly acquired the rhetorical procedural knowledge necessary for competent composition with in a genre. Such "meta-awareness," she claimed, is "empowering, potentially freeing the writer from the assumptions, interpretations, and ideologies that have been tacitly at play" because it "allows for the possibility of dissent and of informed choice" (p. 237). Bazerman (1992), in an argument advocating for explicit instruction in disciplinary genres, similarly claimed that because "explicit teaching of discourse holds what is taught up for inspection," it offers students the "means to rethink the ends of the discourse and offers a wide array of means to carry the discourse in new directions" (pp. 64–65). A. Freedman (1993a) claimed this meta-awareness can only be reached after one has tacitly acquired the formal and procedural knowledge necessary for a writer to produce rhetorically competent discourse in a genre. Yet, because her understanding of competence is lax enough to include merely "passing" performances, perhaps the level of familiarity with the target genre may be rather minimal before explicit instruction proves useful in raising students' awareness.

Thus, another way of describing the objectives of our study's experimental curriculum would be to say that we sought to raise students' nascent awareness of the genre of literary analysis. Since most entering college students have previously experienced writing some form of literary analysis, however different from what is expected of them in college, our attempt to bring to light special topoi conventional to this genre may resemble A. Freedman's (1993a) description of "reflexive consciousness" raising. A. Freedman seemed primarily concerned that explicit instruction would be most ill-advised in situations where novice writers have never before encountered or practiced the target genre, such as might be the case if a first-year composition class was to tackle genres engineers use in their workplaces. While it is questionable just how widespread such cases may routinely be, WID research leads me to suspect that the situation A. Freedman described in the law class she studied represents more typical practices of rhetorical instruction in disciplinary courses. If the law course's assignment instructions and oral discourse were sufficient to support students' acquisition of competent genre knowledge in A. Freedman's sense, then presumably explicit instruction to productively raise their meta-awareness of genre could follow shortly after, even for genres with which students have less previous experience than literary analysis. While A. Freedman treated teaching for genre acquisition as a "separate issue" (p. 237) from teaching for genre awareness,[4] in actual efforts to explicitly impart rhetorical procedural knowledge it may be difficult to disentangle the two. One issue I believe both sides of the debate can agree upon is the need for students to gain repeated experience composing in the target genre in order to fully attain genre knowledge. It is hard to imagine the techniques of explicit instruction making any impact—or having much purpose as coaching—if students are not concurrently involved in the processes of composing. Thus, I doubt few could disagree with A. Freedman's assertion that "full genre knowledge (in all its subtlety and complexity) only becomes available *as a result of having written*" (p. 236, emphasis in original).

Furthermore, it is unclear whether the special topoi of literary analysis we focused on imparting match the types of genre conventions critics of explicit instruction like A. Freedman (1993a) and Spellmeyer (1989) have in mind as potentially inhibitive of either more accurate genre knowledge or creativity and expression. Despite their differences, A. Freedman and Spellmeyer seem to agree that problematic genre conventions are primarily formal features. For instance, A. Freedman (1993b) distinguished between explicit instruction in "procedural strategies," which she grants may be profitable, and "the explica-tion of features or rules characterizing the crafted product" (p. 274), which is the target of her objection. Among the procedural strategies that may be beneficial to explicitly teach, she included "heuristic or invention strategies" (1993a, p. 237). Because it appears A. Freedman may see these procedural strategies as broadly applicable in any writing context—she gave the example of a teacher advising students to use a word processor's cut-and-paste applica-tion to revise a text's organization (1993a, p. 237; 1993b, p. 274)—rather than as specifically tied to certain genres, it is unclear whether special topoi would be included among the abstractions she admitted in the category of invention strategies suitable for explicit instruction. Regardless, analyses of experts' use of special topoi complicate A. Freedman's sharp distinction between process and product. Special topoi function as both textual features that characterize a specific genre, as my analysis in chapter 1 and the work of Fahnestock and Secor (1991) show, and as inventional strategies experts wield when composing, as Warren's (2006) think-aloud protocols demonstrate. I suspect that beyond some general composing strategies, such as the advice on using a technological tool to support revising organization that A. Freedman specified, invention strategies quickly become tied to specific contexts, perhaps especially disciplinary contexts where the invention of new knowledge is crucial. A. Freedman (1993a) appeared to acknowledge this in her observation that the writing by law students she studied marked itself as appropriately distinctive of the discipline by enacting "certain modes of reasoning which privileged some warrants, not others" (pp. 228–29), yet she does not explore how these warrants might function in the classical sense as inventional strategies tied to specific contexts and genres that can be explicitly taught. Rather, by reducing understandings of "convention" to purely formal textual features, she and other detractors of explicit instruction in genre downplay both the socially situated nature of these privileged modes of reasoning and the dynamic possibilities for cognitive apprenticeship in classrooms.

Instructors' Reactions to Teaching the Topoi

Though opportunities for repeated practice in writing literary analyses were integral to both the experimental and control curricula we studied, "turning up the volume" on the genre's special topoi produced noticeable effects. It kept the course consistently focused on procedural knowledge, perhaps at the expense of domain knowledge. As one of our control instructors explained to us, "You teach *writing* about literature, and I teach writing about *literature*." The instructors who implemented the experimental curriculum perceived this shift in emphasis as well. When I interviewed them during the course of our study (in November 2006 and January 2007), they described their difficulties in overcoming the pull of the familiar: their tendencies to revert to leading discussions of literary texts in ways that only implicitly guide students to use the special topoi because this is how they previously taught the course and because this was their own experience of literary instruction as students.

Because of their previous experience with traditional literature instruction, these experimental instructors could comment on the differences they perceived explicit instruction of the special topoi of literary analysis to bring. While not all reacted favorably to the differences they perceived (see chapter 6 for a thorough discussion of resistances one encountered), most plan to continue to weave explicit instruction of disciplinary topoi into future literature courses. Several shared their perceptions on how emphasizing teaching the special topoi differs from emphasizing "the terms." Though at first glance explicitly teaching the special topoi may simply appear to replace one list of terms with another, these instructors found a significant difference to be the ends to which each list was used. They contrasted the "generative" capacity of the special topoi to the

> focus on "theme" and "is this character flat/round." So, at the end of the day, the character's flat, the character's round, so what? [. . .] When you go to construct an analysis, so you think that Matilda's character in "The Necklace" was flat, how does that help you get to constructing an argument that is interesting or useful? And I think this [the topoi approach], sort of, more globally, is more helpful.

Another of their criticisms of "the terms" approach was that the emphasis placed on memorizing the definitions of an amorphous list of literary vocabulary may be misdirected because the specific terms students need to know at any given moment vary greatly depending upon the specific texts and disciplinary subfields they are studying. For one course to fully prepare for all such possible contingencies seems unrealistic. One experimental professor's admission that she often has to "look up" the definitions of some literary terms suggests that one's area of specialization within the discipline may greatly influence the specific literary terms one has at the tip of one's tongue. This realization led her to suggest that appropriate and relevant terms should be taught in all literature courses when they emerge as germane. This suggestion would seem to be in line with A. Freedman's (1993a) emphasis on the importance of learning genre features in temporal proximity to authentic opportunities to rehearse using them.

This professor was equally concerned about the primary emphasis on discussion in traditional approaches to WAL, especially with attempts to impart the "notice what stands out to you" strategy that the former WAL students I spoke with also described (see chapter 5). She felt this strategy, in contrast to the special topoi, left students with a flimsy "scaffold" to carry with them into their attempts to write on other literary texts:

But my concern, especially after the first half of that semester [her first semester teaching WAL] was that once students left a particular assignment [. . .] after we talked about it [a literary text] in class, and they got a sense of "Oh, these are the major themes, these are some of the ideas that comes out of this text, oh, now I can write a paper," they would move on and not be able to sort of reconstruct any of that when they went to the next paper. . . . One of my colleagues said, "Oh, you know, what I do is, you know, Try this: I go in and say how does this text make you feel, how do you respond to it?" . . . Which is nice, and that's a great conversation starter, but they can't sort of literally take that with them to the next text. It's as if they're starting all over. They had no scaffold. And so, the topoi, I feel, gives them some scaffold. It gives them some tools to take with them.

Because it posed a significant shift in teaching technique for them, the transition to explicitly teaching special topoi prompted a good deal of reflection on traditional practices of literary pedagogy among our study's instructors. In their experience, making the special topoi of literary analysis explicit in their teaching practice enabled them to work with students on developing a set of generative, transferrable "tools" for writing in this discipline.

Transforming Precept into Practice

Although our in situ quasi-experiment indicates that explicit instruction in the special topoi can lead some students to write in more disciplinarily appropriate ways than they would have without it, we have a much harder time determining what students do with this explicit instruction. In the next chapter, I present findings from my interviews with students conducted in the years after the completion of our study during which I asked them to reflect on their experience of this instruction and what, if any, use they found for it as they continued to work towards completing the requirements of the English major. While illuminating in many regards, these student reflections are limited in their subjective ability to recount how—or if—students transform the precepts of explicit instruction into applied writing practices.

In an attempt to shed some light on this important and mysterious transformation process, we recruited some study participants at the conclusion of their semester in WAL from both experimental and control sections to perform a think-aloud protocol as they read a short story unfamiliar to them (Leslie Marmon Silko's "Man to Send Rain Clouds") and began to compose a short analysis of it. Geisler (1994) made a persuasive case that think-aloud protocols have the potential to reveal a great deal about sociocognitive writing activities, but as Smith (1992) discussed, they are troublesome tools for assessing the impacts of different instructional techniques. Nonetheless, we hoped a pilot study of a few such protocols might suggest where we ought to be looking to see the ways in which explicit instruction in embedded genre conventions affected students' writing practices in that genre.

As expected, the transcripts of all of the protocols we conducted with student volunteers, regardless of whether they experienced an experimental or control section of WAL, evidence of use of at least one or two of the special topoi. However, protocols and reflective interviews conducted immediately after the protocols tantalizingly indicate that some students who just experienced a semester of explicit instruction in the special topoi made conscious efforts to apply this instruction.

For instance, while reviewing what he had just drafted, one student made explicit reference to the label for a topos his WAL class used: "I've noticed that the things that I saw, read on the surface, these are a little bit of appearance and reality." During his reflective interview, he explained how he decided what to write about using the distinction between surface and depth that his WAL instructor had used to explain the appearance/reality topos as well as the distinction between literary analysis and other genres that his instructor also used:

> It comes down to knowing that I had to write something and trying to find something there that I didn't think was right on the surface, that I could maybe make something out of that people, somebody might find interesting to read. Umm, someone who had read the story and wanted an interpretation of it maybe. Or, ahh, not so much a book report or summarization but something that was below the surface.

Additionally, he also explicitly named the context topos to explain his decision to read first the biographical information about the author that prefaced the story. And although he didn't explicitly name the ubiquity topos, he described his search for patterns in terms that his instructor used to encourage him to use the ubiquity topos, explaining that he sought to find "evidence that isn't immediately obvious." More than many others with whom we conducted think-aloud protocols, he exhibited a willingness to playfully pursue multiple leads in his quest for interpretations: he underlined terms in the text related to color, he noted terms and concepts he would like to research, and he connected images from disparate parts of the story into an interpretation that provided a paradoxical explanation for one of the story's ambiguities. In the excerpt below from his think-aloud-protocol transcript, we can see him employ all of these strategies. He vocalized this section of the transcript as he approached the end of his first reading of the short story. Italics indicate text of the story the student read aloud; underlining indicates text the student wrote down as well as spoke aloud. In this segment of the transcript, the student does not read linearly from the short story but rather reads aloud passages from throughout the text of the story and a prefatory author biographical note.

"For a Christian burial it was necessary." His voice was distant and Leon thought that his blue eyes looked tired. So he is trying and trying and trying to convert these Indians and just not getting any good, not doing any good so. . . . The priest is a failure to convert Indians to Christianity. Here in the desert . . . umm, I really need to look up "arroyo." . . . I think that's like a canyon or. . . . a *cottonwood tree.* . . . I'm not sure what a cottonwood tree is, if it needs a lot of water, if this is a, in this desert, I don't have the same feeling of desert as you see in the movies. I don't see tumbleweeds. They want rain so they've had some drought and they need the rain. They're shepherds themselves—that's an interesting parallel. Taking care of sheep and ahh, the priest is a Christian and there's something about a lamb on a door—*the old carved door with its symbols of the Lamb.* Maybe they're, maybe I could ahh talk about their, their old or their religion is older, they really are shepherds, they really, let's see. . . . [Pause] . . . *gray feather,* the colored gray feather, humm. That's pretty interesting, I like that. Let's see what I can make of that. Didn't get that right away myself so, the fact that they're umm shepherds and that, that imagery with Christianity and the carved door with the symbols of the Lamb so I wonder, I wonder if the priest is trying to convert them to something that they know more about than he does. Umm, the imagery of Christianity is the Good Shepherd. There's really not much talk about the sheep, it's just that that's what they do. They were just out to the sheep camp where they found him. Umm, I'm not sure what kind of Indians these people are. Now *the author,* it says, *mixed American history, Christian theology, Southwestern Indian myth, and botany to create an extravagant family chronicle*—that was in her ahh, her second novel, *Gardens in the Dunes.* This is a little like that, it looks like. Umm, because we have Christian theology being mixed with Southwestern Indian myth.

This thought process led him to compose an opening for his draft that begins to develop his essay's application of the paradox and social justice topoi:

> Father Paul, a missionary, is guilty of the sin of all missionaries—he is unable to fully comprehend and respect the culture & beliefs of the society he is trying to convert. As a Christian, his desire is to be a shepherd, but the people he wants as his flock are themselves shepherds already.

After writing these sentences, he paused to evaluate them, "Both [sentences] are arguments, not too terribly bad." In contrast, although there were some stellar think-aloud performances among students from control sections, other students who experienced traditional WAL pedagogies tended to plow through reading the story, seldom pausing to try out emerging interpretations or use any other topoi beyond appearance/reality and ubiquity, and then summarize the story in their essay.

This preliminary evidence of a student's conscious application of topological instruction suggests that he may be in the process of transforming explicit guidance into what Flower (1989) called an "automated process"—a process at first learned consciously that drops out of awareness with experience. However, Flower pointed to research indicating that a distinguishing characteristic of "expert" writers is their tendency to consciously articulate and actively employ strategies for solving rhetorical problems. In contrast, "novice" writers appear to rely more heavily on tacit and automated processes, making fewer conscious choices in their writing. By naming and deploying a cluster of strategies, some of our students who experienced explicit topological instruction may be more quickly moving to this "active awareness" level of rhetorical expertise, leapfrogging to some degree the traditional long-term immersion and tacit absorption that an expert presumably reflects upon to develop active awareness of strategies for rhetorical problem solving.

Conclusion

It is important to question whether speeding up the process of acquiring disciplinary expertise is desirable. Beyond the recurrently difficult question about whether disciplinary enculturation should be a goal of instruction, we should ask when ideally, in terms of students' cognitive and social development, such genre awareness should be explicitly fostered. However, it seems clear that expectations for college student writing are shaped by disciplinary topoi even in their introductory coursework, as can be seen even in A. Freedman's (1993a) findings from the introductory law class she studied. Several studies also now point to the potential for explicit instruction to neutralize some of the advantage that already-privileged students bring to college classrooms by naming, sharing, and developing the tacit knowledge these students possess. Supporting college instructors' awareness and application of disciplinary topoi in their pedagogy seems a crucial next step for WID.

In literary studies, this next step seems primed by professors themselves who are hungry for methods to clarify and impart what they know to be powerful tools of analysis and argument. Although many literature professors resist seeing their pedagogical practices as supporting disciplinary enculturation (see chapter 2), several literary scholars have called for their colleagues to overcome this resistance and seek to more conscientiously impart the interpretive and argumentative strategies that distinguish good work in their field (Graff, 1992, 2003; Scholes, 1985, 1998; Showalter, 2003; Shumway, 1992). For instance, Shumway (1992) critiqued literary scholars' propensity for tacit instruction in procedural knowledge because it unfairly favors seemingly "natural" students from socially privileged backgrounds: "More than any other academic ideology, humanism has valued the ease and grace of expression that come from early exposure to a particular discursive practice. . . . We need to break down our prejudice in favor of the 'natural' student and tell students how they can learn to learn this stuff" (p. 106).[5]

WAC and WID seem best poised to support instructors' efforts to break down this "prejudice" and reconfigure traditional undergraduate education to include instruction in rhetorical procedural knowledge. Lave and Wenger (1991) described such efforts to apprentice learners in the "know how" of the disciplines as typically deferred until graduate school, prompting situated learning advocates to see undergraduate writing as exercises in institutional disciplining rather than as novice attempts at participation in the disciplines. But WAC and WID from their inception have held out an enticing promise for change, suggesting we need not accept the status quo "banking concept" model of education Freire (1993) potently critiqued. Geisler (1994) similarly challenged the received view that it is "natural" to learn a discipline's domain knowledge before its rhetorical procedural knowledge by exposing the links between this practice and the maintenance of unequal power dynamics within society. Spellmeyer (1996) likewise critiqued traditional approaches to introductory disciplinary instruction focused on content rather than procedural knowledge as best suited to "persuade another generation of nonspecialists that [a] subject should be left to those who know it best" (p. 42). However, whereas Spellmeyer (1996) and "postdisciplinarity" advocates seek to explore possibilities for "uncoercive" and "equitable" learning outside the confines of the disciplines (p. 44), WID advocates can be seen taking this shared point of critique as provocation for changing disciplinary enculturation practices. Geisler (1994), for instance, invited us to conceive "of expertise in academic literacy as the ability to negotiate among multiple worlds of discourse" (p. 240), a shift in the understanding of expertise with implications not only for what instructors might set as goals for their students but also for how instructors themselves may need to develop new expertise at communicating with students. WAC and WID programs seem uniquely positioned to address both these needs, though as I discuss in chapter 6, they also face daunting obstacles.

Yet, such a profound shift in educational practice may yield unforeseen consequences. While our study found that explicit instruction in disciplinary topoi generally supports students' acquisition of useful genre knowledge, it did have rare unintended effects, such as occasional students' misapplications of topological instruction generating new forms of genre error. A. Freedman's (1993a) warning coupled with our study's drawing attention to this possibility may help instructors and WID proponents develop methods for productively handling new forms of error. Elimination of all error may not be possible, or the point, of instruction in procedural knowledge where some degree of coaching through experiences of trial and error may be necessary. Instead, perhaps approaches to genre instruction may be productively compared on the basis of the resources they provide students to recognize and address errors themselves.

Likewise, the impact of making disciplinary special topoi explicit on evaluation practices deserves further research. A. Freedman (1993b) noted that "because one goal of school is to rank students, it is not clear how any kind of teaching can ensure that all students get high grades" (p. 281). Pedagogies that make explicit procedural knowledge may over time lead to reshaping the criteria by which students are so ranked, but these revised criteria need not ultimately reflect the goals of social equity that first motivated the change in teaching. Sternberg (1999) acknowledged this possibility when he claimed that the tacit knowledge that is valued in a field will, once made explicit, cease to be important in distinguishing the more and less successful among individuals in that field and that, like quicksilver, knowledge that still remains tacit will take "its place as an important source of individual differences" (p. 232). Suggesting this possibility, one of the experimental instructors in our study described the special topoi curriculum as enabling her to grade student work with greater rigor now that she could more easily discern which student essays "really weren't anywhere on the mark." The apparent contradiction in this instructor's satisfaction in increasing rigor in her classroom while she sought to reduce gaps in the relevant tacit knowledge her students possessed may point to ways in which making special topoi explicit has the potential to promote a more "level playing field" without diminishing challenges that stretch all students' rhetorical skills. Russell's (1995) stress on the social web of shared understandings necessary for rigor to have meaning—"rigor is the result of a history of using tools in certain ways for common goals, a tradition of shared expectations" (p. 64)—suggests that tools like topoi may help her and other instructors uphold standards while more clearly communicating them.

5

"Other Professors, They Assume You Already Know This Stuff": Student Views of Disciplinary Enculturation and Explicating Conventions

The study described in the previous chapter provides compelling evidence that explicit instruction in a discipline's special topoi can help students learn to write in ways that established members of the discipline are more likely to recognize as "good writing." However, this finding does not address concerns like Spellmeyer's (1989) that WID instruction in disciplinary conventions places inordinate emphasis on conformity and inhibits students' creativity and voice. Spellmeyer sees in WID pedagogies a "tacit demand for 'submission'" (p. 266) and an insistence that students "earn" the "right to speak" through "the effacement of subjectivity" (p. 265). Whereas WID proponents "typically invoke the ethos of 'empowerment'" to justify teaching discourse conventions, Spellmeyer sees instead a pedagogy of "pragmatic accommodation" (p. 267) with effects that belie WID proponents' best intentions. According to Spellmeyer, typical instruction in disciplinary conventions leaves "no place" for "originality," asks students "to suppress feelings and beliefs for the sake of public approval" (p. 267), discourages "any sense of inquiry as conversation" (p. 271) and "thinking that might culminate in necessary social change" (p. 269), and generally encourages "passivity" (p. 272) and "an absence of personal commitment in the creation of a text" (p. 269).

As she neared graduation, two years after she completed a writing about literature (WAL) course in which her instructor sought to explicitly impart procedural knowledge for using special topoi of literary analysis, Eve[1] indicated that she sees validity in WID's claims for the empowering potential of instruction in disciplinary rhetorics. She recommended that professors seek to make their expertise more available to students even as she recognized that many may lack a ready awareness and vocabulary necessary for doing so:

EVE: The professors. . . . it seems like they're looking for a level that's so high, that if a student has never done it before, they don't get it. And you're [professors] going to have to really explain that to them [students], and just help them to understand where you're coming from. And you could probably bring in something that you've written, like something that you wrote early on, and then something you wrote later, and say, "OK, this is what got published, and this is what didn't. And this is why." That might be helpful for a student to understand what the professor is really trying to do with their class.

LW: That's an interesting idea. It makes me want to ask you a question about how do you think the professors learned how to write in their ways, in what ways they internalized these ideas about writing?

EVE: I bet the professors didn't have these titles [gestures to the list of special topoi on the table before us] when they were going through school.

LW: How did they learn how to do it then, do you think?

EVE: They were just taught by other people, without these names, and they were taught to do that. And that may be why some of them achieved higher than others because they didn't have names. And the other people, who didn't achieve, maybe needed these names, and the professors learned by trial and error.

Eve speculates that implicit instruction in disciplinary rhetorical practices places at an advantage those students more adept at learning on their own "by trial and error," such as the students Eve suspects her professors once were. She also suggests that students' attempts to infer where these professors' expectations for student writing are "coming from" may incline them to spend greater efforts struggling to pragmatically accommodate and conform than on developing original, personally committed inquiries.

A survey administered as part of the study described in the previous chapter indicated that students who experienced an experimental explicit special-topoi curriculum felt as free and encouraged to express themselves or connect personally with the literature they read as those students who experienced traditional WAL curricula. Yet, such a blunt instrument for assessing affect cannot adequately address the concerns Spellmeyer articulated. In order to learn more about students' perspectives and experiences with the experimental and traditional WAL curricula they experienced as part of our study, I interviewed a subsample of participants twice over two years. Interviews allowed me to learn more about students' subsequent experiences with writing in their major. Further, I was able to share with them findings from the study in which they participated and seek their input in interpreting them. From students who experienced the experimental special-topoi curriculum, I was also interested to determine if they retained and transferred this knowledge to appropriate new settings.

Interview Procedures

"Transfer of learning" has become a provocative and thorny issue in composition research. Determining what, if anything, students go on to apply in other contexts from what they learned in a writing course has proven notoriously difficult (Ackerman, 1993). Recent studies of this issue, especially as it relates to first-year writing instruction, have placed greater value on students' reflective self-reports via surveys and interviews (James, 2008; Thaiss & Zawacki, 2006). This method seems well suited for assessing the impact of explicit rhetorical instruction because it solicits what individuals can consciously verbalize and recall about their learning. Similarly, longitudinal studies have contributed to our understanding of the role writing instruction plays in students' development as writers over their college years, especially as they encounter and wrestle with the increasingly specialized rhetorical practices of their chosen majors (Beaufort, 2007; Carroll, 2002; Haas, 1994; Herrington & Curtis, 2000; Sternglass, 1997).

Borrowing methodologically from these studies, in this chapter I present findings from eighteen, hour-long interviews I conducted with twelve English majors, seven who had experienced the experimental special-topoi curriculum as taught by three different instructors (described in chapter 4) and five who experienced traditional WAL pedagogies (described in chapter 2) as taught by four different instructors. Six of these students (four from experimental sections of WAL and two from control sections) I interviewed twice over the course of two years, once during their junior year (a year after they completed WAL) and again during their senior year.[2] These interviews were our only interactions. Participants knew me as a researcher from another institution interested in techniques for improving learning and teaching writing about literature. As described in greater depth in the analysis below, I asked participants to describe their general methods of writing literary analyses, advice they would give to beginning English majors on writing such papers, and their experiences writing in this genre before coming to college. I asked several questions about what they learned in WAL, what, if anything, they were continuing to apply in their other courses, and if there were any elements of instruction that conflicted with their later experiences writing in their major. I also inquired about their willingness to challenge professors' viewpoints in their writing and break with established conventions. I asked students to bring to each interview a recent paper written for an English course that they felt was representative of the kind of work they have been asked to do as an English major since taking WAL. Several of my questions explored decisions they made in writing these papers, and with their permission I collected and later rhetorically analyzed these papers. As I explain below, during the second interviews I sought to prompt the experimental students' recall of the special topoi and control students' impressions of the special topoi. I concluded the second interviews by asking participants for their interpretation of some of the key findings of the study they participated in (see chapter 4) and for their take on the debate among compositionists on the ethical issues at stake in explicitly teaching genre conventions such as the special topoi.

Retention and Transfer of Learning

The interviews suggest some range of retention and transfer of knowledge of the special topoi that the experimental curriculum sought to impart. During the first interviews, conducted one year after students had taken WAL, some of the six experimental students readily used the labels for the special topoi when describing for me how they now approach writing a literary analysis or what they learned about this process in WAL. Other experimental students did not use the labels at all, though they described some of the strategies these labels represent (as did some of the control students). There was some range of unprompted recollection: one student, Eric, named five of the special topoi; two students described only two of the special topoi and mentioned none by name.

Some students who experienced the experimental curriculum may have consciously avoided using the names of the special topoi with me, an English professor whom they had just met, because they likely had the experience of moving on to other college English courses and never hearing these labels again. They may understandably, and not incorrectly, have avoided using the names of the special topoi in other contexts after inferring that this was a terminology applied only in their WAL section. Seeking a more direct way to ascertain if students recollected the special topoi, I presented the experimental students with a list of the names of the seven special topoi at the end of the second round of interviews and asked if they could explain or define any of them that looked familiar.

Four students who completed experimental sections of WAL two years earlier recalled the special topoi remarkably well: two students (Ed and Eric) readily defined them all, one student (Eve) defined six out of seven (all but social justice), and another (Emma) correctly defined three (appearance/reality, social justice, and paradox) and confused the "ubiquity" name with the "context" strategy. Ed's definitions of the special topoi are in table 5.1. A student who took an experimental section of WAL three years earlier (Eileen) correctly defined appearance/reality and confused paradigm for paradox, but otherwise the vagueness of her explanations supported her own assessment that although she had heard the terms before, she no longer recalled their meaning.

Performing perhaps a more relevant indication of their retention and transfer of rhetorical knowledge, several students accurately pointed to examples of their use of these strategies in the papers they brought with them. Not only did they use the special topoi in their papers for more advanced English courses but they also readily *recognized* that they applied these strategies, suggesting the kind of active awareness Flower (1989) claims is characteristic of writing expertise. For instance, my rhetorical analysis of Ed's paper on *The Passion of SS. Perpetua and Felicitas* fully supports his own analysis of it:

> I definitely used context. I talk about the life of St. Perpetua's during Roman times. She was imprisoned and asked to fight in the coliseum, and so I just talked about the anti-Christian sentiment that was growing and how she kind of overcomes that and becomes something greater, which also relates to surface/depth. And I also used paradigm to see it as a feminist piece. I don't think it was originally written as a feminist work. It was almost like a narrative, so I definitely used that and linked to the conversation, for sure, bringing in what other scholars have considered to be the beginning of the feminist movement and things like that.

Ed begins this paper with the mistaken-critic topos (or "linking to the conversation"),[3] claiming that previous feminist critics have too often overlooked Perpetua and described the earliest beginning of feminism historically centuries later, a claim he supports with quotations from two scholars. He then

Table 5.1

Definitions of the special topoi Ed provided during our second interview

Topos	Ed's Definition
Appearance/reality (or surface/depth)	It seemed to be the basic one that everybody would use in a paper, as far as seeing what happened on the surface of a novel, like the plot, and seeing how that relates to something greater and how it could be metaphorical or allegorical, and how it says something more than just the words on the page and just the story that's told.
Ubiquity (or everywhereness)	Ubiquity or everywhereness I remember as just being elements of that novel that are seen throughout, almost like recurring motifs or imagery.
Context	Context, which was the actual context in which that novel or piece was written and the historical context or the religious context or any kind of time and space that would affect the overall aim of the novel.
Paradigm	From my understanding, paradigm was like taking a Marxist perspective to a piece or a feminist perspective to a piece and applying the tenets of that ideology or thought, and seeing how it reacts with the piece and how certain aspects would be feminist aspects and how sometimes maybe it would detract from a feminist ideology or how it would support Marxism or how it would support capitalism or put those two together.
Social justice (or social relevance)	Social justice. That, to me, was just what that story gave as a reevaluation of society or breaking down of social norms or accepted policies, such as like civil rights, slave narratives, things that would counteract the given, social accepted policies.
Paradox	I think paradox was the comparison or relation to two different things, bringing in one issue and then kind of placing it with another and seeing how they relate and how it's kind of like a dilemma that one would have to choose between, I guess.
Mistaken critic (or linking to the critical conversation)	To me, that means engaging other peer-review journals, maybe seeing what other people have said, bringing their arguments into their paper and then maybe using that as support or using it to disagree with, just so you're involved with the academic community, in some degree.

NOTE: Alternate topoi names reflect changes to the topoi labels instructors made for pedagogical purposes (see chapter 4).

establishes the feminist paradigmatic lens through which he will look at her text, using this lens with the appearance/reality topos (or "surface/depth strategy") to see suggestions of feminism in the ways Perpetua followed "a subtle tradition of gender equality found in the Bible." To Ed's analysis of his own paper I would only add that his paper's feminist stance also clearly exemplifies the social justice topos.

Recognition of Tacit Knowledge Made Explicit

Students who completed experimental sections of WAL tended to portray the special topoi to me in one of two ways: as knowledge they held tacitly until WAL made it explicit or as knowledge previously foreign that WAL made accessible. To varying degrees, five students claimed that several of the special topoi were familiar to them from previous English courses they completed years before taking WAL, as far back as high school or even earlier. Those named as familiar were routinely the appearance/reality and ubiquity topoi, and some added social justice and context to this list. The image Ed paints of a typical class meeting underscores his awareness of how thoroughly embedded such topoi have been in his experience:

> Context and surface/depth [or appearance/reality] seem to be something that cover generally like in the everyday class setting. The professor usually brings in some kind of historical backing or you read some kind of excerpt that will tell you in what time period, what was going on when this piece was written, and then surface/depth seems to be what is discussed on a regular basis, how the metaphor that you pull apart and examine, and how that narrative operates on another level.

These students felt that WAL simply gave a label to rhetorical strategies they already were familiar with. Several echoed Eve's recollection of her reaction to encountering these special topoi in WAL: "I was like, 'Oh, yeah. I've used this before, but I'd never given it any name.'"

Perhaps not coincidentally, these same five students described their previous encounters with the special topoi in exceptionally advanced high-school coursework such as advanced placement or international baccalaureate English courses. In this regard they appear similar to "Sandy," the highly successful student in Herrington's (1988) case studies of students writing in an introductory literature course whose "strong literature program in high school" (p. 155) appears to have equipped her to enter "the course knowing 'how to read [and write] like an English major'" (p. 156). Though Ed described his experience in WAL as taking the knowledge he obtained in an AP English course into greater "depth," he nonetheless felt that he "had already learned basically how to formulate a literary analysis. [WAL] just taught me the formal names of certain things" like "paradoxes and paradigms and . . . social context—that was something that I had already, like, been taught and used fairly often in writing analysis papers but wasn't necessarily called social context."

Their purported familiarity with these disciplinary special topoi raises several important issues: (1) It calls into question the arguments for seeing undergraduate literary study as "predisciplinary," (2) it appears to have limits that point to crucial distinctive features of expectations for student writing in postsecondary literature courses, and (3) it may nonetheless be enhanced by explicit instruction aimed at raising students "genre awareness" (Devitt, 2004; A. Freedman, 1993a). These students' adamancy that the topoi were familiar to them would seem to challenge critics of instruction in disciplinary conventions who claim that such instruction presents too advanced or too narrowly professional material too soon (Fleming, 2000; Hedley & Parker, 1991; Ohmann, 1996; Trimbur, 1995). They felt this knowledge was recognizable from and expected of them in even their most introductory English coursework. To deny the disciplinary situatedness of such introductory courses would contradict these students' reading of the implicit values embedded in them.

However, though these students adamantly maintained their acquaintance with several key disciplinary topoi, other topoi appear to have been less familiar to them yet pivotal in their transition into college literary study. In particular, the paradigm and mistaken-critic topoi continued to pose challenges for students as they approached graduation, and most students I spoke with pointed to WAL as where they first became aware of these topoi that subsequently proved to be important strategies in their later coursework. Eve's perception of a hierarchy of difficulty in the layout of the list of special topoi we discussed underscores that some of the special topoi were less familiar and particularly challenging. Eve divided the list into two groupings, the first of which contained appearance/reality, ubiquity, and context and signified to her "the lowbrow ones, the easy ones, like anyone should be able to do those." But paradigm, social justice, paradox, and mistaken critic

> get a little harder, and if you can prove you can use these, then you can prove to the professor that you know what you're talking about. You're

a better writer than someone who can only use appearance/reality. . . . But . . . if you can take that mistaken critic, and if you can make that your own and really build on what the previous writer said, the professor is going to grade you higher, I think. . . . If you can reach that higher end, you're proving that yes, you can do theory, and yes, you can write for college-level courses.

Eve's assessment resonates with Scott's (2002) depiction of the significantly different expectations for writing about literature that students in England encounter at the university level. Whereas literature students enter English universities familiar with an approach to literary texts steeped in I. A. Richards's "practical criticism" that in my reading of Scott's analysis support their use of the appearance/reality and paradox topoi, the new disciplinary expectations students encounter in university literary study stem from other theoretical approaches that tacitly demand they apply the paradigm, context, mistaken-critic, and social justice topoi. College-level literature courses in the United States appear to similarly privilege diverse theoretical perspectives beyond only the New Critical. Considering that for Eve (and others), WAL "added the theory portion . . . I'd never really dealt with that," our experimental pedagogy appears to have both made explicit some highly embedded disciplinary topoi that transcend markedly different theoretical approaches in the discipline and explicitly introduced topoi tied to the theoretical approaches encountered at more-advanced levels of literary study.

Additionally, though WAL may have merely made explicit the topoi such as appearance/reality and ubiquity that many students had already been using, the act of making this rhetorical procedural knowledge explicit had beneficial effects according to several students. Greater clarity may have been attained through explication of the sort recommended by Blakeslee (1997) and Lingard and Haber (2002), allowing students to validate, organize, and refine their inferences and avoid some errors in application. Elisa indicated that her WAL professor "laid it out a little bit clearer than previous English professors had." For instance, though she claimed the ubiquity topos was familiar to her, she previously "didn't really know what to do with" the "themes or ideas or even like symbols or objects" that she noticed recurring in a literary text. Thus, explicitly learning the special topoi filled in gaps in her procedural knowledge for enacting the rhetorical strategy.

An Underprepared Student's Experience of Explicit Instruction

As proponents of explicit instruction in disciplinary conventions on social-equity grounds may anticipate, not all students described even appearance/reality and ubiquity as disciplinary topoi familiar from their previous schooling experiences. Eric and Eileen described the special topoi as entirely new concepts they encountered in WAL for the first time. Because I interviewed Eric twice—once in each of the two years following his completion of WAL—I was able to learn more about his initial reactions to and subsequent reflections on his experience of explicit instruction in the special topoi than I was from Eileen, whom I spoke with once three years after she completed WAL.

Eric closely matches the type of student proponents of explicit instruction hope to benefit: students whose previous experiences have not included frequent and full opportunities for reading and writing in different genres (Russell, 1995). Near his completion of his WAL semester, Eric indicated on a questionnaire that he strongly disagreed with this statement: "I think my previous high school and college English and literature courses [prior to WAL] prepared me to write successful arguments about literature or literary analyses." He was the only student I interviewed who had done so; the others had responded to this statement with responses ranging from "neutral" to "strongly agree." In our subsequent interviews, he described his previous educational experiences in English as inadequate, largely preparation for taking multiple-choice exams with little to no essay writing. As he put it, in high school "we read stories, and we just took tests, which taught us to look closely, but we never really wrote about any book or anything." He felt that prior to WAL he had never been asked to "interpret" literary texts before. Despite the initial setbacks he perceived he faced in comparison to his peers, Eric completed his BA with plans to pursue graduate study in English. In comparison to the other students I interviewed who had completed advanced English coursework in high school, Eric seems to have traveled the furthest in his acquisition of disciplinary rhetorical knowledge. He appears to have started WAL with preparation similar to "Kerri," a student from Herrington's (1988) ethnographic analysis of an introductory literature course who "did not have a strong background in English" and "was not confident in her abilities" (p. 158). However, unlike Eric, Kerri ended the semester of her first college literature course still writing largely plot summaries and with "little sense of how to go beyond her initial sense of liking a work or not understanding it" (p. 160). Like many literature instructors, Kerri's literature professor provided predominately implicit instruction in the methods and strategies for reading and writing "like an English major," though Herrington concludes that Kerri "probably needed more guidance as to *how* to go about formulating an issue and working out an interpretation to resolve it" in order to "make an argument of some sort and 'get it right' with herself and other readers" (p. 160). Eric's WAL professor attempted to provide just this type of explicit guidance, particularly by making the special topoi of literary analysis explicit.

Once in his WAL classroom, Eric perceived that others there were better prepared to write in the genre of literary analysis but also that some students shared a level of preparation similar to his: "We got into groups and all discussed our papers anonymously, and you could tell that some people were similar to me. They didn't know a whole lot, and others were ahead." However, his instructor's approach alleviated some of the understandable anxiety this perception caused him. Eric sensed that his WAL instructor anticipated working with students at his level of preparation: "The professor . . . she seemed like she was prepared if we did not know anything, and I felt like no, I didn't know anything. I wasn't equipped to be ahead in the class, but she had to start from scratch with somebody like me."

Eric credits WAL with informing him of much of what he knows about writing in this discipline, and over the course of our interviews, he repeatedly stressed to me how the course felt profoundly enlightening to him. Eric's description of what made the paper he brought to our first interview representative of his writing in English courses after having taken WAL underscores his perception that it represents his acquisition of rhetorical procedural knowledge that others "take for granted":

> I've pulled evidence out of the text in quotes. I mean, a lot of people take it for granted, but coming from where I was coming from before [WAL], this is a prime example of how I've learned to pull quotes out to support what I'm arguing for. And a thesis statement at the beginning. I mean, I'd been told what a thesis statement was, but I'd never had to apply it. Anything that makes any sense in this paper is an example of what I've learned in [WAL], really, because I felt like I was that far behind from high school. And throughout most of the paper, you can see the sentences alternating between an argument and evidence, argument and then evidence. I mean, there's some occasions when it didn't work, but throughout maybe 90 percent of the paper, that's the way things are, and that's an example of [WAL].

Eric had excellent recall of the special topoi during both interviews. He readily used them to describe what he learned in WAL, to explain how he begins to write literary analyses, and to give advice to college students encountering a literary-analysis assignment for the first time. During the first interview, when I did not explicitly prompt students to recall them, Eric referred to more special topoi than any other student (five: appearance/reality, ubiquity, paradigm, social justice, and context). He peppered our conversation with references to the special topoi. For instance, he said his WAL instructor "showed us things like everywhereness [or ubiquity], is what she called it. [. . .] All those things that are everywhere in the text might [indicate] [. . .] the author's trying to say something." She also exemplified "how someone might be trying to express something about social justice. And she showed us ways of using paradigms [. . .] as a lens to see through maybe this short story we're reading." He included several unprompted references to the special topoi during our second interview, too, and when finally shown the list of topoi, he readily defined them all, often with examples from papers he remembers having written or with examples from the paper he brought with him. Though he claims the special topoi were entirely new to him in WAL, he seems to have retained them and continued to find them useful in explaining the reading, interpreting, and writing acts associated with this discipline, perhaps more so than his peers who felt they had encountered many of these strategies previously and only found the labels presented in WAL to be novel.

Eric's reaction to the professional debate regarding the ethical ramifications of explicit teaching of disciplinary conventions highlights his awareness that there could have been another way for him to learn the special topoi of literary analysis—the traditional pathway of long immersion in their use:

When I took [WAL] . . . actually, before I took [WAL], I had no idea what a literary analysis was. I had no idea what criticism was. I mean, I thought it was really saying the work was bad because of these reasons, and coming in having no idea how to do something like this, these things [gestures toward list of special topoi] just made it so much clearer for me to understand. They're great teaching methods. Without them, I don't know how a professor would have taught me how to do an analysis, *unless I just read criticism all the time and merely imitated what they did*. But these were so helpful for me to learn about literary analysis. (emphasis mine)

The traditional pathway of long immersion and imitation that Eric alludes to would seem, however, to leave him perpetually behind many of his peers. Explicit rhetorical instruction in the topoi, matched with Eric's interest and motivation, appears to have helped Eric "catch up."

Eric's analysis of his writing suggests his conscious awareness and application of the special topoi contributed to his successful manipulation of them. When examining the list of special topoi during our second interview, Eric readily recalled the final paper he wrote for WAL two years earlier in order to exemplify the ubiquity topos. The first thing he said on looking at the list was, "Ubiquity stands out. Everywhereness. In William Faulkner's 'A Rose for Emily,' there's all kinds of images about the things that are past, like archaic writing, for example. And I used that in a paper I wrote to suggest that he's speaking of the past." This paper was one we collected and analyzed as part of our study, and in it Eric used five of the special topoi, as the excerpts in table 5.2 illustrate. It had received the highest possible ratings for the two topoi that are central to its argumentative strategy, appearance/reality and ubiquity, and rather high ratings for social justice and context (it also exemplifies the mistaken-critic topos, though we did not rate students' use of this topos due to the overall rarity of its use).

Table 5.2

Excerpts illustrating Eric's use of five special topoi in his final paper for WAL

Appearance/ reality	The story, "A Rose for Emily" is about Miss Emily Grierson, who is reluctant to accept change. Her impervious mind is like steel, and no words of change can penetrate it. Beneath the obvious, though, this story represents the South's unwillingness to give up a tarnished way of life that should have fallen into ruin after being defeated in the Civil War. Many images within the story are suggestive of the past. Some of the images represent slavery, and others just suggest decay, as if something is old. The story also illustrates desires to prevent progress. These desires are illustrated through images of holding on to the past.
	[...]
	By showing the reader Miss Emily has an invisible watch in the beginning of the story, he shows that time will be hard to see throughout the story. Furthermore, by placing the invisible watch in Miss Emily's pocket, who is a southern lady, he is representing the South's inability to discern the chronology of real life. Consequently, they are left in the past and unaware of passing time.

Ubiquity	There are many phrases and words in this story suggesting the past still lingers. Miss Emily is referred to as a "fallen monument" (2017), a representation of a past that has fallen—but still lingers. Her house, which is in "decay" (2017), shelters leather furniture that has "cracked" (2017). The condition of these objects suggests they are old and from the past. The story reveals that Miss Emily writes a letter in "faded" ink (2017), on "paper of an 'archaic' shape (2017)." The ink represents a past that has faded with time, and her paper represents a way of life that is seldom used any longer. These objects signify the South's old way of life that remains, despite being faded and cracked by time.
Context and social justice	Faulkner is not a stranger to sympathizing with the southern blacks. He had more than likely seen many blacks mistreated, because he grew up in the heart of the south—Oxford, Mississippi (Martin 608). Moreover, Faulkner also sympathizes with blacks in his other works. In *The Unvanquished*, he retells the horrifying events of the Civil War. Interestingly, though, he retells the story partly through the eyes of negroes (Glicksburg 153). In addition, Faulkner shows that white people live about the same kind of life the Negroes of Mississippi did in his book *Absalom! Absalom!* (Glicksburg 154). This information increases the probability that Faulkner would be using the chronology of "A Rose for Emily" to sympathize with the black inhabitants of the south by depicting the white inhabitants as individuals who could not discern the chronology of time in real life.
Mistaken critic	Many critics have suggested different thoughts about the chronology of the story. However, many critics overlook the symbolic meaning of time and the chronological order. They tend to focus closer to the surface by attempting to figure out things such as Miss Emily's age at certain points in her life, and when exactly her father died. They put forth ideas like "Miss Emily could not have been 'about forty' at the time, but would instead have been about 50" (Moore 5), and "[...] the chronology deliberately manipulates and delays the reader's final judgment of Emily Grierson by alerting the evidence" (Getty 1). Though possibly important to understanding the story, these pieces of information seem useless to show the symbolism that time is used for. The chronology, without closely examining Emily's age or her father's death, still shows an important illustration of time. It suggests that the South's inhabitants had time mixed up; that they did not realize the times had changed after the Union won the Civil War many years prior. Since they had difficulty discerning the chronology of actual life, they continued to live in the past and refused to make progress towards a new way of living.

NOTE: Spelling, syntax, and punctuation are as in original.

Eric's discussion of the paper he brought with him to our first interview, a paper from a course on nineteenth-century fiction, reveals his firm understanding of several of the special topoi, and the paper itself exemplifies well the appearance/reality, ubiquity, context, and paradox topoi. Eric explained that in this paper he directly challenged the assignment prompt, which asked him to choose which lifestyle, the contemplative or the active (each represented by an opposing character), Chekhov supports in his story "The House with the Mezzanine." Instead of making a selection, Eric used one of Chekhov's letters stressing the importance of objectivity in storytelling to argue that Chekhov reserves judgment in the story and "illustrates that either person—or lifestyle—could benefit from the other by accepting the positive things they offer," thus, "in effect, he forces the reader to actively contemplate which way of life appears better." When asked if he used any strategies that he learned in WAL in writing this paper, Eric indicated he consciously used the ubiquity, appearance/reality, and context topoi and accurately pointed to examples of each in his paper. He further explained that his use of sources in his application of the context strategy had not been influenced by an assignment requirement but instead by what he learned in WAL. When I pointed to the phrases he used to begin his second paragraph ("on the surface of the story") and third paragraph ("below the surface, however") and asked why he chose to begin these paragraphs this way, he answered:

> "Below the surface," using things like that to, I don't know, as maybe like a start before you jump off of a cliff of interpretation. [. . .] Using simple words like "however," and especially using words like "appears" and "seems" and "suggests" and "illustrates" because I found myself before that class [WAL] saying, "He obviously shows this," or "It's clear that he says this," and if it's really a deeper interpretation, it can't be obvious, or it can't be clear. And I learned things like that in [WAL]. So anytime you see a word like "seems," "below the surface," or "however," "suggests," that's something I've learned from [WAL].

Eric here credits WAL for clarifying the value in moving beyond the "obvious" in rhetorical terms—a reading would be considered "obvious" not only by an individual writer's standards but also by his audience's, a community that approaches the text with similar purposes.

Eric was similarly aware of his use of the social justice, appearance/reality, and context topoi in the paper he brought to this second interview from an advanced special topics course. Of this paper, on "Imperiled Men" from Andre Dubus's memoir *Meditations from a Moveable Chair*, he said, "I know that I did this one based on what was called 'social justice,' that I learned in [WAL] . . . because it was about homosexuality in the forties. And it just seemed to work well with it." In this paper, Eric uses the appearance/reality topos to argue that Dubus's confinement to a wheelchair colors his recollections of a gay military officer and facilitates his shift from indifference to empathy towards him. When shown the list of special topoi, Eric chose to point to this paper to explain the appearance/reality topos to me with an example:

> The sentence says, "The flight deck was 1,000 feet long. The ship weighed seventy thousand tons, and I rarely felt its motion." And to me, that suggests that it was like the commanding officer's homosexuality. It was a huge deal, like the flight deck, 1,000 feet long. But like the ship, he didn't know it was there. He rarely felt its motion. And I used the appearance of that sentence, on the surface. And then interpreted it to mean something else beneath the surface.

The section of his paper he pointed to reads:

> Dubus suggests the magnitude of not knowing CAG when he recalls the ship he was on. He tells us "the flight deck was a thousand feet long, the ship weighed seventy thousand tons, and I rarely felt its motion" (34). This description appears to speak about CAG, because his homosexuality was an issue that was as large and as powerful as a naval carrier; but like the ship, Dubus was not aware it was there. He tells us this when he writes, "Then I knew what I had not known I knew, and I said: 'Was he a homosexual?'" (43). CAG's homosexuality was important enough for his superiors to force him into resignation, to force him to take his life, but—like the ship's movement—Dubus did not realize it at the time.

Additionally, Eric recognized that he used context in this paper: "in the context of the forties and the ways things happened then" as well as how the emergence of empathy for another in "Imperiled Men" can be understood in the context of similar insights in Dubus's other essays in *Meditations from a Moveable Chair*. And though he didn't draw my attention to it, this paper also uses the ubiquity topos, with its multiple examples supporting his appearance/reality claim.

Though one topos, paradigm, did not turn up in any of the three papers written over two years that Eric shared with me (and Eric correctly indicated that he did *not* use this topos in these papers), he explained he did use this topos in WAL and in papers for subsequent classes. He described his use of the paradigm topos in a paper he wrote for WAL that examined two poems through a psychoanalytic lens as "kind of a bold attempt for me to use a paradigm because I'd never done it before." During our first interview, he indicated he had "used that strategy one other time" when writing about *Uncle Tom's Cabin* through the lens of a historian's comments on religion in the North and South: "everything I looked at in the story, I looked at it through that book [by the historian]." The professor had not explicitly asked that he do so; Eric "just saw that it worked well." By our second interview when explaining the paradigm topos to me, Eric claimed he "often used [published] papers written for psychology to kind of do a psychoanalytical approach to something," and "after recently taking critical theory classes," he has "been using those as paradigms."

Several other students with whom I spoke claimed they observed classmates like Eric who experienced similar positive results from explicit instruction in the special topoi. Eve and Emma claimed they saw the experimental curriculum equip other students with previously unfamiliar procedural knowledge. For instance, Eve recognized that her exceptional high-school experience was not widely shared and that other students reacted differently to instruction in even the more "basic" topoi:

> I really do think that if I had not had such good English teachers in high school, that [WAL] would have made much more of an impact. But, as it was, it was kind of like an add-on to what I'd learned before. [. . .] I noticed it was very useful for some of the other students in the class. Until they had a name to it, they were having difficulties with that style or that method. . . . And I guess, depending on what style of learning you have, putting a name to it really helps and really solidifies that thought and helps you to use it later on.

Emma similarly distinguished her preparation from her peers' and claimed she "definitely saw improvement through peer reviews of other classmates." These observations suggest that making disciplinary special topoi explicit in WAL was not uniquely helpful to Eric. They also underscore the wide disparities in experience and exposure among entering college students. A survey that ninety-two students completed asking them to evaluate their experience in WAL at the conclusion of their semester in an experimental section of the course suggests that Eric's experience may be more common. Whereas six of the thirty-three students who opted to make open-ended comments on this survey indicated that the special topoi codified much of what they had already learned in other English classes, fourteen students indicated that they found the instruction in the topoi clarified disciplinary practices that were previously opaque to them.

Recognition of Explicit Knowledge Returning to Tacit

All the students who experienced the experimental curriculum claimed to be continuing to use the special topoi in their other English courses. None reported that what they learned or practiced in WAL conflicted with advice they received in other English courses on their writing or made it difficult to write papers in other English courses. On the contrary, they were unanimous in their sense that most of the special topoi represented interpretive and persuasive strategies that their literature professors were pleased to see them use. Eric assessed their positive reactions to the topoi this way: "it seems like when I apply the strategies, I usually get graded well." Emma, after reviewing the special-topoi descriptions during our second interview, declared, "I can say that I've never had a teacher who wasn't very happy to see any of these in my writing."

Of course, the rhetorical terminology these students encountered in WAL was not repeated, or repeated in the same way, in their subsequent English courses. Such a dynamic is similar to the transition to tacit rhetorical instruction students experience on completing a general first-year writing course after which they may no longer hear terms such as "genre" or "audience" that their former writing instructor hoped would be useful in new contexts. This lack of shared vocabulary to describe procedural knowledge could pose challenges to transfer of learned writing skills (Beaufort, 2007; Carroll, 2002).

The students I spoke with demonstrated their awareness of this transition to tacitness. Eric complained during our first interview that "other professors, they assume you already know this stuff." Ed spoke of the special topoi as relating to his subsequent literature coursework

> without necessarily [. . .] being named, like you don't necessarily talk about the surface/depth, but that's what we're doing. It just isn't given a name. [. . .] Yeah. I think they [his English professors since WAL] look for them, and they want you to do things a certain way, at least engage the material in a certain way. They don't necessarily give everything the same name, but they are looking for basically the same elements.

Some described this transition as making the recollection of explicit knowledge difficult, impeding their ready recollection of the names of the topoi. For instance, during our first interview when I asked her to describe the strategies for writing literary analysis that students learned in WAL, Eve replied, "I don't think I can *name* them now because [. . .] nobody else has brought them up."

Some students singled out the mistaken-critic and the paradigm topoi as strategies that not all their subsequent literature professors wished them to use. They encountered some professors who would discourage using scholarly sources beyond an assigned literary text for fear that a student would rely on, as Eric put it, "their ideas, instead of trying to work with your own." Yet, rather than signal that the emphasis placed on the mistaken-critic and paradigm topoi in their WAL course was professionalizing too soon, they also encountered professors who tacitly expected students to know how to use these topoi. Experiencing their professors' opposing views on the merits of these topoi appears to have led to confusion for some students. For instance, Eve appeared to realize only during our second interview that a professor who assigned a great deal of scholarly criticism was probably encouraging students to use the mistaken-critic topos: "The mistaken critic/linking to the conversation . . . I think that not only did I hear about that in [WAL] but I think that's what she was trying to do in the Austen class, since we were looking at so many critics. [. . .] I guess. I don't know." Eve attributed the difficulty she experienced recognizing this expectation when it could have been more helpful to her—when she was enrolled in the Austen course—to an intervening course in which the professor actively discouraged the use of sources beyond the primary text. The lack of an explicit connection in her Austen course to relevant rhetorical knowledge she had already acquired amounted to a missed opportunity to trigger and activate this knowledge. The promise of transfer of rhetorical knowledge may remain untapped if, as Beaufort (2007) speculates, instructors across courses within a discipline do not make an effort to cue it (p. 150). Eve's analysis of her own experience suggests that transfer may be made even more challenging when intervening instruction has actively discouraged application of the relevant rhetorical procedural knowledge.

In contrast to Eve's inability to recollect the mistaken-critic topos when it was again relevant, several students claimed that using the special topoi now comes "naturally" (Evelyn) or even "subconsciously" (Ed) to them when writing papers for their literature courses. Eileen saw this automatic application as grounded in the explicit instruction they received:

There's things that float around inside your head as you're writing. When I write, I don't think, "OK, I have to talk about context. I have to use social relevance." I don't think that, but I think it plays in the back of your mind, as something that you've been taught, and if you understand them, you can pull them all together without necessarily thinking about them.

During our second interview, even Eric, who initially found all the special topoi novel, suggested that the topoi may have "become almost unconscious" operations for him. He stressed that he keeps these strategies "in his head" as he writes: "They're always in my head, and unconsciously, I think I pick up on different things in the text that relate to the things like this I've learned." He suggested this move to a mental storehouse of strategies one can automatically activate may be necessary to succeed in this field: "All these things are so relevant that to do well, you need to use them in every paper you write, so even though it was two years ago [since he took WAL], I feel like if you're trying as an English major, all these things should stay in your head, as much as possible." Eric's and Eileen's sense that using the topoi they were explicitly taught has become almost automatic supports Young's (1980) sense that the process of learning heuristic procedures involves initially carrying "out deliberately and rationally" what eventually will become "habitual way[s] of thinking" (p. 345), Flower's (1989) description of the shift from learned knowledge to automated processes, and Russell's (1995) portrayal of neophytes moving from conscious to unconscious manipulation of tools such as genre conventions on their way to becoming full participants in an activity system.

Creativity and Freedom of Expression

Because debate over the merits of teaching disciplinary discourse conventions often hinges on the issue of students' expression and creativity, during the second round of interviews I directly asked if students ever self-censored their views in their papers. Likewise, because objectors to explicit teaching of disciplinary genre conventions often claim this instruction unnaturally treats these conventions as static and unchanging, I also asked if the students felt it would be possible to change or challenge conventions such as the special topoi. At the conclusion of the second interview, I also shared a condensed version of some of the key ethical issues in the scholarly debate over explicit instruction in such disciplinary conventions and asked for their reactions to these issues. As was the case with the survey that found comparable levels of personal engagement and expression among students enrolled in experimental and control sections of WAL, I could not discern any distinctly different reactions to these queries from the students I interviewed who had taken experimental or control sections of WAL. Instead, students from both experimental and control sections expressed a range of views on the constraining character of academic discourse, though most affirmed a "creativity within constraint" commonplace.

Like the students in Carroll's (2002) study who felt constrained by the pressure of grades to conform to their professors' views and never question disciplinary conventions, many of the students with whom I spoke, both those who experienced the experimental and the traditional WAL curricula, emphasized the power and influence their professors have over them. They cited both their desire to earn high grades and the extensive training and expertise of their professors as reasons they chose to largely conform to their expectations. As did the students in Thaiss and Zawacki's study (2006), several described the importance of the first paper assignment when taking a course with a professor for the first time because any feedback they receive on this assignment gives them important clues for how to perform for this professor in the future. When I asked how they would advise a beginning English major about to begin a first writing assignment, several stressed ascertaining—through careful reading of the assignment prompt, through visits to the professor's office, and through close observation of the professor during class—exactly what the professor expects. Sometimes this advice appeared to border on determining not only a professor's goals for the assignment but also determining and echoing the professor's stance on the topic. As Emma put it, "If you listen carefully, you know exactly what points they want you to hit. . . . You obviously can't argue the polar opposite of what the teacher was saying and still make the teacher happy."

But more often the students suggested that they did not self-censor under the gaze of a professor as much as allow their professor's views to be so influential that they essentially shaped their views. Rather than hold back a viewpoint differing from their professor's, they may never have formed such a different viewpoint. Their experience lends support to interpretations of college classrooms as predominantly foregrounding school discourse community practices over those of particular disciplinary discourse communities. As A. Freedman, Adam, and Smart (1994), Nelson (1990), and others noted, the power dynamic inherent in grading practices and tendencies to see a course as fulfilling an institutional requirement work powerfully against students' participation as legitimately peripheral to a disciplinary discourse community's work.

However, Ed, Eileen, and Cal indicated they felt free to disagree with professors in their papers. While Eileen described herself as being somewhat deferential in her approach toward such disagreement, explaining she would not "full-out make my paper a disagreement, but to say, 'You know, this was said, but I'm wondering . . . ,'" Ed claimed a student could reject the foundational premise on which a professor interpreted a text "as long as you can support it. [. . .] You can take any stance you want." Cal saw his professors' reactions to his challenges to their views in his papers as "pretty fair. [. . .] They'd let me know they disagreed with me, but they would still grade the paper fairly." Beaufort (2007) argued that it may be possible to structure a course to move legitimate peripheral participation in a disciplinary discourse community into its foreground. Eileen seems to suggest that her experimental WAL section may have helped her to see such a purpose for her writing beyond typical classroom goals when she claimed that WAL encouraged her to see

> that maybe some papers are more than just a paper. [. . .] In lower-level English and other courses, you do your paper. . . . I mean, you do it correctly, and you follow the guidelines and everything, but sometimes it requires a little more "in-depthness," and that class [WAL] just kind of showed me how to approach it I guess more scholarly, instead of just doing the work.

That Eileen sees her "scholarly" work in WAL as "more than just a paper" suggests that explicit acknowledgment of this disciplinary discourse community lent classroom projects greater meaning, motivation, and even freedom of expression.

Challenging the views of classmates rather than a professor appears much less daunting, and students could see the benefits of doing so in terms of forging "original" claims. Calling to mind the mistaken-critic topos, some described advantages to taking a risk and deliberately writing against the grain of class discussion or the views of the majority of students. This type of originality was extolled by Evelyn, Emma, and Christine. They described using class and online discussions and workshops of drafts as opportunities to learn the views of their classmates in order to strategically strike out against them. As Christine put it, "If I have access to other people's papers or insights, then I would probably chose something that isn't being talked about. [. . .] If everybody else is writing about the green light in *The Great Gatsby*, then I'm going to write about something else." Emma saw her employment of this strategy in the paper she brought to our interview as related to the A grade it received and her own evaluation of it as the "best paper" she had written for a class: "I kind of had a different opinion on my interpretation on this story than the rest of the class did. . . . It might have benefited me to be a little bit different from everyone else."

Yet, understanding a disciplinary discourse community as an open forum for argumentation did not necessarily lead to seeing its preferred genre as unconstraining. Though one of the most vocal believers in students' freedom to express themselves through effective argumentation, Ed was also one of the most vocal critics of the limitations he perceived in literary analysis and other academic genres. Over the course of our interviews, Ed repeatedly expressed his disappointment that the academic genres he encountered have inhibited his creativity. He did not point to the special topoi his WAL instructor emphasized as inhibitive but rather the genre for which they are conventions:

> I don't think necessarily the strategies per se [inhibited]. But I kind of feel sometimes that the analytical essay, in general, kind of detracts from personal creativity, almost. It may just be inherent because you're writing an academic paper, but it just seems that sometimes it just gets too dry and boring, and you have to make your point, and it's all laid out and almost seems like there's no way to really engage the reader anymore, outside of just following your theory and giving evidence and things like that.

Ed emphasized the potential for other genres to reach a wider audience with his concerns:

> I feel like there is another way to present the same information, almost. Not that the way things are done now are necessarily bad, but I just feel like there's another way that you could somehow make a paper more interesting, make it more like a narrative and less like a research or almost like a court document, where you're laying out evidence for a certain idea of yours, but I think that may detract somewhat from the acceptance it would have in the academic community, but at the same time, it would make it more approachable for a wider audience.

Like Spellmeyer (1989), Ed senses that disciplinary genres such as literary analysis discount pathos and promote a false objectivity:

> I think it also does inhibit creativity and, in my experience, you just seem to not want to appear biased in any way. I mean, it's almost like you're treading a thin line. You don't want to make your voice heard, almost, in the paper as much as you want to show your understanding, not . . . necessarily emotion, I guess. That's probably what it seems to me to limit because you're sticking to what you see, what evidence there is, what support there is. . . . So you just want to seem to be an unbiased person, I guess.

Interestingly, though Ed appreciated that literary analysis provided a forum for him to freely argue his views as long as he employed effective argumentative techniques, he recognized constraining effects of this genre and felt powerfully discouraged to challenge its conventions. When I asked if he ever tried the kind of genre switching or mixing he describes above, he answered, "Kind of incorporated some of the elements but just the fear of getting a good grade is a strong motivation."

Christine expressed a similar exasperation with disciplinary genres. Like Ed, she described the genre of literary analysis as potentially limiting and lacking in "personality," in contrast to "creative writing":

> I haven't taken a single creative writing course at all, ever. And I . . . this [pointing to the literary analysis she brought with her] is all the writing that I do. And so I think that for me [. . .] if I'm given any leeway, I'm going to not write this [again pointing to the paper she brought with her] way. I'm going to write something that's more pleasurable to read, in meaning that it's interesting because it has personality. And this type of analytical paper [again pointing to the paper] is going to be very argumentative.

In Ed's and Christine's experiences, despite the relative lack of formal rigidity in its predominant genre, especially in comparison to predominant genres in other disciplines that follow rigid structures such as IMRD (introduction, methods, results, discussion), literary studies rigidly encourages students to compose in only one genre.

While Ed and Christine find the conventions of academic argument in genres like literary analysis to be constraining and uncontestable within the power dynamic of a classroom, others either are satisfied with and unmotivated to challenge the genre's conventions or claim they feel empowered to challenge conventions. Like the students in Carroll's (2002) study, some seemed contentedly unable to imagine a need to challenge the status quo. For instance, Emma finds the special topoi to "have always been pretty faithful" to her own goals in writing about literary texts:

> I've never really looked at "context" and said, "Oh, this author didn't pick this time and this place to show this." That doesn't make any sense. I do believe that there are authors who just write stories and that sometimes we find these things, and they're contrived and manipulated by the critic instead of intended by the author. But, at the same time, that can just simply be a form of interpretation. I mean, because we found a context doesn't mean that the author defines that context. It means that possibly the reader defined it, which is OK. That's what writing is for. So I've never been frustrated by these terms because whether they're defined by the author or defined by the reader, they're usually present.

While the evolution of rhetorical practices within this discipline supports Emma's suggestion that the special topoi are flexible and resilient to changes in theoretical perspectives (see chapter 1), this history also supports the views of those students who could imagine cause and context for transforming disciplinary discourse conventions. For instance, to exemplify her claim that a student could productively and effectively challenge disciplinary special topoi, Eve pinpointed a tension between the ubiquity topos and valuing the singular or unique: "I think that if you feel that this word, here, being in only one place in the entire book, is important, and if you can back that up, you should be able to talk about it in your writing and not get penalized for it." The subtle shift in topological conventions over time in literary studies exemplified in the move away from adherence to the contemptus mundi topos and towards the social justice topos supports Eve's assertion that it is possible to move a disciplinary community from support of a long-held value to its binary opposite through argumentation (in fact, I noted signs of the very tension she points to between valuing the ubiquitous and the singular in my rhetorical analysis of recent journal articles in literary studies). While Eve's choice of the term *penalized* highlights the power of the professor as evaluator, her awareness of the penalties for defying audience expectations is not incongruent with the risks present in any broader disciplinary discourse community when scholars defy convention.

In contrast to the complaints students like Ed and Christine lodged against what they saw as the oppressive confines of argumentative academic genres, a commonplace asserted enthusiastically by most of the students I spoke with was that creativity thrives within constraint. Most indicated they detected the value professors place on originality as characterized by the literature professors I interviewed (see chapter 3). For instance, Emma stressed that her professors value "something that sets you apart from every other cookie-cutter writer in the class," and she felt this particularly in her WAL course that sought to explicitly impart conventional topoi:

> That was one of the things that I liked about it the most, was the discussions were always very interesting because we would talk about these tools, but we would talk about them from our individual perspectives, and so they're always a little bit different. And we would almost argue sometimes, and it was fun, to see how different people interpreted [with] these tools.

When asked if he felt being taught the special topoi in WAL inhibited his creativity, Eric responded:

> No. I think . . . as an example, this may sound crazy, but I like to play the guitar, and I never did know how to use scales, but when I used scales, I think that just structured my creativity and made me better. And I think these are like those scales. They just structure your creativity and make things more coherent to read and make things better.

Evelyn described how she saw the special topoi used in her WAL section to cultivate students' development of original ideas while navigating the demands of persuasive argumentation:

> We would read each other's paper, and they'd be like, "Well, I think this is a little obvious," or maybe, "This is a little far-fetched," and you have to go back and find that median where it's still being, maybe, original and creative, but it still can be found multiple times within what you're reading, so it kind of encouraged me to do that.

Evelyn repeatedly stressed that her experience of explicit instruction in the special topoi "encouraged my creativity in my analysis a lot" by providing constraints or "boundaries" upon it, especially the constraint that her analysis not be obvious.

Interestingly, students like Evelyn who had taken several creative writing courses and even identified as "creative writers" held a very different perception of conventions of analytic writing than did Ed and Christine. Complicating tendencies to oppose expressivist pedagogies and social-constructivist pedagogies, Emma claimed that since taking WAL, she has become aware that she uses the special topoi in her creative writing courses. She explained she not only uses the special topoi as interpretative tools for reading her classmates' stories for workshops but is aware she also uses the special topoi "in my trying to create that kind of a background in my own writing, my own creative writing," by which I understood her to mean that she takes into consideration the critical-reading practices of her readers—the ways in which she may be able to encourage certain appearance/reality readings, for instance—as she composes. Seemingly paradoxically, she described how the lack of explicit constraints in her creative writing classes ("the only requirements I've had are length, that's it") led her to feel inhibited because she perceived her creative writing teachers as using her choices in "subject matter" to "judge the kind of person I am." She did not feel this kind of inhibiting personal scrutiny in her literature courses, where she felt judged on the strength of her arguments.

Students reacted strongly when presented the viewpoint that explicit instruction in disciplinary conventions such as special topoi could inhibit students' creativity and encourage formulaic writing. While some such as Evelyn and Eric adamantly disagreed and saw such conventions as encouraging the opposite of formulaic thinking and writing, others described disciplinary conventions as inescapable parts of the reality in which writers work. Emma found the concern for inhibiting students "valid" but claimed professors who express it are "contradicting themselves" and "not realistic" because in her experience so many professors reward students for using the special topoi. Similarly, Caitlin, one of the students from a control section of WAL who nonetheless readily recognized the special topoi when I presented them to her, claimed that professors who critique explicit instruction in disciplinary conventions on these grounds are "in deep denial if they think students don't already have to adhere" to special-topoi conventions.

Students' Interpretations of Findings and Recommendations

At the end of the second interview, I shared with students some findings from the study described in chapter 4 that they had participated in and asked for their input in interpreting them. Students who experienced explicit instruction in the special topoi tended to interpret our finding that the more of the special topoi students used in their papers, the more highly a group of English faculty rated them as evidence that professors prefer to see students use the rhetorical practices of their disciplinary discourse community. For instance, Eric speculated that literature professors preferred student papers that contained more of the special topoi because "these are almost like a professional language critics have, and it's just noticeable for them. [. . .] And it seems like you're trying to take part in what they do." Emma related an interesting theory to explain the professors' preference that I read as an attempt to explain how members of the same discipline come to share values and expectations. Drawing from her observations as a clerical worker for the AP College Board one summer, Emma postulated that perhaps this organization was instrumental in shaping the common values of literature professors. She speculated that the findings from our study may reflect the uniformity of the "checklist" of criteria the College Board uses to ensure that professors use fair grading practices and not rely on mere "opinion" when evaluating AP exams. She sounded convinced that the tendencies we observed in our data reflect standards instituted by a governing body like the College Board yet typically—and almost conspiratorially—kept hidden from students:

LW: Do you think that your professors here have this kind of checklist that they're using?

EMMA: Absolutely.

LW: Do they share it with you?

EMMA: No, but I've written papers with these kinds of tools, and I've written them without, and I've noticed what you've noticed, that the grades are all higher when I use those tools.

I am struck by Emma's sense that professional organizations and common training may promote common standards and expectations beyond an individual's idiosyncratic "opinion" on whether a paper is "good" or not. Of course, Emma speculates that the process of acquiring and applying such standards occurs far more uniformly and explicitly than is routine in disciplinary enculturation practices.

Students who had completed a control section of WAL were more likely to explain our findings by claiming that when students use more of the special topoi their papers are "better" in a seemingly general sense. At the conclusion of the second round of interviews, I presented control students with brief descriptions of each topos (similar to the list presented in the introduction to the current volume) to facilitate our discussion of the study they participated in. The four students who had completed control sections of WAL that I spoke with during these interviews readily recognized the special topoi as present in their English coursework. Although we did not take a great deal of time to discuss each topos or even look at examples of them in use, several signals indicated that these students correctly understood what I meant by the special topoi. For instance, the three who brought sample papers identified some of the key topoi that they used in these papers (confirmed by my later analysis). Further, their descriptions of how they came to be familiar with the topoi plausibly characterized their implicit presence in their classrooms. For example, several recognized that the paradigm topos would facilitate their using the theories they were learning in a required, upper-level literary-theory course in their papers, and Camilla described her observations of her professors' use of the appearance/reality and ubiquity this way: "If we're discussing a piece of literature, they're like, 'Look below the surface,' or 'This is something that was on page twenty, and it appears again in page fifty-three and three more times on that particular page.'"

Though as seniors these students could readily recognize the special topoi as crystallizing strategies they had observed and been encouraged to use over the course of their years as English majors, they tended not to discuss them as discipline-specific conventions but rather features of "good writing." Interpreting the results of our study, Christine explained that using the special topoi would make an argument more specific, which she understands as a good feature of any critical argument, but she also indicated that she sees the special topoi as "methods that are accepted by the university," suggesting they are tools for effective argumentation broadly applicable across disciplines. Cal signaled that he may have already internalized the values of the discipline of literary studies in his assumption that a more complex argument would be a better argument: "If they're not only using more but they're coming up with more complexities, more sophisticated, of course those would get rated more highly than one that was simpler, maybe not as in-depth, maybe didn't use as many theories." In their assumption that discipline-specific rhetorical practices are universal, these students are not unlike the professors I interviewed (see chapter 2) as well as professors in other disciplines (Thaiss & Zawacki,

2006). Such a universalizing tendency may thus be an understandable outcome of tacit acquisition of a discipline's rhetorical knowledge.

In light of our discussions of their experiences, the study findings I shared with them, and the scholarly debate over the ethics of explicitly teaching disciplinary discourse conventions, I asked students to make their own recommendations on how to best prepare students for the challenges of writing in the English major. Ed's concern that academic argument inhibits student expression and his impression that WAL redundantly covered writing skills he had already mastered earlier made him reluctant to recommend the approach his WAL course took to other students. When presented with the view that not all students enter college as prepared to writing literary analyses as he did, Ed acknowledged that some students might benefit from such explicit instruction: "I'd say definitely if you're struggling to write a paper, these will definitely help you to produce something. If you're unfamiliar with writing on a college level, I guess, it definitely helps you have a fallback, at least, to follow these strategies into a paper, and it will help you generate some kind of ideas."

Most students stated that the special topoi should be taught explicitly, though they had specific suggestions for how they should be taught. Eileen stressed that this instruction should provide models that demonstrate the topoi in use. Eve stressed that such instruction should focus on what she had described as the more advanced topoi because those such as appearance/reality and ubiquity should already have been "learned" in high school, and, thus, inordinate focus on them would not sufficiently challenge students. She appears to suggest that her own experience of moving from a context that implicitly values the special topoi to a context in which the topoi are explicitly acknowledged is ideal:

> It might be good if they tried to teach them without the names, at first, just to try to get the students familiar with them. I don't know how you could do that, but after you do get to [WAL], I think that this is where you can learn the names for the topics. And it's kind of like the light bulb goes off. If you haven't realized that's what they're called before, "OK, that's got a name. Sure. I understand that." And sometimes putting a name with it helps some of the other students to understand it a little better. [. . .] It depends on your learning style.

In contrast to Eve's implicit recommendation that instructors work to replicate her own experience, Camilla directly referred to her own experience of never having been explicitly taught to use the special topoi in her recommendation that they should be explicitly taught. As she put it, in her experience, the special topoi have "never really been touched on," she feels that some guidance beyond her "own trial and error" would be "helpful," and "it would probably make sense to have it in the [WAL] curriculum. Perhaps it is already there, and I was taught all of this, and I didn't realize it."

Students' Perceptions of Traditional WAL Instruction

I asked all the students I spoke with, not just those who experienced experimental sections of WAL, about strategies for writing literary analysis that they recalled practicing or learning in WAL. The responses of control students suggest what has "stayed with them" from the various traditional approaches to WAL and differ in important ways from what students from experimental sections said they retained from WAL. They uniformly told me they enjoyed WAL, felt they benefited from its opportunities to practice writing and ask questions as they entered their more challenging upper-level courses, and described their professors as "warm" and approachable. Yet, Cailtin's response to my question on whether any advice she received in WAL contradicted advice on writing she received in later literature courses captures a dissatisfaction with implicit rhetorical instruction shared by some of her peers: "You've almost got to teach yourself sometimes. [. . .] I don't remember getting any advice that conflicted. I just remember wondering if I was given an easy way to go, if I wasn't critiqued enough, if I needed some more constructive criticism." Students who experienced "the terms," "theory overview," "expressivist," and "civic discourse" approaches to WAL characterized and critiqued the strategies these approaches imparted in the following ways.

Learning Literary Terms Will Help Unlock Meaning in Literature

Some students were grateful for the opportunity to clarify the meanings of literary terms they had heard in contexts where they felt understanding of the terms was assumed and they were embarrassed to ask for clarification, yet they had a difficult time recalling more than one or two such difficult terms that WAL clarified for them. For instance, Christine stressed her gratitude for WAL shedding light on "existentialism" but could not now explain the term, suggesting she did not retain this knowledge, and she could not recollect any other terms she learned in WAL. However, naming terms covered in WAL that felt more like review of familiar knowledge to her came more easily: "I would say like 'metaphor' and 'simile.' Those are really pretty elementary, in that they're not as relevant or even . . . I felt like in high school, we spent a lot of time on 'allusion' and 'hyperbole' and that those, to me, are not really what I'm going to end up writing about." Cal similarly described a limit to the usefulness for his writing of this literary terms pedagogy: "We did spend a significant amount of time in class talking about 'character,' 'plot,' 'this,' 'that,' which was less relevant to the writing we did, and I thought we were beyond that." Unlike several of the experimental students who attributed their prior familiarity with some special topoi to their exceptional high-school English instruction, Cal did not attribute his sense that he was beyond "the terms" to his exceptionally good high-school experiences. In fact, he described his high school as an "inner-city school" in which "there was no [. . .] critiquing literary stuff. I mean, in high school, I didn't even read that much." Yet, during our second interview when I asked him if he continued to draw on anything he learned in WAL in his subsequent English courses, he said, "Not really. [. . .] I don't think I learned that much new." Smith (1992) and Franzak (2008) both observed an inordinate emphasis on understanding such literary terminology over richer practices of interpretation and writing in high-school literary instruction. Though this sense of familiarity echoes the familiarity many students from experimental sections claimed they felt towards several special topoi, a key difference is that students found "the terms" to be of little use as inventional aids to composing. Cal and Christine support the experimental instructors' sense (see chapter 4) that translating understanding of these terms into rhetorical knowledge applicable to writing their papers is not an obvious process.

"Notice What Stands Out to You"

Students who named noting whatever "stands out to you" as a central strategy echoed a concern raised by an experimental instructor who worried this advice does not support the development of transferable rhetorical skills (see chapter 4). Christine explained that a drawback to this strategy is that it "is really, really vague as to what becomes important and what is worth developing an entire argument and thesis and paper on." She went on to explain that she has a hard time moving from the prewriting activities associated with this strategy (such as class discussion and journaling) to the type of analytic argument she knows her English professors who use this strategy ultimately expect from her. She described this type of instruction, "'Read this and find something that stands out to you, and pick a point, and kind of talk about that.' [. . .] If someone gives you an assignment like that, it's going to become like a journal entry, you know?" She gave the example of issues related to marriage particularly interesting her now that she is about to get married, and so she may choose to write on anything she could find related to this topic in her reading. And yet, because she feels that a "journal entry" is not ultimately what her professors are looking for, she finds this instruction misleading.

Use Literary Theories as "Lenses" through Which to Read a Text

Though two students reported being advised to use literary theories as lenses through which to read texts, both also reported feeling unsure *how* to apply this advice (Carrie described her introduction to how to do this in WAL to be "fuzzy"). Several students reported finding greater clarity when they took a required, senior-level literary-theory course. Though in WAL they had been shown model analyses that applied the paradigm topos, like the students in Charney and Carlson's (1995) study they needed further instruction to learn how to apply this strategy effectively.

Use Class Discussion to Complicate and Develop Your Initial Ideas

While this strategy was also used in the experimental curriculum (and likely any literary pedagogy), some students I spoke with pointed to its limitations as a primary technique for writing instruction. Christine described a WAL class she had taken at another university during her first year of college that had a heavy reading load and used discussion as the primary technique for teaching writing that led her to believe that "the emphasis was on I need to be able to talk well. I need to be able to discuss these books [. . .] in class." However, she discovered her grade was actually based on papers for which she felt she received "no instruction whatsoever." She found the move from discussion to writing to not be a clear path, and the use of one medium to evaluate learning in the other felt mismatched to her ("looking back, it was nuts"). Cal similarly felt that the amount of reading assigned and discussed in his WAL course de-emphasized writing instruction. At the end of our second interview, he recommended WAL instructors assign "less reading of the text and maybe more writing, more class discussion about things like this on the paper [gesturing to the list of special topoi used during second interviews]. There was a lot of reading, and [. . .] we just didn't talk that much about the writing of the papers or concepts like this [the special topoi]."

Integrate Quotations, and Use Correct MLA Style Citation

Handling quotations and citations was of course addressed in all sections of WAL. However, some control students described some problems with limiting instruction in handling quotations to issues of integration (the three-step "introduce, quote, and explain" strategy that more than one of them described to me as key) and proper citation. Camilla described a focus on concern for attribution of ideas and avoidance of plagiarism as making developing her own voice and views challenging:

> I guess I feel a little ill prepared. [. . .] I have a hard time putting in my own voice when I have to use something where I have to have citations because I feel if I say something in my own voice that I run the risk of it sounding very similar to an author's idea, that maybe I didn't quote. There's that whole plagiarism thing that's in the background, that I think I (and every other English major) am terrified of, so I guess I didn't really learn how to sort of meld the two together.

She also recognized that her literature professors value her original thinking when they criticize her for "relying mostly on what the work itself says or what critics [who] have responded to the work" have said and "not putting enough of my own ideas into it." Neither she nor the other students from control sections described learning rhetorical techniques for developing and inserting their views into published discussion on literary texts. Instead, instruction focused on formal matters of quotation and citation.

Two students from control sections pointed to unhelpful gaps in their WAL experience. Cal singled out one paper assignment informed by the "civic discourse" approach to WAL, a proposal argument about whether *Huckleberry Finn* should be banned in schools, as calling for a genre he has not been asked to compose in again since taking WAL. While such an assignment may provide an opportunity to rehearse civic rhetorical practices of deliberation, Cal experienced this assignment as an odd deviation from the rhetorical practices valued in his major. Even within his WAL course, it was the only time he was asked to compose in this genre, and this lack of recurrent practice (Wardle, 2009) would seem to undercut the rehearsal of civic discourse practices that may have been his instructor's goal. Likewise, Christine noted the absence of examination of models that she feels would have been productive but "is something that never happens, never happens" in her literature courses. Though she had experienced peer-review sessions, no distinctions were made between "which papers are getting As and which papers are not." She understands that one reason instructors might not assign models is "probably" because "there is no complete formula for an A paper," but she claims that on the contrary it is helpful "to see what someone who is at my level, in my major, is capable of doing." She also speculated that another reason instructors shy away from using models is that they have "expectations [. . .] that they may not even realize."

Conclusion

A distinguishing feature emerged between the experimental and control students during my analysis of interview transcripts. Students who had taken experimental sections of WAL made notably more references to argumentation as the task of literary analysis. Only one of the five students who had completed control sections of WAL readily described the writing she did for her major as argumentative, whereas all of the experimental students repeatedly used variations of terms such as "argue," "claim," "evidence," and "support" to indicate their understanding of literary analysis and their paper assignments as argumentative, using such terms three times as often as control students.[4] In this way, the experimental students I spoke with (and one control student) appear to be more like the students who earned As in the introductory American literature course I observed who were more likely to describe persuasion as the purpose of their writing for this course than their peers who earned lower grades (Wilder, 2002).

Though these students may have developed this sense of the importance of argument in other ways, the explicit instruction they experienced in WAL was designed to heighten their awareness of the transactional and persuasive purposes this genre serves within a disciplinary discourse community. This instruction may have cultivated a more rhetorical outlook on school discourse, foregrounding the work of the disciplinary discourse community and encouraging students to see their writing as "more than just a paper." In contrast, students I spoke with who completed control sections of WAL, even as they approached graduation two years later, repeatedly described discerning their professors' expectations for their writing as a guessing game. Keeping disciplinary rhetorical procedural knowledge tacit throughout their undergraduate experience appears to have contributed to their tendency to see features of the predominate genre in their discipline as universal qualities of good writing and their tendency to attribute some professors' expectations as informed by idiosyncratic whims rather than disciplinary discourse community practices.

Explicit instruction appears to have contributed to validating and organizing into useful heuristics the tacit knowledge students already possessed. Because the rhetorical context this instruction sought to prepare students for was encountered repeatedly in their later coursework, students appear to have largely retained and transferred this learning. As James (2008) found to be the case for second-language learners, the perception of task similarity seemed key to successfully triggering these students' transfer of learning from WAL to their later literature courses.

However, some students felt on reflection that the lack of explicit cues for this learning in their later coursework inhibited their ability to transfer it into situations where it would have been useful, such as Eve's return to a classroom that valued her use of the mistaken-critic topos. In that case, Eve explained that the problem of transfer was compounded by intervening instruction that had actively discouraged use of the mistaken-critic topos. Topoi like mistaken critic and paradigm that require a writer to engage with published scholarship would seem to be more obviously disciplinary than other topoi because using them involves overt acknowledgment of the existence of the discipline—its publications, its hierarchy of scholars to which one makes appeals to authority, and its citation conventions. As a result, instructors' preference or distaste for these topoi may be a consequence of their position within the debates regarding disciplinarity in undergraduate literary study, with instructors aligned with "pre-" or "postdisciplinarity" positions discouraging use of these specific topoi. What becomes important to note, however, is that these instructors do not appear to discourage but rather are gratified by students' use of disciplinary topoi that do not so clearly announce their disciplinary affiliations.

Indeed, one possible conclusion to draw from these student interviews is that the constraints this discipline places on discourse are subtle yet profound and likely greater than many "pre-" and "postdisciplinarity" advocates realize. Outside of elective courses in creative writing, literary analysis was the predominate, if not the only, genre these students wrote for courses in their major. Thus, although it may lack rigid formal constraints, this genre nevertheless may serve an extremely conservative disciplinary function, restricting discourse to primarily addressing one conventional stasis issue (the interpretive or definitional stasis that all of the students I spoke with readily described as the central, guiding concern of literary analysis). Schmersahl and Stay (1992) found in a survey of faculty at a liberal arts college in the early 1990s that literature professors were unique among those surveyed not because the genres they assigned "consistently imitate professional genres" (p. 142) but because, unlike other professors who similarly expected students to approximate professional genres, they were not "self-conscious" (p. 143) or aware of this preference. These interviews suggest that students at a midsize, public, metropolitan university might similarly describe their literature professors' expectations today. In contrast to Thaiss and Zawacki's (2002, 2006) findings that professors in other disciplines may encourage "alternative" forms of discourse more frequently than WID critics tend to acknowledge, literature professors appear less likely to assign "alternative" genres. Or if they do, as in the case of the civic discourse argument proposing action in response to a controversial text, such a genre is unlikely to be called for again, encouraging students to see it retrospectively as an odd deviation from standard disciplinary practice.

However, many students who had been taught to recognize and use special topoi associated with literary analysis described how they experienced this disciplinary procedural knowledge as enhancing their creativity. Their adamancy of this complicates WID critics' conflation of this type of instruction with the inhibiting qualities of disciplinary discourse. Many of the students I spoke with described how treating the special topoi in WAL as explicit strategies opened up rather than limited possibilities for their writing. Rather than "reading between the lines" to discern the implicit rhetorical curriculum, they could redirect this energy to applying strategies for producing interpretive arguments that pushed class discussion and even occasionally current scholarship in "original" directions. Explicit genre instruction appears to have supported the value members of this discipline place upon originality and complexity and, most important, supported students' acquisition of rhetorical procedural knowledge necessary for appealing to these values in their writing.

Responding to Spellmeyer's (1989) concerns regarding the potential for explicit instruction in disciplinary discourse to inhibit student expression in light of these interviews is thus not a clear-cut matter. Several of the students I spoke with from experimental and control sections described their reluctance to disagree with their professors and recounted their strategies for inferring the stances they believe their professors wish to see them take. Others, however, pointed to adhering to conventions of "good" argumentation as a successful strategy for taking on viewpoints they know to counter their professors', and they felt able and even encouraged to do so. Yet, Ed, a vocal adherent to this latter view, reveals how conflating an unwillingness to oppose authoritative viewpoints with inhibition may be inappropriate with his adamant assertion that the genre of literary analysis constrained his expression. While no student described learning and practicing the special topoi as inhibiting their expression (and most described it as supporting their expressive goals), Ed portrayed the predominance of the genre of literary analysis as oppressive.

Thus, explicit instruction in disciplinary conventions such as special topoi, linked as they are to disciplinary habits of mind (Francoz, 1999) and inventional techniques, does not seem to inhibit but rather supports students' expression and creativity, though within a specific, socially sanctioned recurrent rhetorical situation that students may find constraining. One recommendation for practice literature instructors may thus take from these students, then, may be to become more open to alternative forms of discourse (Schroeder, Fox, & Bizzell, 2002) in their classes. A positive aspect of the predominance of literary analysis is the repeated opportunities for practicing it that students are provided, making genre knowledge much more likely to be acquired accurately and with a high degree of refinement and awareness of its options, perhaps much more so than students in other majors who only get one small taste of a discipline's key genre when writing a senior thesis. Nonetheless, I think that Ed's and Christine's fatigue with this genre could be alleviated with opportunities for expression in other genres and for other purposes. Pope's (2003) call to treat literary texts as invitations to respond in literary genres by rewriting them from different perspectives, for instance, may provide these students with the desired outlet and simultaneously build their knowledge of literary technique. Though Pope would prefer that such assignments not be treated merely as "prewriting" leading to traditional essays, the attention to subtle textual details the assignments cultivate may nonetheless support students' use of topoi like appearance/reality, as Emma became aware when she took creative writing courses after her experimental section of WAL. The potential for useful knowledge transfer from such assignments make them a particularly attractive option for "alternative" forms of discourse literature instructors may wish to pursue.

I was impressed by the candor and ingenuity of all the students with whom I spoke. While, of course, their comments to me may have been inhibited by social pressures I could not account for, because I was not one of their instructors or even on the faculty at their institution, I believe they felt little pressure to please me or conform to my views and instead took quite seriously my stated goal to advance research that could be used to improve writing instruction in their major. As a result, I think we should take seriously the concern expressed by experimental and control students alike that a course like WAL could and should do more to challenge them. Because literary analysis is a genre several of them had previously encountered, they desired to expand their knowledge of this genre. Several experimental students described how they entered college familiar with some topoi like appearance/reality and ubiquity, while topoi such as paradigm and mistaken critic continue to challenge them as they approach graduation. Likewise, "the terms" emphasis of many WAL sections seemed largely redundant to control students because this approach dominated their high-school literature instruction. While one could find ever-more-esoteric literary terms to emphasize in WAL in order to avoid this sense of redundancy, this would only further reinforce learning Applebee (1996) characterized as the dead-end of "knowledge-out-of-context" (p. 25) rather than enabling "knowledge-in-action" (p. 23). Instead, the students with whom I spoke suggested a more productive way of challenging them: support their development of knowledge of how to use topoi they are unfamiliar with while working to create a classroom environment connected to the work of the larger discipline that promotes their development of original arguments in this social context. As part of efforts to promote this environment, I would recommend exploring reasons and techniques for defying convention as well as attendant risks, perhaps to a greater degree than did the instructors who taught the experimental, special-topoi curriculum many of these students experienced. In this way, explicit instruction in disciplinary conventions can be seen as increasing complex challenges for students rather than as remediation.

While explicit instruction in disciplinary special topoi thus may challenge the best-prepared students, it must also to address the needs of students like Eric who come to college having never before written in the predominant genre of their major and uncertain of even where to begin tackling the rhetorical demands of that daunting undertaking. Eric's instructor sought to confront rather than resign herself to perpetuating her students' disparities in exposure and preparation. Eric pointed to his own experience as the best evidence he could think of to support the stance of WID advocates who claim it is both possible to explicitly impart conventional rhetorical practices in the context of meaningful disciplinary activity and important to do so on social-equity grounds. What helped validate and organize the tacit procedural knowledge several of his peers already possessed simultaneously appears to have filled in gaps in his procedural knowledge, effectively allowing him to "catch up." While, of course, a host of other factors beyond his instructor's approach to WAL, such as his high level of motivation, likely influenced Eric's success in his major, he greatly credits the course with providing access to knowledge he was aware others possessed but that he had not previously been exposed to, an experience that may not only have increased his genre knowledge but also his motivation and belief in his abilities.

Although Eric claims explicitly learning special-topoi conventions helped him to confidently navigate disparities in power and express himself, the form his expression took clearly does not challenge the existence of conventions or disciplinary hierarchies, and as such it may sound like a hollow achievement to those who feel such a challenge ought to be the imperative of all writing instruction. Yet, I think it is important to recognize, as Eric did, that although this rhetorical instruction certainly guides students to use some inventional tools and not others, students must provide the insights, the stances, the observations that make up the arguments they construct, especially if they are to approach the valued "originality" within the context of class discussion or broader researched scholarship. Eric claims his deliberate use of the special topoi facilitated his bringing his perspective into disciplinary conversations or, as he put it, "made it more clear to them [his professors] what *I* was doing." Although becoming a member of this discourse community undoubtedly began to shape Eric's goals, he also brings insights and perspectives to this community that would be poorer without them.

6

"There Were Negative Results for Me": Faculty Resistance to Explicit Instruction in Disciplinary Rhetoric

Though many of the students I interviewed found illuminating the efforts made in a writing-intensive course in their English major to explicitly impart rhetorical strategies conventional to literary scholars, not all of their instructors found these efforts easy or desirable to make. Everyone who taught the experimental sections of writing about literature (WAL) (for the purposes of the study described in chapter 4) recognized that to fully integrate such explicit instruction into the course, they had to disrupt familiar patterns of teaching that they had largely picked up in a manner they found personally and professionally influential: the implicit example of their own former college instructors. Although most ultimately came to share several students' sense that explicitly teaching special topoi was more effective and fair than their previous approaches to the course—so much so that they continue to use the experimental curriculum's major features when teaching WAL and other literature courses—this conversion experience did not occur for all of them. One instructor in particular came to hold strong reservations about the experimental approach. This chapter discusses his concerns as well as those of two other professors: one of his colleagues who encountered elements of the experimental curriculum and implemented them in her section of WAL and the professor whose course I observed (see chapter 2) and with whom I shared my analysis of the ways in which I saw disciplinary rhetorical practices permeating his instruction. Though attention has been given to faculty resistance in WAC and WID scholarship, the concerns of these three professors are not fully reflected in this work. WAC proponents have tended to emphasize the enthusiasm of faculty "converts" (Walvoord, 1997) to "writing to learn" techniques following sometimes only a few WAC faculty workshop sessions (Fulwiler, 1988a; Herrington, 1981; Prior, Hawisher, Gruber,

& MacLaughlin, 1997; Thaiss & Zawacki, 2006; Walvoord, Hunt, Dowling, & McMahon, 1997). Discussions of resistance to WAC or WID pedagogies have tended to emphasize the impediments institutional arrangements present to tapping this enthusiasm rather than the ways such configurations of power and values have been internalized and cemented by individual faculty.

Before proceeding, I should comment first on my use of the term *resistance* because the term has been criticized as unduly emphasizing WID or WAC proponents' pedagogical goals over those of the faculty they collaborate with (Walvoord, Hunt, Dowling, & McMahon, 1997, pp. 8–13) and implying a "colonizer's" attitude towards other disciplines (Farris, 1992). Use of the word *resistance* has been said to reflect "an outsider's attempts to describe an insider's response to change" and present "a perspective that views teachers' responses negatively, a perspective that views these responses as reactions against, rather than as commitments to, proposed [curricular] changes" (Swanson-Owens, 1986, p. 72). Swanson-Owens (1986) conceded that as a proponent of social-constructivist views of knowledge and writing-to-learn pedagogical strategies, she was an "outsider" among the two high-school English teachers who held very different views of knowledge and pedagogy and with whom she collaborated as a WAC consultant. As a result, she described their resistance to her suggestions as "natural" and "appropriate" reflections of their "commitments to effective practice as they know it" (p. 72), thus attenuating the term's negative connotation. Further, Mahala and Swilky (1994) called into question the appropriateness of the "metaphor of WAC as a 'colonization' of the disciplines" because they claimed it "misrepresents the real power relations surrounding writing instruction, which has long been viewed as a 'service function' and has long been carried out, disproportionally, by women and low-ranking faculty" (p. 49). Rather than sidestep the topic of resistance, as some WAC proponents have advocated (Walvoord, 1992, p. 21), in this chapter I address the views of faculty who elect *not* to work further in WID collaborative research or who outright reject recommendations based on WID research and theory. Their reactions have much to teach scholars of disciplinarity about the function and transmission of disciplinary authority through discourse. *Resistance* may prove an apt label for marking faculty concerns that otherwise would be overlooked by WAC and WID proponents. Indeed, *resistance* and related terms denoting hesitation, unease, opposition, and ultimate refusal were terms introduced during our interviews by the three professors whose views I discuss here.

I have already discussed some of the previously identified resistances to making explicit disciplinary rhetorical practices in WID instruction, such as the view that in introductory or "gen. ed." coursework, a "predisciplinary" approach is favorable (Diller & Oates, 2002; Fleming, 2000; Hedley & Parker, 1991; Ohmann, 1996; Trimbur, 1995) or the view that we have moved or should move beyond the confines of rhetorical practices of the disciplines that valorize argument and perpetuate prevailing power structures so that a "postdisciplinary" pedagogy is now more appropriate (Downing & Sosnoski, 1995; Spanos, 1993). Other resistances identified in WAC and WID literature stem from institutional and academic structures that privilege research over teaching (Boice, 1990; Donahue, 2002; Halasz, Brinckner, Gambs, Geraci, Queeley, & Solovyova, 2006; Patton, Krawitz, Libbus, Ryan, & Townsend, 1998; Swilky, 1992; Walvoord, 1996). Until such structures are revised, the additional effort and time needed for faculty to implement pedagogies unfamiliar to them will likely and understandably be seen as too great a professional risk to take. Similarly, the structures of disciplinary specialization and expertise can deter professors from working to clarify the conventions of writing in their discipline when such work is seen as the purview of the writing specialist (Boice, 1990; Halasz, Brinckner, Gambs, Geraci, Queeley, & Solovyova, 2006; Mahala & Swilky, 1994; Patton, Krawitz, Libbus, Ryan, & Townsend, 1998). In this instance, the professionalization of rhetoric and composition and WAC specialists ironically works against WAC goals. This type of resistance can even be detected among high-school English teachers who have been strongly influenced by their university training to see reading and writing as basic skills best addressed by specialists prior to students' entrance to their classrooms (Franzak, 2008; Hamel, 2003, pp. 77–79).

Although many of these forms of resistance deter faculty from ever attempting WAC or WID pedagogies, Geisler (1994) provides one of the more nuanced explorations of resistance based on a professor's attempt to implement WID goals. Her qualitative study of an advanced writing course in which the professor sought to impart the rhetorical procedural knowledge common to scholars of philosophy uncovered several powerful reasons why this professor often retreated from this aim. In particular, she charted the pressure students exerted on the professor "to separate rhetorical process and domain content and attend to them in an order that matched their expectations: domain content first, rhetorical process later" (p. 228) and the pressure the professor exerted on students stemming from his expertise, which "seemed to make him unable to imagine his students taking any position [. . .] other than his own" (p. 226) and, thus, unable to fully allow them to take up and apply domain and rhetorical knowledge as fellow experts. Despite the professor's efforts to do otherwise, these pressures encouraged the integration of rhetorical process and domain knowledge in his classroom to remain largely "at the tacit level" (p. 230). At this level, the professor modeled for students expert integration of rhetorical and domain knowledge by repeatedly demonstrating how he revised his own analysis of course texts, but this public "back pedaling" left the professor worried he "might seem inept" (p. 223). Though his students seem instead to have learned from his behavior valuable lessons about how experts work, Geisler concluded that attempts like his to "open up" expert practice for students pose too many challenges for them to be made institutionally programmatic:

> This study suggests that such simple prescriptions for reform are problematic. In particular, experts who attempt to teach an integrated practice ultimately have an unsatisfying experience. They feel accountable when they do not live up to their students' demands to pass on knowledge and seldom persist in this effort. With no metalanguage with which to rise above their own convictions, they have no way to teach their practice except through actual demonstration, but this very demonstration often puts them at risk in the classroom—at risk of losing face, at risk of losing control. We cannot expect too many to be willing to take these risks. (p. 231)

Geisler's provocative conclusions based on one professor's experience suggest the need to explore further the bases for such resistances. Particularly because our experimental curriculum sought to provide instructors with the kind of "metalanguage" Geisler describes, faculty reactions to the curriculum suggest that their resistance to WID pedagogies extends beyond perceived risks of revealing the messiness of expert practice and losing face.

Faculty Interview Participants

Professor Evans

At the time of our study, Professor Evans[1] was a visiting assistant professor of contemporary poetry and critical theory. He originally participated as a control instructor, teaching WAL as he had previously done and allowing us to invite his students to participate by allowing access to their final papers and by completing questionnaires. But in a subsequent semester of our study, he volunteered to participate as an experimental instructor because, as he told me later, "I was a little bit set in my ways" and

> It is a writing course, and I figure if it's a writing course, then I guess I should talk about writing in ways that I haven't been talking about it before. I will admit that I am a literature person so I am not interested in the compositional aspect as much.

Like the other experimental instructors, he was provided with support for teaching in this new way in a variety of forms, including peer mentorship, scholarly articles explaining the special topoi and methods for teaching them (Fahnestock & Secor, 1991; Wolfe, 2003), sample course materials, and a small stipend made possible by a research grant to partially compensate for the time and effort required to modify his usual teaching practices. He also was supported by a teaching assistant, a graduate student in rhetoric and composition who led some class discussions on using the special topoi with his students. Despite this pedagogical support, in the end Professor Evans confessed that he felt that his switch to a new approach to WAL was rather perfunctory and that he had not integrated the special topoi into his teaching practices as much as he recognized could be possible. More than simply fighting a tendency to stick with the familiar, he found himself actively resistant to making these changes. I interviewed him to discuss his experience and reactions in November 2005, during the semester following his experience teaching WAL with the experimental curriculum.

Professor Caldwell

I also interviewed the other instructors who led our control sections, including Professor Caldwell, who was also then at the rank of visiting assistant professor. During this interview, I learned that Professor Caldwell had come to hear through word-of-mouth about one of the study's experimental teaching methods and had subsequently appropriated an assignment sheet used in experimental sections on using the mistaken-critic topos to engage published criticism in a research paper. Though this encounter made our distinctions between experimental and control sections somewhat less tidy (and sheds light on some of the challenges of in situ quasi-experimental research methods), it also provides another opportunity to learn about an experienced literature instructor's reactions to making special topoi explicit for pedagogical purposes. My analysis of both of these professors' views on their routine objectives for WAL is included in chapter 3; here I seek to understand their reservations about making explicit for literature students the special topoi conventional to the genre of literary analysis.

Professor Gregg

For this same purpose, I also include in this chapter analysis of portions of my interactions with Professor Gregg, whose introductory literature course I observed (see chapter 2 and Wilder, 2002). He raises somewhat different objections based on a different manner of encountering WID research on the rhetorical practices of literary scholars. After the semester I spent observing his class, I shared with him a full draft of my analysis of the role disciplinary special-topoi conventions play in his classroom. He generously shared his reactions to my findings and manner of viewing his course goals during interviews and in written comments on my draft. Chief among these reactions is his reluctance to acknowledge the presence of disciplinary rhetorical practices in his teaching, a reaction that suggests that motivating changes in classroom practices may not be accomplished simply by unmasking for professors the ways in which disciplinary rhetorics function.

Interview Findings

Professor Evans's and Caldwell's Reflections on Explicitly Teaching Special Topoi

Although both professors candidly shared with me reservations about explicitly teaching the special topoi of literary analysis in WAL—reservations so strong that they likely will never teach in this way again—they both acknowledged several positive aspects of teaching the special topoi. Professor Evans indicated that he thought the special topoi were welcome additions to his class discussions of published literary criticism, helping the class analyze critics' arguments. He estimates one-third of the class "really got it," using the topoi enthusiastically to not only analyze published criticism but also to brainstorm for their own arguments. He said these students pushed conscious use of these analytic and inventional tools much further than he did in his own course preparation:

> I would incorporate them [the topoi] into informal writing assignments and in class activities to tease out the topoi, and they, they really did it, much more so than I did in my own preparation. They really took to it.

He claims he saw no effect, positive or negative, on the remaining two-thirds of the class, though he acknowledged that "just because I couldn't discern whether other students were taking to it, that doesn't mean that it didn't help them." Thus, his perception that this teaching methodology benefitted a significant portion of his students without drawbacks for others led him to question why he found himself rejecting the teaching methodology. As he put it, "I don't think there were any negative results for them, but there were negative results for me. [...] I spent the entire semester trying to figure out why I was resisting."

Professor Caldwell found similarly positive outcomes in her class when using the assignment for working with the mistaken-critic topos, yet also similarly she reported she would not be using this assignment again. She said that previously, when she gave "no direction" in strategies for using published literary criticism, her WAL students' attempts to incorporate research in their papers were "a disaster." Echoing the students I interviewed who singled out the mistaken-critic topos as particularly challenging (see chapter 5), Professor Caldwell said, "They need some guidance. This is very difficult for them to go from their paper to incorporating outside.... This is a very sophisticated thing to do." She found the mistaken-critic assignment to provide this needed guidance. This handout outlines a series of exercises to be conducted over two weeks of the semester. It walks students through the process of locating, assessing, and summarizing sources and then using the mistaken-critic topos to indicate how a student's early draft of a literary analysis engages with this previous criticism. The assignment illustrates five ways a writer can engage previous criticism including the corrective aim the name "mistaken critic" implies as well strategies for seeking to fill gaps in previous criticism, offering another layer of meaning while maintaining the integrity of previous interpretations, and building on or extending previous criticism. Though she describes this assignment as "fantastic" and one that helped her students meet the challenge of using sources in their papers, like Professor Evans she found the approach taken in the assignment so contradicts her teaching philosophy that she will not be using it in the future.

These professors' resistance to a pedagogy that seeks to demystify disciplinary rhetorical conventions is not, then, a knee-jerk reaction based on a first impression of a WAC administrator's attempt to persuade (or compel) faculty to change their classroom practice but instead is thoughtfully based on an extended, voluntary attempt to implement this goal in their classrooms. Further, both indicated that they recognized that the special topoi describe not only what professional literary scholars do in their writing but also what their best, most advanced students have tended to do as well. As Professor Evans told me, the students in his class "who get As do have [thesis] statements that are . . . much in line with [the] topoi." However, Professor Evans and Professor Caldwell enumerated several often-overlapping reasons for their resistance to making explicit these rhetorical practices in their classrooms:

Professionalizes students too soon. Echoing the criticisms advanced by advocates of "predisciplinary" pedagogy (Hedley & Parker, 1991; Ohmann, 1996; Trimbur, 1995), Professor Evans raised concerns that teaching the special topoi professionalizes students too soon. As he put this concern,

> If [students] had completely internalized these topoi by the end of the term, then they should be writing like a professor, where this is old hat to them. And in my opinion that's professionalizing them way too soon.

While this seems a too-simple conflation of the special topoi with all aspects of professional rhetorical practice and domain knowledge, he clearly does not support what appears to him to be an attempt to "speed up" the traditional pace of acquisition of disciplinary rhetorical process knowledge. Thus, he shares with predisciplinary advocates a desire to maintain a space for students' encounters with a discipline's domain knowledge without, or with lesser, concern for mastery of disciplinary rhetorical and procedural knowledge. However, while many predisciplinary advocates speak of this space as ideally located in general education coursework suited for nonmajors, Professor Evans desires to maintain this space in a "gateway" class for majors designed to focus on the writing practices they will encounter in this discipline. As a result, the kind of deferral of instruction in disciplinary rhetorical process knowledge that Geisler (1994) described may be maintained even by a WID course that proposes to provide it.

Saps the fun and pleasure from reading. Professor Evans's desire to defer this instruction appears related to the kinds of distasteful, bureaucratic, and dehumanizing qualities that Ohmann (1996) associated with "the discipline" and "the profession." Both Evans and Caldwell are concerned that such explicit teaching of professional rhetorical strategies might sap the fun or pleasure out of their class or the reading of literature. Aligning himself with the critics of WID like Spellmeyer (1989), Professor Evans described the special topoi as potentially hampering students' "emotional" engagement with literary texts because they are "almost like a formula":

> I don't want to say that it [the approach to teaching the special topoi] takes the pleasure out of the text, out of the reading process, but it might. It might point too heavily toward the end product as opposed to the process.

Here compositionists may hear echoes of their debates on the pedagogical soundness of developing students' writing processes over concentration on the correctness of their final products, debates that Evans is aware of from his exposure to rhetoric and composition during his graduate training. However, what Professor Evans means here by "process" is "the reading process," indicating his preference like so many of our control instructors to focus on reading over writing in WAL (see chapter 2). The inventional, "prewriting" playfulness that rhetoricians associate with topoi is obscured in Evans's apparent focus on the audience-centered persuasive capacities of the special topoi. As a result, he sees them vacating both "process" and "pleasure" or diminishing the potential for "fun":

> My approach to literature is that it should be wrestled with, and there are other professors that "no, you master it, you control it, you articulate your argument in this completely polished form." Even at the undergraduate level. I mean, you should have fun when you're an undergraduate.

Similarly, Professor Caldwell sees the value she places on students' excitement and enjoyment with literary texts as oppositional to her department's, and perhaps the profession's, dominant culture of scholarly argumentation (see fuller discussion of her expressivist approach to WAL in chapter 2).

"Boxes in" and limits creativity. Professor Caldwell believes her students' excitement is promoted by the freedom she gives them to "do their own creative thing." She is thus very concerned that listing strategies in the manner of the mistaken-critic-topos assignment sheet "boxes in" students and limits their creativity. In this way, her views echo Spellmeyer's (1989) concerns as well as those of some literature faculty Sullivan (1991) interviewed who fear that explicit instruction in the processes of inquiry and genre conventions of the seminar paper would inhibit students' creativity and "induce them to write 'formulaic stuff'" (p. 294). Caldwell distinguished the responses of her students by her perception of their skill level and ability. She thinks articulating topoi "works with the top student, makes it easier for the top student" because she perceived them to be better able to use the topoi flexibly. However, for weaker students, she feels making such topoi explicit "limits

them" because "they're not good enough to break out of the box." And "middle" students, she says, "just slavishly follow" the explicit guidance given. It appears that Professor Caldwell's adherence to the disciplinary value of originality—ironically, a value that literary scholars highlight through their use of the mistaken-critic topos—leads her to denigrate as uncreative attempts by struggling students to imitate unfamiliar discourse practices.[2] By contrast, although Professor Evans expressed concerns that this pedagogy might diminish students' pleasure in reading, he did not find the special topoi to inhibit students' creativity. When I specifically asked him if this was a concern of his, he replied, "Creativity? No, because my understanding is that [. . .] these topoi give all the possibilities, and the students still have to work through and figure out which one is the best."

Too much guidance means not enough struggle. Because Professor Caldwell appears to measure students' creativity by how far they depart from guidance, it may not be surprising that she chooses to provide little guidance. While she emphasizes collaborative brainstorming and peer review, she does not "give them a lot of guidance for what the paper's supposed to look like." She believes that by doing so, she resists pressure from students and encourages independent thinking: "Some students really don't like it because they want more guidance, but . . . I try to be really nondirective." And she clearly feels that making the special topoi explicit provides too much guidance. Of the mistaken-critic-topos assignment, she said, "I don't like to give this much direction. That's against my strategy, my philosophy." Professor Evans appears to share this philosophy. A term he used repeatedly when describing what he wanted to see students do with literature is "wrestle," and he clearly feels that making the special topoi explicit provides a shortcut around this struggle.

Conflicts with discipline's value of complexity. Echoing Professor Caldwell's contention that the experimental curriculum may be at odds with a core philosophy, Professor Evans sees teaching the special topoi of literary analysis as conflicting with his values, or as he put it, "my literary worldview." He even speculated that the third of his class who really "took to" the special-topoi instruction may have an overall "different approach to literature than I do." Rather than promoting the "wrestling with ideas" he so esteems, the special topoi, as he understands them, reduce complexity in the interest of rational, clear argument. As he explained to me, the topics he addresses in this course (dreams, coming-of-age anxiety, existentialism) are all "I don't want to say nebulous, but they're topics that people in the field spend years and years and years" working to unravel and understand because they deal with the unconscious. In contrast,

> These topoi, and my interpretation of [. . .] rhetoric and composition studies in general, [try] to articulate from a rational, persuasive standpoint what is happening in the topic under discussion, be it literature or be it, you know, whatever. And I think that what I'm trying to get at is the unconscious, is some kind of irrational project that is going on in literature, and [. . .] I don't know how well that jibes with the special topoi.

These explanations suggest that Professor Evans's resistance to making the special topoi explicit in his classroom may be rooted in the kinds of cultural differences that contribute to distinguishing the rhetorical practices of different disciplines. For instance, he sees rhetoric and composition as maintaining values that oppose not only his own but also those of other "people in the field" he works in. Similarly, he recognizes that some students in his classroom may come from different discourse communities and hold different values. However, he appears unwilling to acknowledge the ways in which his field's values manifest as provisionally definable social conventions, whether rational or not. For instance, Professor Evans requires his students to produce what he called "standard," thesis-driven "five-hundred-word essays." But for these he insists that his students'

> theses are always going to point to an unresolvable conflict in the text. And I basically tell them, I don't care if you resolve the conflict, I just want you to show me all the aspects of it, and if it'll make you feel better, come to a tentative conclusion about which side you pick. But I don't want them to choose a side. I don't specifically tell them to pick unless they need it. 'Cause some students need it. Some students just do not want to have anything to do with my approach to literature.

Thus, he is able to describe and in fact prescribe a conventional value of his field, a thesis that reflects the preference for the irreducibly complex, a value my rhetorical analysis of professional discourse in this field reveals to be conventional (see chapter 1). But the articulation and exemplification of further steps writers can take to explore and support such a thesis he views as conflicting with his valorization of irresolution, complexity, and irreducibility. Due to this conflict between the reductions necessary for pedagogical clarity and the desire to maintain complexity, the call for explicit instruction in genre conventions may raise distinctive resistances for instructors of literature and other disciplines within the humanities.

Overwhelms students. Whereas Professor Evans is concerned that teaching the special topoi might encourage students to bypass necessary wrestling, Professor Caldwell seems more concerned that guidance of this sort on writing would "overwhelm" students: "If [my students had] been given six strategies, they just would have cried and be done." Thus, while Evans is concerned that making the special topoi explicit reduces difficulty, Caldwell worries it unnecessarily increases difficulty and anxiety.

Facilitates B.S. Perhaps related to his concern for bypassing complexity and struggle, Professor Evans is concerned that knowledge of the special topoi might assist students in deceiving their professor: "If you use them, you can essentially B.S. your professor, and that kind of disconcerted me." In this fear, Evans appears to articulate the popular association between academic writing and bullshit described by Eubanks and Schaeffer (2008) as well as ancient charges against rhetoric as trickery.

Provides an unfair advantage. Professor Evans feels to some degree it is unfair to give his students advantages he did not have himself as a student:

> These topoi are basically saying, "Here are the six or seven ways, in general, that you can talk about literature," and I want to say that that's something they [students] should figure for themselves. Because that's how I did it. I didn't have someone say, "Here are the six, seven ways you can talk about literature in every single paper."

While reminiscent of the rationale behind hazing traditions, his comment does resonate with the insight a student, Eve, came to at the conclusion of our interview: that her professors likely learned the special topoi through "trial and error" and that the implicitness of the special topoi may in fact have given them an advantage over many of their contemporaries who were less adept at intuiting such rhetorical conventions and their importance (see chapter 5). By Evans's logic, the implicit rhetorical curriculum may serve as an effective filter for the discipline, facilitating the admittance of the right individuals to its higher ranks—people who share his knack for discerning and employing such conventions. Thus, while he presents his concerns in terms of fairness, WID proponents who see explicit rhetorical instruction as an attempt to redress social inequities among entering college students would likely see Professor Evans as overlooking social factors that gave him an advantage in acquiring the rhetorical process knowledge of his discipline.

Professor Gregg's Denial of Disciplinary Influence on Favored Rhetorical Practices

Unlike Professor Evans and Professor Caldwell, Professor Gregg rejects my and other WID researchers' claims regarding the existence of discipline-specific rhetorics. Gregg strives to make his introductory course relevant to the diverse students who take it by imparting skills for argumentation that they can transfer to other rhetorical contexts. Although he agrees that the rhetorical strategies I observed were in fact used by himself, TAs, and students, he disputes my categorization of these strategies as disciplinary in a number of ways.

Like several of his colleagues (see chapter 2), Gregg repeatedly associated disciplinarity with an older, outmoded version of his discipline. I presented the special topoi to him as markers of disciplinarity, and he responded by associating several of them, specifically the paradox and appearance/reality topoi, with New Criticism, hinting that I may be searching for discourse practices in his classroom that he feels are no longer viable or perhaps lingering aspects of his students' former educational encounters with literature.

Another mode of his disputation was to universalize the rhetorical practices of literary scholars, a tendency I also observed in his colleagues. For instance, his reactions to the results of a questionnaire I administered in his class indicate that he prefers to understand the special topoi as widely applicable critical-thinking tools rather than rhetorical strategies unique to the discourse of literary scholars. The questionnaire asked students to distinguish whether different passages were from "arguments about literature" of the kind appropriate for this class. Some of these passages were from professional literary analyses and exemplified scholars' use of the special topoi, some were summary passages from *CliffsNotes* treatments of literary texts, and some were from statistical analyses of literary texts conducted by linguists. On first learning that students who were more adept at recognizing passages that employ the special topoi as valid arguments tended to earn higher grades in his course, he replied:

> I think you can argue in terms of ideas of textual power or doing things with a text, these [the passages that exemplify the special topoi] are the ones that do things with them, so that would be then a nice result,

they recognize that this is what I'm supposed to do, I'm supposed to do something with this, not simply kind of say what's happening or make some kind of statistical . . .

Here he references the concept of "textual power," one that he had stressed in his training of his TAs as a concept he derived from Scholes (1985). In his book *Textual Power*, Scholes (1985) urged literature instructors to accept that "our job is not to produce 'readings' for our students but to give them the tools for producing their own" (p. 24). Professor Gregg equated the special topoi with the kind of tools Scholes wishes to see students master. In this sense, he agrees with Fahnestock and Secor's (1991) discussion of the way special topoi function as logos: "From one point of view the special topoi are the logos of literary arguments and are thus the very constructs which enable scholars to operate on literature" (p. 91). He was pleased to see that students who did well in his course appear to understand that using these tools produces valid arguments in contrast to summaries, which merely "say what's happening," and linguistic treatments of literature, which "make some kind of statistical" argument. However, despite his gratification on seeing evidence that his best students not only distinguished literary analysis from summary but also from a type of argument suitable in another discipline, linguistics, he rejected seeing the special topoi as unique to his discipline. Rather than regarding them as exemplifying different disciplinary approaches to analyzing a shared object of study, he regards the passages by literary scholars as the correct way to argue, and the passages by *CliffsNotes* writers and linguists as incorrect ways to argue, or at least incorrect ways for his students to argue.

Perceiving the special topoi as specialized rhetorical knowledge would undercut his goals to promote generalizable rhetorical skills useful to students in numerous contexts:

It would be important to me that these [the special topoi] not be distinctive. It would be bad for me if these were say highly distinctive of literary critical arguments but that you don't really find this form of argumentation outside of literary criticism.

He thus rejects seeing the special topoi as the locus of "the interaction between arguer and audience, between logos and ethos," in ways that announce an arguer's "membership in the community of literary scholars who in turn will listen most attentively to the speaker with such credentials" (Fahnestock & Secor, 1991, p. 91). Instead, he prefers to see topoi such as paradigm as general strategies that are not "especially literary but rather [. . .] at the heart of most critical thinking" and "central to nearly every discipline I can think of." In this way, he appears to see critical-thinking and writing skills as lying outside and prior to the specific work of academic disciplines. He thus echoes the "predisciplinary" advocates Hedley and Parker's (1991) claim that "we should not be inviting undergraduates to begin to be sociologists or art historians before they have begun to be reflective, critical thinkers" (p. 27). This objection to WID appears rooted in a dichotomous view of writing and critical-thinking skills on one hand and disciplinary rhetorical and procedural knowledge on the other.

Conclusion

Understandably, memories of their own experiences as undergraduates seem often to have been guiding forces behind many of these professor's current decisions about teaching undergraduates. Having never experienced an approach to literary study that sought to make explicit and offer conscious practice in conventions of literary analysis, these professors can only observe student reactions and infer what this experience is like from the other side of the desk. Professor Caldwell clustered students into high-, middle-, and low-skilled groups and projected different reactions from each group, from ease to tears. Professor Evans speculated about both the pleasure and the struggles his students experienced while completing assignments for his class. In this, these professors are no different from many other faculty across campus whose explorations of pedagogy are largely drawn from inference and personal experience. A potential problem with personal experience as a primary source of pedagogical theory, as several scholars interested in tacit knowledge have discussed, is that professors tend to have been among the "best" students, those "natural" students Shumway (1992) and Bourdieu, Passeron, and de Saint Martin (1994) described as likely favored as much or more by social circumstances as by nature. Hamel's (2003) research indicates that teachers' rely on their memories as "naturally" good readers and writers rather than assessing their current students' understanding when making pedagogical decisions in high-school literature courses as well (pp. 61, 68). Simply put, there is reason to believe these memories and projections based upon them do not fully reflect the experiences of many students currently in these instructors' classrooms.

For instance, the student voices represented in the qualitative research described in earlier chapters counter several of the professors' assumptions about how students react to explicit instruction in the special topoi of literary analysis, suggesting that students' enjoyment, creativity, and intellectual and emotional challenges may not be hampered in the ways that Professor Evans and Professor Caldwell fear. Students who experienced a WAL curriculum that sought to make explicit the special topoi were just as likely—and sometimes more likely—than students taught using traditional WAL pedagogies to describe themselves as personally engaged with and interested in the literature they were reading. None of the students I interviewed described being overwhelmed or puzzled by the attempts of their WAL professors to make the special topoi explicit. On the contrary, a self-described underprepared student, Eric, was effusive about how clarifying and enabling he found this instruction. In fact, the only students who expressed confusion were students who experienced traditional approaches to WAL. Ed, a student who experienced the special-topoi curriculum in WAL, was, however, vocal about his frustration stemming from the creative confinement he felt when writing in genres of academic argument. The kind freedom from the constraints of such genres that Professor Caldwell allowed may have appealed to him. But other students like Eric and Evelyn reported that as inventional tools the special topoi enabled their creativity.

The number of students who described the special topoi as merely providing labels to strategies they either had already intuited or recognized as implicit in their previous literature courses call into question Professor Evans's concern that making the special topoi explicit professionalizes students too soon. Evidence that college literature instructors already prefer student writing that exhibits the special topoi (see chapter 3) also complicates faculty desires to forestall professionalization. Simply put, evidence from a variety of sources indicates these professional conventions are already thoroughly embedded in students' experience of academic literary study. Explicit acknowledgment of this would not be the impetus behind such professionalization, then; rather, it would oblige instructors to become more aware of this tendency. If in fact this is a tendency that Professor Evans and others, such as advocates of post- or predisciplinarity, wish to stem, such awareness could help them modify the values and conventions they have intuited from their disciplinary training and tacitly come to see as signs of "good writing."

However, such a redirection of the goals of a course like WAL may prove to be much more complex. I recognize that a possible interpretation of Professor Evans's and Professor Caldwell's concerns is that they more fully embrace expressivist "writing to learn" goals of WAC pedagogy than rhetorical "writing to communicate" WID goals. However, both indicated that they see WAL as preparation for the major in English, and to meet this goal, both routinely make certain aspects of professional discourse the explicit object of instruction. Both, for instance, teach vocabulary for literary analysis. Professor Caldwell is quite adamant about this, encouraging students to consult regularly Abrams and Harpham's *Glossary of Literary Terms*. As she said, "I'm assuming with the English majors, this should get them used to the vocabulary, the conventions." Thus, their resistances do not stem from a complete rejection of WID goals. Both indicated that teaching the special topoi might be appropriate for advanced students, perhaps in an advanced research and critical-writing course. However, both agreed that their best WAL students already figure out how to use many of these special topoi on their own, as Professor Evans recognizes he had done when he was a student. When acknowledging that his A students already use the special topoi in their writing, Professor Evans said,

> I don't know what to do with that. I mean, you obviously want everyone to get to that stage, but I don't know. I don't know if you can get to that stage in an introduction to literature course. And I don't know if I would want them to.

That his resistances stem more from his own values than his students' experiences was candidly acknowledged by Professor Evans. This makes responding to his concerns with descriptions of students' experiences a problematic tactic. For instance, he raises a valid concern that the techniques necessary to make the special topoi explicit to students may conflict with his and his discipline's valorization of complexity. Attempts not only to teach such conventions but also to codify them in rhetorical analyses such as the one presented in chapter 1 inevitably reduce complexity for the sake of analytical and pedagogical clarity. This has led some rhetorical scholars to question the efficacy of such explicit instruction in helping students achieve genuinely effective versions of the target genre (A. Freedman, 1993a, 1993b) and others to ask what less-conventionalized and more experimental, alternative, or marginal aspects of a discipline's discourse may be overlooked (Herndl, 1993; LeCourt, 1996; Mahala, 1991; Mahala & Swilky, 1994). However, neither of these concerns captures the reservations raised by these three literature professors. Instead, the issue appears to be the confrontation of one value, complexity of meaning, with another, the provisional clarity required to impart understanding to a novice. It appears that codifying formal conventions that appear more on the "surface" of the genre of literary analysis, such as specialized vocabulary, the MLA citation style, or use of the present verb tense, pose less of a value conflict for literary scholars than codifying special topoi, which critics use to craft not only the logos of their argument but also their ethos and pathos appeals. However, such surface conventions appear to be ones that students have less trouble identifying and applying without explicit instruction (MacDonald, 1987, p. 315).

Professor Evans's worry that explicit instruction in the special topoi would disconcertingly implicate him in facilitating students' ability to "b.s." their professors is also not as easy to dismiss as it may first appear. It is certainly a charge against rhetorical instruction with a long history, reminiscent of Plato's Socrates's separation of dialectic, and by extension invention, from the realm of rhetoric, a separation made further indelible by Peter Ramus in the sixteenth century (Kennedy, 1999, p. 250). A consequence of this separation, which twentieth-century revivalists of the rhetorical tradition found themselves repeatedly rebutting, is that rhetoric is understood to denote only arrangement, style, and delivery, discourse features thought to beautify, mask, or distort substance rather than *be* substance. Professor Evans appears to be concerned that his students might use the special topoi to dazzle him with professional-sounding arguments that mask a lack of serious engagement with the literary texts he assigns. Indeed, even in their recent attempt to understand and reclaim "bullshit," Eubanks and Schaeffer (2008) concede that when students are insincere and disengage in this way, they aim "to get by with something worse than a lie," which the authors see as a problem rhetoricians and writing teachers should address (p. 386). However, Eubanks and Schaeffer do not indicate how instructors can distinguish this apparently egregious form of bullshit from the type they describe as "benign" and even "productive" and leading to "better thought and better selves" (p. 387). This productive form is affiliated with a student's attempts to craft an ethos within a discourse community new to them, no small task. As Eubanks and Schaffer put it,

> composition theory explicitly advocates that students do just what makes academic writing seem to many like bullshit: to develop an identity within a community of discourse—that is, to gain "genre knowledge." [. . .] Whether we liken today's students to those of Isocrates,

who were encouraged to create a persona that they wanted to inhabit, or whether we think of student writers along the lines of Lave and Wenger's apprentices, good writing is inseparable from the context in which it arises—and thus from the manipulations of self that contexts foist upon us all. Along the way to professional writing competence, there is bound to be some bullshit. (p. 385)

Perhaps, Professor Evans is uncomfortable becoming purposefully involved in his students' rhetorical manipulations of identity, preferring instead to focus in the abstract on philosophical discussion of the logos of their interpretations of literature, or what he calls their reading process. Gregg appears similarly uncomfortable with the relationship between the special topoi and ethos. He is satisfied that the special topoi function as the logos of arguments in his classroom but displeased that using them signals a rhetor's standing within a specific disciplinary community.

Nonetheless, Professor Evans's recent work with the special topoi appears to have made him aware that he more highly regards the work of those students whose projections of ethos resonate with his professional and disciplinary assumptions. This recognition ought to make his reservations stemming from a desire for fairness particularly troubling to WID advocates motivated by concerns for social equity. Professor Evans invokes the value of equity to argue for maintaining the system of granting greater status and further access up the rungs of disciplinary hierarchy to those students who are adept, like he was, at discerning the implicit rhetorical curriculum of their major. That so much evidence suggests this adeptness stems from the uneven social and educational contexts students navigate long before they enter a college classroom leads many compositionists, including myself, to claim the status quo is far from fair. His reaction suggests the powerful ways in which aspects of disciplinary enculturation may be seen as initiation rites. Changing these rites may literally change the culture. Preserving them maintains the community one has worked so hard to enter.

Segal, Paré, Brent, and Vipond (1998) counseled that professionals' resistance to rhetorical interpretations of their discourse practices are likely related to the hierarchal distribution of power within professions. They claimed that the resistant reactions their analyses of professional discourse communities have received often stemmed from anxiety that such analyses unmask, and therefore diminish, key markers of professional power:

The resistance we meet when we share our rhetorical interpretations [. . .] often occurs because we have challenged someone in power, sometimes inadvertently. Those who suffer as a result of unfair, unequal, or oppressive discourse practices may have no difficulty understanding and appreciating our critical analyses, but those who benefit from those practices are often quite resistant. (p. 87)

However, they acknowledged that such resistance may be even more complexly motivated:

We have learned, too, that even the apparently powerful may be constrained by institutional or disciplinary forces we cannot at first perceive or appreciate. And those who are placed at some disadvantage by professional discourse practices may reject or resist our criticisms or suggestions for change, since such changes might expose them to further and worse controls and jeopardize their positions. (p. 87)

This perspective suggests that Professor Evans's motivations for maintaining the status quo are likely too complex to be understood on the basis of our one conversation. As a professor in a non–tenure-track appointment, he may have found objectionable and unfair actions that support making the climb up the disciplinary hierarchy easier or swifter for those behind him. Additionally, given his tenuous status in the professional hierarchy, Evans may have felt the risks that Geisler (1994) observed in a similar case—the "risk of losing face" and "risk of losing control" (p. 231)—even more acutely. The rhetorical metalanguage provided by the special topoi seems to have done little to alleviate sources of resistance related to power dynamics and face-saving.

From this perspective, one may interpret as the luxury of a power holder within the discipline the lack of inclination exhibited by Professor Gregg to acknowledge that his favored discourse practices were influenced by his discipline. Previous studies of students struggling to meet the genre expectations of different disciplines (Beaufort, 2004; Carroll, 2002; McCarthy, 1987; North, 2005; Thaiss & Zawacki, 2006) and the students who related their cross-disciplinary writing experiences during their interviews with me offer a contrasting perspective.[3] One consequence of this professor's emphasis on the commonality of critical-thinking and argument strategies is a tendency to see general admonitions to "write arguments" as sufficient rhetorical instruction in the context of disciplinary coursework. While some students may have stubbornly doubted or ignored his recurrent descriptions of their papers as arguments, others may have lacked a clear understanding of what argumentation looks like when the subject is literature and the audience is a professor of literature. Thus, for them his direction "to argue" may have been insufficient.

I am also struck by what appears to be a trend among some literary scholars in associating disciplinarity with an older, bygone era of literary studies. The same poststructuralist theoretical developments that have led literary scholars to interrogate disciplinarity often motivate WID work such as mine. However, we appear to differ on our perceptions of the degree to which we are capable of "getting outside" of disciplinary discourse. My research and rhetorical training inform my perception that while theoretical developments and the inclusion of new members and perspectives do indeed lead to radically altered discourse practices within disciplines, these new practices solidify into conventions used alongside many older conventions. In fact, I argue this is how an established discourse community must change—a slate is not wiped clean but instead long-standing conventions are used to leverage new ones and oust others (see chapter 1 for a discussion of the social justice and contemptus mundi topoi as examples). I, thus, tend to see a continuity of rhetorical practices where it appears some literature professors see rupture and radical innovation, with the persistence of older conventions remaining largely transparent to them. Perhaps as a result, the professors I spoke with tended to describe disciplinarity as a state their profession, or they themselves, had moved past, whereas I see them still thoroughly situated within the disciplinary discourse community.

Fish (1985) similarly characterized such suspicion of disciplinarity and professionalism as inconsistent with poststructuralist developments in literary theory. Although he saw disdain for professionalism exhibited by the discipline's conservative traditionalists as consistent with their essentialist view of Truth, the censure of professionalism by the discipline's vanguard, Fish argued, contradicts a view of knowledge, truth, and selfhood as socially constructed. He saw this contradiction, for instance, in Ohmann's (1996) desire for access to and transmission of a "literary culture and consciousness" unmediated by professional discourse. Although these scholars are strikingly adept at untangling the impact of social context and convention on the texts they study, like the scholars in the sciences (see Charney, 1993), they are much less aware—or even suspicious of—the rhetoricity of their own discourse. Fish suspected that the assumption that the artificial conventions and social motives of professional discourse are in some way subversive of real, genuine truths and selves, may in fact be a hallmark of disciplinarity and professionalism. Belief in an autonomous, entirely free self, Fish claimed, is part of "the story the rising or bourgeois class tells itself" (p. 105) and one that the professional continually attempts to "mediate and ameliorate" while in "the context of purposes, motivations, and possibilities that precede and even define him" (p. 106). Thus, "far from being a stance taken at the margins or the periphery, anti-professionalism is the very center of the professional ethos" (p. 106).

Whereas Fish's characterization of antiprofessionalism may suggest little possibility for effectively motivating change in a professional's understanding of the rhetoricity of their professional discourse,[4] I find fissures and opportunities within the candid words of the literature professors with whom I spoke. For instance, Professor Gregg's desire to have his students practice argumentation skills that they will use in other contexts outside of his classroom and his discipline is one I not only sympathize with but share. However, we differ greatly in our sense of whether specific disciplinary contexts for argumentation impede or enable this goal. I am, of course, hopeful that students who are provided guidance in disciplinary topoi conventions will go on to use them effectively in other courses within that discipline (as suggested by my interviews with students in chapter 5). But like a growing number of proponents of genre-based first-year composition courses (Beaufort, 2007; Carroll, 2002; Devitt, 2004; Downs & Wardle, 2007), I also find compelling evidence that suggests the most-useful knowledge students can learn in any introductory writing course is rhetorical awareness of audience, purpose, and genre, knowledge they can build upon later and adapt in new situations. Highlighting these features in gen. ed. courses may help students develop rhetorical awareness and genre analysis skills in the truly complex discourse-community environments of the disciplines in ways they can carry with them into new contexts. Thus, what Gregg might characterize as a too-narrow focus on the rhetorical practices of one discipline may in fact present the most effectively transportable rhetorical knowledge.[5]

Professor Caldwell's experience with explicitly teaching the mistaken-critic topos did inspire her to alter her pedagogical practice in the future. Although she will abandon the assignment that provides explicit guidance in the mistaken-critic topos, she does plan to incorporate models to teach the rhetorical strategies of this topos:

I'm thinking of bringing in papers that use the strategies I think are right and don't give them any of this. And just give them the model papers and then have them look at that and then tell me, tell each other, what [the paper] has done. And then I don't think that would box them in as much.

By incorporating such rhetorical analysis into her pedagogy, she may encourage her students to become active agents in investigating the rhetorical practices of the discipline in a way advocated by several WID and genre-theory proponents (Beaufort, 2007; Devitt, 2004; LeCourt, 1996). However, in a study of students' acquisition of genre knowledge appropriate to the discipline of psychology, Charney and Carlson (1995) found that "students wrote more successful products and reported using more active and evaluative writing strategies when given models in conjunction with some other instruction than when given models alone or guidelines alone" (p. 115). Caldwell's future plans keep the rhetorical conventions implicit in her teaching, though the explicit invitation to look for strategies may help many students recognize that this is a productive way of reading examples of the target genre. Professor Caldwell's plans suggest that her experience with a pedagogical tool that sought to make disciplinary conventions explicit has deepened her commitment to the WID goals of her department's WAL course and encouraged her to adapt the tool in a way she finds does not conflict with her teaching philosophy.

However, Professor Evans plans to make no such modifications to his usual approach to WAL, despite his realizations that the rhetorical practices of his "best students" more closely matched the conventions of his discipline. He plans to return to his usual practice of assigning a lot of B grades at semester's end, reserving Cs and Ds to those infrequent students he claims truly do not wrestle with ideas and instead try to get away with handing in plot summaries. I cannot help but wonder whether the process of determining the degree to which students truly "wrestle" with course texts might not present a problem parallel to the "b.s." that concerned him: How does one determine the "true" intent behind students' performance for evaluation? Because he ultimately assesses his students' degree of wrestling from their written texts, some of the plot summaries he receives may likely be evidence not of some students' failure to "wrestle" but of their lack of understanding the motivations, identities, tools, and processes of writing in literary studies. In which case, their wrestling may remain unseen, unaccounted for.

Recommendations for WID Proponents Facing Resistance

The kinds of resistances described in this chapter suggest some of the reasons why courses labeled by universities as WID have typically been characterized by little more than a cap on class size and requirements mandating a minimum number of pages of student writing. Like Russell (2001), I hope to see "the fruits" of WID research "inform educational practices across disciplines and institutions" (p. 291). However, given WID proponents' concern for bridging rhetorical divides between novices and experts and among disciplines, it is painfully ironic that chief among the causes for resistance to WID may be the difficulties WID researchers face in persuading colleagues in other fields about the validity and applicability of their findings. As Segal, Paré, Brent, and Vipond (1998) have argued, to do so effectively, WID proponents must aim to be rhetors who understand their audiences.

One practical suggestion for WID proponents that emerges from these interview findings is the need to share research on disciplinary rhetorics not only among rhetoricians and not only among the professionals from the disciplines with whom we collaborate and study (Segal, Paré, Brent, and Vipond, 1998) but also among professionals in other fields in order to more clearly bring into relief their own conventional practices. In my discussions with Professor Gregg, it quickly became apparent that a likely effective way to persuade him of the existence of discipline-specific rhetorical practices in his own field and teaching would be through contrasting them with the rhetorical practices of other disciplines he is less familiar with. He raised this suggestion himself when he asked me, "What would be the commonplace arguments in science?" The descriptions of most WID-inflected WAC faculty workshops indicate that facilitators focus on helping faculty to identify the tacit conventions of and expectations for writing in their field (Carter, 2007; Magnotto & Stout, 1992; Thaiss & Zawacki, 2006; Walvoord, 1992). The use of cross-disciplinary rhetorical comparisons is seldom mentioned and must seldom emerge since facilitators typically conduct these workshops with faculty from the same department. The inclusion of cross-disciplinary rhetorical analysis in these workshops may help faculty understand the need to teach disciplinary rhetorics, since this should help clarify that not all effective writing skills will be—or can be—imparted in a general first-year writing course. Such comparisons should bring into clearer view the struggles of students in their classrooms who may be more familiar with rhetorical practices valued in other disciplines or who may be struggling to infer conventions across a wide array of disciplines. For example, Professor Gregg's perception that special topoi of literary analysis are widely applicable to academic discourse could be partially validated but also called into question by a cross-disciplinary comparison. From a distant vantage point, a topos such as paradigm is indeed widely shared: scholars in many disciplines ground their observations in explicitly stated theoretical constructs. However, seen up close, scholars often apply theories in rhetorically diverse and specialized manners. MacDonald (1994), for instance, illustrated how disciplines within the humanities differ in their understandings of what counts as evidence and how these understandings are reflected even in their conventional patterns of sentence structure.

We need not only further WID research that draws out and takes seriously the concerns of faculty across the disciplines but also WID outreach that uses what we learn about the values that inform disciplinary discourse when attempting to influence such discursive practices. Literary scholars' own context topos could be invoked in appeals to them to see student discourse as occurring within overlapping disciplinary and institutional contexts. Calling into question the possibility that writing and critical-thinking skills might be segregated from these contexts (let alone from one another) may prove an effective response to those who claim a predisciplinary space for their pedagogy but who adamantly argue for the importance of literary, historical, or political context for understanding the texts they study. Likewise, in an appeal to the appearance/reality topos, WID advocates could encourage literary scholars to look beyond such surface conventions as the MLA citation style to identify those more-embedded conventions and values that give shape, meaning, and exigency to the collective projects of their discipline or subdiscipline. Turning the appearance/reality topos on the discipline itself in this way could help make the case that such embedded conventions—which can be uncovered even by disciplinary experts only through close reading and thoughtful reflection—present daunting challenges for beginning students, who are routinely expected to intuit them on their own, often simultaneously facing parallel challenges in different disciplines.

Pursuing this vein of invention with special topoi still further, we might call on the paradox topos to frame a suggestion that literary scholars consider holding simultaneously what appear to be contradictory pedagogical goals because both are helpful, indeed because the one illuminates the limits and possibilities of the other. Professor Gregg's desire for a widely applicable rhetorical pedagogy and a pedagogy that highlights the disciplinary specificity of audience, purpose, and convention may not be as contradictory as first meets the eye. Or Professor Evans's desire to promote interpretations that revel in irresolution may be supported by reductively characterizing for his students strategies for achieving this goal. Similarly, WID proponents may find appeals to the social justice topos resonate with their own concerns for equity and access in higher education. Again, the task for the WID proponent becomes turning many literary scholars' outward-looking concerns inward, asking them to consider how the same social arrangements they critique influence the jumble of discourse practices in their classrooms and building on the activist impulse of this topos to encourage faculty to question what they could modify in their writing instruction to ameliorate these arrangements.

Reflection on the faculty concerns discussed in this chapter suggests to me two further ways WID proponents could appeal to the values of this disciplinary discourse community. Concerns that explicit instruction in disciplinary special topoi requires a reductive oversimplification of disciplinary discourse could be met with examples of useful simplifications already widely employed in the discipline. For example, course catalogs and professional job listings regularly rely upon distinctions of periodization and nationality (e.g., Elizabethan literature, American literature to 1865, African drama). In fact, many departments' requirements indicate that undergraduate English majors should become conversant with some of the features that demarcate different periods and national literatures. And yet, just as literary scholars view this knowledge as integral and helpful, they also recurrently work against these categorizations, calling into question the reductive oversimplification of periodization and national boundaries. Special topoi could be presented analogously as usefully reductive yet necessarily complicated in specific contexts.

Similarly, Professor Caldwell's concern that making special topoi explicit in her teaching would hamper creativity, a concern echoed in critiques of WID such as Spellmeyer's (1989), might be addressed effectively through discussions of the role that conventions and constraints play in more obviously creative endeavors, such as poetry writing or filmmaking. Several students I spoke with made this connection, likening the special topoi to the conventions trained musicians learn to work within and around. The opposition of the creative to the formulaic seems to resonate strongly in suspicion of WID among literary scholars (see also Sullivan, 1991), suggesting that there may be an opportunity for a lively if less-romanticized examination of writing process research in discussions of writing instruction with literature professors. The weight given to this value also suggests that WID proponents may be more successful emphasizing the inventive play facilitated by awareness of topoi over the persuasive capacities of topoi within a particular disciplinary context.

But likely more important than this inventional exercise in drawing on a discipline's favored topoi to invent arguments its members may find appealing will be reassuring resistant faculty that WID aims not to transform their goals, values, and conventions but instead aims to make more readily apparent the goals, values, and conventions that already underpin their teaching and professional discourse. In recommending this, I am aware that I appear to align with the linguists and EFL specialists working under the English for academic purposes (EAP) and English for specific purposes banners who advocate for a genre approach to disciplinary discourse that is purely descriptive and does not seek to challenge or reframe the work the disciplines do (see, for instance, Barton, Aldridge, & Brown, 2004; Hyland, 2000; Swales, 1990). I am also aware of critiques by critical cultural studies composition (CCS) scholars who disparage such an approach as entirely too accommodating to oppressive configurations of power. However, the views of the faculty I present in this chapter persuade me that taking this stance is at once more radical and less accommodationist than either EAP or CCS arguments have previously acknowledged. On the one hand, my reassurances to resistant faculty about WID neutrality may be viewed as somewhat disingenuous as it should by now be clear I firmly believe that making the values and conventions of the disciplines apparent and guiding students in their use offer radical potential for transforming the disciplines and unmasking the illusion of purely meritocratic academic success. On the other hand, the research I discuss in this chapter makes me more convinced that persuading faculty to adopt values and discourse practices perceived as imported from the discipline of rhetoric and composition will be met with such resistance that the goals of CCS and many WAC compositionists will ultimately be thwarted. While there may always be a few gung-ho early "converts," enacting broader WAC and WID goals in meaningful ways will require steady engagement with objections raised by faculty such as those I discuss in this chapter. The perception that I was seeking to impose goals foreign to their discipline or pedagogies presented a prohibitive obstacle to the faculty I worked with. Their concerns impressed upon me all the more the importance of "knowing your audience": despite my analysis of professional discourse, immersion in published debates on literary pedagogy, and previous training and work within English departments, my sense of the discipline could be dismissed as out-of-date and retrograde (Gregg's reaction) or as in conflict with the discipline's core values (Evans's reaction).

However, I would much rather continue to confront this rhetorical challenge than cede WID as a pedagogical project enacted by faculty in the disciplines. Our experiment in making the special topoi explicit in WAL found that instructors trained in rhetoric and composition were both more comfortable and more adept with this approach (they readily embraced the approach, and the papers written by students in their sections were rated more highly by literature professors).[6] One possible interpretation of these results, then, would be to suggest that WID instruction may be best performed by rhetoric and composition specialists rather than by instructors in the disciplines themselves. I believe, however, that this interpretation should be resisted for several reasons. In this instance, the discipline in question happens to be institutionally situated very close to rhetoric and composition; in fact, all our experimental instructors had previous experiences with literary studies as both students and faculty. The same cannot be said for the relationship most rhetoric and composition scholars have with other disciplines, and I hope WID research projects such as this one clarify why a writing instructor's close familiarity with a discipline's genres would be so useful to students. But beyond the uniqueness of this case, in order for WID to have any of the positive and radical impact on the disciplines that I claim for it here, the discipline's faculty must be involved. Otherwise, the traditional divide between domain knowledge and rhetorical procedural knowledge Geisler (1994) describes will only become further reified, with separate faculty assigned to each. Frankly, I also hold out more hope, despite the resistances described here, of persuading disciplinary faculty to embrace and adapt WID goals than I do of recruiting rhetoric and composition faculty to support the aims of other disciplines; after all, faculty have a vested interest in helping their students join their disciplinary conversations. The pull of a unique disciplinary identity, with its attendant discourse practices and sociorhetorical need to recruit new members, marks rhetoric and composition as not terribly different in this regard from other disciplines with longer histories. That said, I suspect some of the best, most productive WID arrangements will thrive where rhetoric and composition specialists collaborate with faculty in other disciplines since each group's need to explain its practices to the other should make more apparent to all involved the disciplinary rhetorics that are otherwise treated as transparent and "natural" as air.

Notes

References

Index

Notes

Introduction

1. More recently, Eberly (2000) has advocated, over "traditional literary criticism and English studies pedagogies," using literary texts as "inventional prompts for discussion about various publics and their possible reactions to the texts in question" (p. 170) in order to facilitate students' participation in the deliberative public spheres of discourse concerning the literary texts. However, several new anthologies that address the relationship of literature to composition announce their less-radical intention to address the realities of staffing sections of first-year composition with instructors mainly trained in literary studies. Interestingly, the MLA collection edited by Anderson and Farris (2007) indicates that the genre of literary analysis can be treated in such a course as "at once a specialized discourse and an exportable one" (p. 5), whereas the NCTE collection edited by Bergmann and Baker (2006) leaves open not only the question of whether or not literary texts should be used in first-year composition courses but also the question of what genres students should write in reaction to literary texts.

2. Prior to this disciplining moment, "Literature" denoted a far broader category than novels, plays, short stories, and poems. "Literature" meant all letters—the products of the printing press: pamphlets, broadsheets, newspapers, as well as books. What we now demarcate as "literature" circulated among these letters as epideictic discourse intended to teach and delight (Clark & Halloran, 1993, p. 2) but was otherwise largely undifferentiated from political and scientific discourse. "Literature" was what the literate were acquainted with, and their shared "cultural literacy" both prepared and facilitated their participation in a literary public sphere (Habermas, 1991; Ross, 1996; Warner, 1990). Thus, poems, stories, and novels written in English were part of a public realm of letters in the United States, discussed in literary societies and publications but not initially a central concern of schoolwork where Greek and Latin predominated. To understand the role such works played in the public realm of letters, we need to exercise reading strategies different from those we have inherited from our institutionalized study, and such recovery projects attempting to read early American fiction and poetry in the context of the literary public sphere in which they circulated have been undertaken by Tompkins (1985) and Dowling (1990).

The discipline's historians and genealogists have sought to explain the many motivations for submitting literary study to discipline and specialization. McMurtry (1985) and Franklin (1984) attested to the increased need of "men of letters" for institutionalized support in an industrial age. McMurtry argued the rise of science as a separate, specialized study showed the path philology—the form of historical linguistics in which literary study first took shape in the modern research university—should take to achieve legitimization, while Franklin (1984), Eagleton (1983), Ohmann (1996), and Scholes (1998) argued that the weakening hold of religion on the popular mind left a void for English studies to fill. In particular, Eagleton pointed to the desire among a growing middle class for access to the cultural capital familiarity with literature brings, and the desire among an established elite to "humanize" this growing middle class by training them in appreciation of elite discourse. Not only would the vernacular be more practical and efficient than classical languages for this purpose (Eagleton, 1983), proponents of professionalization argued that the philological study of the vernacular could provide "mental discipline" in as rigorous a fashion as the study of classical languages (Applebee, 1974; Franklin, 1984; Graff, 1987). Further, Ross (1996) pointed to the commodification of old texts by deceased authors, encouraged by recently established copyright laws as facilitating the discipline's canon formation. And lastly, Graff (1987), Frantzen (1990), and Horsman (1981) pointed to the desire to celebrate nationalism and racial superiority as a strong motivating factor in the development of a discipline that celebrates a racial heritage in each tracing of an etymology.

3. Coming at the issue of community in a broader sense in *Against the Romance of Community*, Joseph (2002) has critiqued the tendency to idealize community. In particular, she interrogated ways in which capitalism depends upon and generates idealized senses of community in part defensively because of these idealizations' disruptive potential and in part proactively because of their conservative, hierarchal, exclusionary, and disciplining tendencies. Joseph may help interested rhetoric and composition scholars develop an activist stance towards discourse communities, and central to her constructive critique is first a close examination of the ways, complicit and oppositional, in which community is performed.

4. While I generally agree with the stress Beaufort (2007) placed on the usefulness of the discourse community concept, I disagree with her characterizations of rhetorical theory as much more limited in its usefulness, involving only conceptualizing an immediate audience. Instead, as I hope this book shows, I believe much more complexity and conceptual utility are available in classical rhetorical theory than Beaufort acknowledged, especially when the work of the New Rhetoricians is seen as building upon it. This trajectory of work allows me and others, such as C. R. Miller (1994), to see discourse community and genre theory as extensions and refinements of classical rhetorical theory.

5. Devitt (2004) supplemented her description of physically and temporally proximate discourse communities with the concepts of "collectives" and "networks." *Collective* she defined as sharing a common purpose "either for a short time (as in an academic class or task force) or at infrequent intervals (as in a club or interest group)" (p. 44) and not necessarily working in physical proximity. *Network* she drew from the concept of social network developed in sociology and linguistics and used to describe the discourse practices of groups formed through direct relationships and further links based from these relationships with other members, such as recipients of group e-mails. Thus, like collectives, participants in a network need not be physically proximate to one another. Devitt's encouragement to consider alternate groupings and relationships beyond the discourse community should help genre theorists and researchers explain how a range of genres function outside of academic disciplines, but it also seems a weakness of her scheme that a place for academic disciplines cannot be clearly found within the three groupings as she described them.

6. Nadeau (1964) explained that though Hermagoras is frequently credited as its author, rhetorical stasis theory appears inchoately in the work of the Stoics, Aristotle's *Topics* and *Rhetoric*, and the *Rhetorica ad Alexandrum*. The writers of subsequent rhetorical handbooks regularly repeated the theory while somewhat modifying and rearranging stases. Though the handbooks primarily focused on and illustrated the forensic use of the stases, many at least suggested the usefulness of stases in deliberative and even epideictic rhetoric.

7. Perelman and Olbrechts-Tyteca (1969) claimed that "value hierarchies are . . . more important to the structure of an argument than the actual values. Most values are indeed shared by a great number of audiences, and a particular audience is characterized less by which values it accepts than by the way it grades them" (p. 81).

8. C. R. Miller (2000) pointed to recent cognitive research that supports the usefulness of the ancients' spatial conception of discovery and invention.

1. "The Rhetoric of Literary Criticism" Revisited:
Mistaken Critics, Complex Contexts, and Social Justice

1. This assumption of the uniqueness of each literary text is challenged by Moretti's (2005) quantitative methods of "distant reading," perhaps explaining why his work in this vein has been received with great controversy.

2. Butler, Guillory, and Thomas (2000) explicitly acknowledged this development in their preface to the anthology *What's Left of Theory? New Work on the Politics of Literary Theory*:

> The extraordinary interest in social theory and the law that has recently emerged in literary studies has seemed to many to constitute an important redirection of the field toward political themes and active political investments in justice, freedom, and equality. Whereas some argue that literature should remain cordoned off from social science and social theory, others are relieved that literary studies has moved toward a more active engagement with social issues, with race studies, practices of gender and sexuality, colonial space and its aftermath, the interstitial cultural spaces of globalization. It may be that literary scholars make poor social theorists, as Richard Rorty has argued, but it seems more likely that literary scholars bring insightful forms of reading to bear upon social and political texts that have great relevance for the course of our collective lives. (pp. xi–xii)

3. Balocco (2000) similarly found that the epistemic "creating a research space" moves Swales (1990) described appeared in a nonlinear fashion throughout another recent sample of journal articles by literary scholars.

4. Bear in mind, however, that Williams (1999) characterized a recent trend in literary criticism as "New Belletrism." Elder's use of personal narrative, a mode of discourse also used in this sample by Gilbert and Gallagher, and encouragement of literary appreciation, though a throwback to an earlier moment in literary history, may be new directions of the field.

5. Gibbons et al. (1994) and Hyland (2000) suggest that the sciences may simultaneously be moving towards embracing social-justice concerns more familiar in the humanities as public pressure for the social accountability and the relevance of their work increase.

2. "You Wouldn't Want to Introduce That to Undergraduate Students": Literature Professors' Views of Disciplinarity and Student Discourse

1. Downing (2005) later revised his stance on postdisciplinarity. Rather than calling to abandon the disciplines, he has come to argue for the value of "nondisciplinary" practices functioning "beside" the disciplines. Downing described the nondisciplinary as including situated, tacit, and procedural knowledge, types of knowledge that I argue are already an unacknowledged but vitally important aspect of disciplinary knowledge. Whereas I see arguments such as Downing's as working to reshape the disciplinary discourse community to which he belongs, Downing and other critics of disciplines tend to see disciplines as responding too slowly and conservatively, taming members' radical impulses.

2. One interview was conducted by e-mail because the professor was overseas for the semester.

3. Interview participants' names throughout this book are pseudonyms.

4. For instance, scientific discourse communities tend to value the simplest, most direct explanations, and students pursuing degrees in these fields may already firmly hold this value, putting them at odds with literary studies' value of complexity. Linguistic research has uncovered significant consequential differences in rhetorical practices among undergraduates pursuing majors in the sciences and the humanities. For instance, North (2005) found that undergraduates who have taken just a few courses in the "arts" were more likely to present knowledge claims as constructed in their writing for a history of science course, and consequently receive higher grades in this course, than undergraduates who had just begun to pursue studies in science. In a similar vein, Charney, Newman, and Palmquist (1995) found that "epistemological styles" vary across disciplines with, for example, students in the humanities being significantly less absolutist than students studying business. This may create value conflicts in a literature course with students pursuing diverse majors. A tendency to reduce complexity, a tendency I saw among several students in the introductory course I observed (Wilder, 2002), could be an understandable response of a student adhering to a more absolutist epistemological style.

3. "This Is How We Do Things": Professors' Expectations for Student Writing

1. Interview participants' names throughout this book are pseudonyms.

2. I also knew the papers we discussed contained a mix of papers by students who had been explicitly taught the special topoi and by students who had enrolled in our "control" sections, though at the time I conducted these interviews, I was blind to which condition the student writer had experienced.

3. During the course of our study, we conducted two rounds of ratings. During the first round, three of the five professors rated sixty-six papers, and during the second round, three professors rated an additional eighty-two papers.

4. The interrater reliability determined using Cronbach's alpha coefficients were .72 for overall quality, .65 for sophistication of argument, and .66 for organization and coherence. See Wilder and Wolfe (2009) for a discussion of the unlikelihood of achieving higher interrater reliability on this complex and fluid task. In order to encourage these rater's regular evaluation practices, we purposefully did not follow usual rater-training techniques designed to achieve higher interrater agreement or provide a detailed rubric.

5. As reported in Wilder and Wolfe (2009), student papers' use of the ubiquity and appearance/reality topoi were correlated with the evaluations received from the faculty raters. In particular, use of ubiquity and appearance/reality predicted raters' perceptions

of argument sophistication, r = .55 and .50 respectively. Students' use of the social justice topos was weakly correlated with the professors' overall quality and sophistication of argument ratings.

6. The WAL instructors whose views I discuss in chapter 2 also specified that they wish to see students make original arguments in their papers by extending class discussion of texts. The "expressivist" professor, Professor Caldwell, describes A papers in her syllabus as those that "go well beyond the findings of our in-class discussions." Professor Carter, who emphasizes "the terms," told me that though she receives "a lot of paraphrase of class discussion," she strongly prefers for student papers to "do some of their own original work." But she qualified this originality by saying, "This is not a matter of saying something that none of the critics have ever said in a hundred years or whatever's been written." Instead, "in the context of our class," students should add original insights not previously shared in discussion.

7. Compositionists' critiques of traditional views of plagiarism underscore this fraught status of "originality." See, for instance, Buranen and Roy (1999) and Howard (1999).

8. Professor Ross described the ways in which her specialization (women's studies) shapes—and constricts—her understanding of exigency this way:

> Well, I do think that I reacted strongly to the first paragraph in maybe a pissed-off way because I felt that as a women's studies professor, when people want to say, "Oh, no, no, no, it's not about lesbian desire, it's about sisterhood and togetherness, but it can't ever be like a sexual thing"—that sets me off to begin with and again makes me think that this person doesn't understand the distinction that or the fact that maybe there isn't a distinction and so has probably misunderstood, I'm assuming, at some point, you know, a lecture, a conversation, from which this paper attempted to draw. So right away I'm like . . . that cocktail conversation was not accurately being stated.

9. Understandably, one professor indicated that actually knowing the student writers often influences her judgments, and several made clear that knowing the actual assignment requirements that the students were attempting to fulfill would also influence their sense of the papers' merits.

4. "Some Tools to Take with Them": Making Disciplinary Conventions Explicit

1. As explained further in Wilder and Wolfe (2009), the researcher who identified and evaluated students' use of the special topoi did not know whether the papers she read were from experimental or control sections of the course. Furthermore, we checked the reliability of the researcher's identification and assessment of the special topoi in the students' papers by having a second reader apply the same assessment rubric to a random subsample of the papers.

2. Over the course of our study, for which we collected data over four semesters, we slightly modified the terms instructors used to describe the special topoi of literary analysis. A big change was to abandon Greek terminology, which could be needlessly confusing. For instance, we came to replace the term *topoi* with *strategies*. Similarly, because the term appeared to be too unfamiliar to be helpful, we replaced *ubiquity* with *everywhereness*. *Appearance/reality* was changed to *surface/depth* because this seemed a better way to promote the search for and acknowledgment of multiple possible layers of meaning within a text, thus encouraging discourse more in keeping with the discipline's

values. In order to give equal weight to other, legitimate means of signaling how one's essay builds on previous scholarly discourse beyond rebuttal, we replaced *mistaken critic* with *extending the critical conversation*. We replaced *social justice* with *social relevance* for somewhat different reasons, however, because we became concerned that *social justice* too narrowly prescribed the political stance students should take as they developed claims for the contemporary relevance of their analyses. Thus, at the risk of misdirecting students, we decided *social relevance* both retained the spirit of the disciplinary discourse community's practices while broadening the ends to which the rhetorical strategy could be applied. For further description of an instructor's experience implementing this approach to teaching a "writing about literature" course, see Wolfe (2003). For some sample course materials that use the special topoi explicitly, see Wilder and Wolfe (2009).

3. Another assignment I have used to support this goal has students interview literature scholars about their writing processes. While their retrospective accounts reveal fewer finer-grained details than the think-aloud protocols we examine, students claim to be deeply impressed by what they learn about the professional peer-review process and their interview subjects' revision practices. This assignment, of course, depends upon a sufficient number of my tolerant colleagues to agree to be interviewed each semester, for which I am grateful. I recognize this assignment may not work in this form for instructors at all institutions. Wolfe and I are completing a textbook manuscript that supports the explicit approach to teaching the special topoi of literary analysis, including use of transcripts of think-aloud protocols, described here.

4. Devitt (2004) similarly distinguished explicit instruction designed to heighten "genre awareness," which she supports, from explicit instruction intended to promote "genre acquisition," which she fears may lead to "rigid prescriptivism" (p. 212).

5. Though Shumway (1992) described his call for infusing explicit instruction in the discursive processes of "theorizing" in literature courses as "a postdisciplinary practice" (p. 101), he took "postdisciplinarity" to denote issues, such as theory, relevant to multiple disciplines: "In my view, postdisciplinarity does not assume the disappearance of the disciplines. Rather, it would function in their interstices, forging connections between different disciplines but not seeking to combine them into a new discipline" (p. 108).

5. "Other Professors, They Assume You Already Know This Stuff": Student Views of Disciplinary Enculturation and Explicating Conventions

1. Pseudonyms in this chapter beginning with "E" denote students who experienced the experimental special topoi curriculum described in chapter 4; names beginning with "C" denote students who enrolled in traditionally taught control sections of WAL described in chapter 2.

2. For the first round of interviews, I invited by e-mail the twenty-two declared English majors who consented to participate in the 2005–6 year of the study and who were not seniors when they took WAL. Nine students accepted my invitation and were interviewed in January 2007. For a second round of interviews in September 2007, I sent invitations by e-mail to a slightly larger pool (thirty-five) by including English majors from 2004–5 year of our study. Again, nine students responded and participated. Interviews were conducted in a room in the students' main campus library. Participants were compensated $30. Of course, students' reasons for self-selecting to participate in these interviews and the small number of students I spoke with make it unwise to generalize about all students' views from my findings. Furthermore, my questions may have prompted a degree

of "meta-awareness" of issues of writing process and rhetorical contexts for writing in school that may have influenced the experience and views of especially those students whom I interviewed a second time.

3. Over the course of the study, researchers and instructors modified the names given to the special topoi for pedagogical reasons, as explained in note 2 to chapter 4.

4. During the first interviews, the average number of such terms the three students in the control sections used to describe their papers was 3.3, whereas the average number of such terms used by the six students in the experimental sections was 9.3. Removing from the data the transcript of the control student whose use of such terms exceeded even the experimental students, the trend observed during the first interview remained in the second interviews: the average number of such terms three students from the control sections used to describe their papers was 3.6, whereas the average number of such terms used by the five students in the experimental sections was 11.4.

6. "There Were Negative Results for Me": Faculty Resistance to Explicit Instruction in Disciplinary Rhetoric

1. Professors' names are pseudonyms.

2. Some rhetoric and composition scholars such as Howard (1999) present a challenge to this view by arguing that students benefit from learning rhetorical patterns and disciplinary ways of thinking new to them through imitation.

3. Several students I interviewed described what they experienced as differences between disciplines' rhetorical practices. For instance, Carrie and Eve perceived different expectations for their writing in history. Eve listed a number of pronounced differences:

> If you're an English major, you write papers like an English major. I took a history course after [WAL], and history professors do not want English papers. They want something very different. [. . .] I did very poorly in that course because I had such an English background and did not know what else was out there. MLA format for everything, but in history, it's a little bit different. [. . .] You don't use flowery words in history. You get to the point. I know in literary analyses, you get to the point, but you can use metaphor and simile and things like that. I tried to use a metaphor in the history paper, and apparently it went on too long, and she took points off for that. She graded me down, and I was very disappointed. I did not realize that there was such a difference and that you apparently dig right in and pull a lot of things from other [texts]. . . . In English, you can look at a text. You can use a lot of textual references. In history, how my professor described it to me was that you don't use so many textual references. You use them to back yourself up when you need to, but you don't use them like in every paragraph. And I had no idea.

4. Despite his advocacy for the concept of interpretive communities, Fish (1994) described his own pedagogical practice as traditional, noncollaborative, performative rather than interactive and highly influenced by his own educational experiences.

5. For instance, Geisler's (1994) research demonstrated how students further acculturated into an academic discipline are better able to evaluate conflicting opinions in print and insert themselves into debate, even when writing for a broad, magazine-reading public. Seitz (1999) claimed that as a result of their experiments with role-playing in the disciplines, students become attuned to the constructed nature of ethos in texts, even in those texts "that most assiduously attempt to locate themselves in the language of

objectivity—an insight that can direct students toward more perceptive reading in addition to more flexible writing" (p. 9) in other contexts. Bruffee (1993) argued that students' provisional participation in disciplinary discourse communities supports greater linguistic and rhetorical flexibility and is ultimately what makes them "liberally educated" (p. 135).

6. See Wilder and Wolfe (2009) for further discussion of the possible impact of the disciplinary training of this study's instructors.

References

Abrams, M. H., & Harpham, G. G. (2005). *A glossary of literary terms* (8th ed.). Boston, MA: Wadsworth.

Ackerman, J. (1993). The promise of writing to learn. *Written Communication, 10*(3), 334–370.

Albrecht, James M. (1999). Saying yes and saying no: Individualist ethics in Ellison, Burke, and Emerson. *PMLA, 114*(1), 46–63.

Anderson, J. H., & Farris, C. R. (Eds.). (2007). *Integrating literature and writing instruction: First-year English, humanities core courses, seminars.* New York, NY: Modern Language Association.

Anderson, W., Best, C., Black, A., Hurst, J., Miller, B., & Miller, S. (1990). Cross-curricular underlife: A collaborative report on ways with academic words. *College Composition and Communication, 41*(1), 11–36.

Applebee, A. N. (1974). *Tradition and reform in the teaching of English: A history.* Urbana, IL: National Council of Teachers of English.

Applebee, A. N. (1996). *Curriculum as conversation: Transforming traditions of teaching and learning.* Chicago, IL: University of Chicago Press.

Balocco, A. E. (2000). Who's afraid of literature? Rhetorical routines in literary research articles. *ESPecialist, 21*(2), 207–223.

Barnet, S. (1971). *A short guide to writing about literature* (2nd ed.). Boston, MA: Little, Brown.

Barnet, S., Berman, M., Burto, W., Cain, W. E., & Stubbs, M. (2000). *Literature for Composition: Essays, fiction, poetry, and drama* (5th ed.). New York, NY: Longman.

Barnet, S., & Cain, W. E. (2000). *A short guide to writing about literature* (8th ed.). New York, NY: Longman.

Bartholomae, D. (1985). Inventing the university. In M. Rose (Ed.), *When a writer can't write: Studies in writer's block and other composing-process problems* (pp. 134–165). New York, NY: Guilford Press.

Barton, E. L., Aldridge, M., & Brown, R. (2004). Personal statements: A conversation with John Swales and Chris Freak. *Issues in Writing, 15*(1), 5–30.

Bawarshi, A. (2003). *Genre and the invention of the writer: Reconsidering the place of invention in composition.* Logan: Utah State University Press.

Bazerman, C. (1981). What written knowledge does: Three examples of academic discourse. *Philosophy of the Social Sciences, 11*, 361–387.

Bazerman, C. (1988). *Shaping written knowledge: The genre and activity of the experimental article in science.* Madison: University of Wisconsin Press.

Bazerman, C. (1992). From cultural criticism to disciplinary participation: Living with powerful words. In A. J. Herrington & C. Moran (Eds.), *Writing, Teaching, and Learning in the Disciplines* (pp. 61–68). New York, NY: Modern Language Association.

Beaufort, A. (1997). Operationalizing the concept of discourse community: A case study of one institutional site of composing. *Research in the Teaching of English, 31*(4), 486–529.

Beaufort, A. (2004). Developmental gains of a history major: A case for building a theory of disciplinary writing expertise. *Research in the Teaching of English, 39*(2), 136–185.

Beaufort, A. (2007). *College writing and beyond: A new framework for university writing instruction.* Logan: Utah State University Press.

Beck, S. W. (2006). Subjectivity and intersubjectivity in the teaching and learning of writing. *Research in the Teaching of English, 40*(4), 413–460.

Berger, Courtney. (2000). When bad things happen to bad people: Liability and individual consciousness in *Adam Bede* and *Silas Marner. Novel, 33*(3), 307–327.

Bergmann, L. S., & Baker, E. M. (Eds.). (2006). *Composition and/or literature: The ends of education.* Urbana, IL: National Council of Teachers of English.

Berkenkotter, C., & Huckin, T. N. (1995). *Genre knowledge in disciplinary communication: Cognition/culture/power.* Hillsdale, NJ: Erlbaum.

Berkenkotter, C., Huckin, T. N., & Ackerman, J. (1988). Conventions, conversations, and the writer: Case study of a student in a rhetoric Ph.D. program. *Research in the Teaching of English, 22*(1), 9–44.

Berlin, J. A. (1988). Rhetoric and ideology in the writing class. *College English, 50*(5), 477–494.

Bilsky, M., McCrea, H., Streeter, R. E., & Weaver, R. M. (1953). Looking for an argument. *College English, 14*(4), 210–216.

Bizzell, P. (1982). Cognition, convention, and certainty: What we need to know about writing. *PRE/TEXT, 3*(3), 213–243.

Blakeslee, A. (1993). Readers and authors: Fictionalized constructs or dynamic collaborations? *Technical Communication Quarterly, 2*, 23–35.

Blakeslee, A. (1997). Activity, context, interaction, and authority: Learning to write scientific papers in situ. *Journal of Business and Technical Communication, 11*(2), 125–169.

Boice, R. (1990). Faculty resistance to writing-intensive courses. *Teaching of Psychology, 17*(1), 13–17.

Booth, W. C. (1974). *A rhetoric of irony.* Chicago, IL: University of Chicago Press.

Booth, W. C. (1983). *The rhetoric of fiction* (2nd ed.). Chicago, IL: University of Chicago Press.

Bourdieu, P., Passeron, J.-C., & de Saint Martin, M. (1994). *Academic discourse: Linguistic misunderstanding and professorial power* (R. Teese, Trans.). Stanford, CA: Stanford University Press.

Brown, J. S., Collins, A., & Duguid, P. (1989). Situated cognition and the culture of learning. *Educational Researcher, 18*(1), 32–42.

Bruffee, K. A. (1993). *Collaborative learning: Higher education, interdependence, and the authority of knowledge.* Baltimore, MD: Johns Hopkins University Press.

Buranen, L., & Roy, A. M. (Eds.). (1999). *Perspectives on plagiarism and intellectual property in a postmodern world.* Albany: State University of New York Press.

Burke, K. (1973). *The philosophy of literary form* (3rd ed.). Berkeley: University of California Press.

Burton, Stacy. (2001). Rereading Faulkner: Authority, criticism, and *The Sound and the Fury*. *Modern Philology, 98*(4), 604–628.

Butler, J. P., Guillory, J., & Thomas, K. (2000). Preface. In J. P. Butler, J. Guillory, & K. Thomas (Eds.), *What's left of theory? New work on the politics of literary theory* (pp. viii–xii). New York, NY: Routledge.

Cahalan, J. M., & Downing, D. B. (Eds.). (1991). *Practicing theory in introductory college literature courses*. Urbana, IL: National Council of Teachers of English.

Callaghan, P., & Dobyns, A. (1996). *Literary conversation: Thinking, talking, and writing about literature*. Boston, MA: Allyn & Bacon.

Carroll, L. A. (2002). *Rehearsing new roles: How college students develop as writers*. Carbondale: Southern Illinois University Press.

Carter, M. (1988). Stasis and kairos: Principles of social construction in classical rhetoric. *Rhetoric Review, 7*(1), 97.

Carter, M. (2007). Ways of knowing, doing, and writing in the disciplines. *College Composition and Communication, 58*(3), 385–418.

Casanave, C. P. (1992). Cultural diversity and socialization: A case study of a Hispanic woman in a doctoral program in sociology. In D. E. Murray (Ed.), *Diversity as resource: Refining cultural literacy* (pp. 148–182). Alexandria, VA: TESOL.

Casanave, C. P. (1995). Local interactions: Constructing contexts for composing in a graduate sociology program. In D. Belcher & G. Braine (Eds.), *Academic writing in a second language: Essays on research and pedagogy* (pp. 83–110). Norwood, NJ: Ablex.

Charney, D. (1993). A study in rhetorical reading: How evolutionists read 'The Spandrels of San Marco.' In J. Selzer (Ed.), *Understanding scientific prose* (pp. 203–231). Madison: University of Wisconsin Press.

Charney, D., & Carlson, R. A. (1995). Learning to write in a genre: What student writers take from model texts. *Research in the Teaching of English, 29*(1), 88–125.

Charney, D., Newman, J. H., & Palmquist, M. (1995). "I'm just no good at writing": Epistemological style and attitudes towards writing. *Written Communication, 12*, 298–329.

Chin, E. (1994). Redefining "context" in research on writing. *Written Communication, 11*(4), 445–482.

Chiseri-Strater, E. (1991). *Academic literacies: The public and private discourse of university students*. Portsmouth, NH: Boynton/Cook.

Clark, G., & Halloran, M. S. (1993). Introduction: Transformations of public discourse in nineteenth-century America. In G. Clark & M. S. Halloran (Eds.), *Oratorical culture in nineteenth-century America: Transformations in the theory and practice of rhetoric* (pp. 1–26). Carbondale: Southern Illinois University Press.

Comfort, J. R. (2002). Surviving intact: African American women negotiating scholarly identities through graduate school writing. In R. P. Yagelski & S. A. Leonard (Eds.), *The relevance of English: Teaching that matters in students' lives* (pp. 235–256). Urbana, IL: National Council of Teachers of English.

Cooper, M. M. (1989). Why are we talking about discourse communities? Or, foundationalism rears its ugly head once more. In M. M. Cooper & M. Holzman (Eds.), *Writing as social action* (pp. 202–220). Portsmouth, NH: Boynton/Cook.

D'Angelo, F. J. (1984). The evolution of the analytic topoi: A speculative inquiry. In R. J. Connors, L. S. Ede, & A. A. Lunsford (Eds.), *Essays on classical rhetoric and modern discourse* (pp. 50–68). Carbondale: Southern Illinois University Press.

Davies, J. M. Q. (Ed.). (1994). *Bridging the gap: Literary theory in the classroom*. West Cornwall, CT: Locust Hill Press.

De La Paz, S. (2005). Effects of historical reasoning instruction and writing strategy mastery in culturally and academically diverse middle school classrooms. *Journal of Educational Psychology, 97*(2), 139–156.

Delpit, L. (1995). *Other people's children: Cultural conflict in the classroom*. New York, NY: New Press.

Devitt, A. J. (2004). *Writing genres*. Carbondale: Southern Illinois University Press.

Diller, C., & Oates, S. F. (2002). Infusing disciplinary rhetoric into liberal education: A cautionary tale. *Rhetoric Review, 21*(1), 53–61.

DiPasquale, Theresa M. (2000). Woman's desire for man in Lanyer's *Salve Deus Rex Judaeorum. Journal of English and Germanic Philology, 99*(3), 356–377.

Doheny-Farina, S. (1989). A case study of one adult writing in academic and nonacademic discourse communities. In C. Matalene (Ed.), *Worlds of writing: Teaching and learning in discourse communities of work* (pp. 17–42). New York, NY: Random House.

Donahue, P. (2002). Strange resistances. *WAC Journal, 13*, 31–41.

Dowdey, D. (1992). Citation and documentation across the curriculum. In M. Secor & D. Charney (Eds.), *Constructing rhetorical education* (pp. 330–351). Carbondale: Southern Illinois University Press.

Dowling, W. C. (1990). *Poetry and ideology in revolutionary Connecticut*. Athens: University of Georgia Press.

Downing, D. B. (2005). *The knowledge contract: Politics and paradigms in the academic workplace*. Lincoln: University of Nebraska Press.

Downing, D. B., Harkin, P., Shumway, D. R., & Sosnoski, J. J. (1987). A conversation with Gerald Graff. *Critical Exchange, 23*, 1–30.

Downing, D. B., & Sosnoski, J. J. (1995). Working with narrative zones in a postdisciplinary pedagogy. *Narrative, 3*(3), 271–286.

Downs, D., & Wardle, E. (2007). Teaching about writing, righting misconceptions: (Re)envisioning "first year composition" as "introduction to writing studies." *College Composition and Communication, 58*(4), 552–584.

Eagleton, T. (1983). *Literary theory: An introduction*. Oxford, England: Basil Blackwell.

Earthman, E. A. (1992). Creating the virtual work: Readers' processes in understanding literary texts. *Research in the Teaching of English, 26*(4), 351–384.

Eberly, R. A. (2000). *Citizen critics: Literary public spheres*. Urbana: University of Illinois Press.

Eisenhart, C. (2006). The humanist scholar as public expert. *Written Communication, 23*(2), 150–172.

Elder, John. (1999). The poetry of experience. *New Literary History, 30*(3), 649–659.

Eubanks, P., & Schaeffer, J. D. (2008). A kind word for bullshit: The problem of academic writing. *College Composition and Communication, 59*(3), 372–388.

Fahnestock, J. (1986). Accommodating science: The rhetorical life of scientific facts. *Written Communication, 3*(3), 275–296.

Fahnestock, J. (1993). Genre and rhetorical craft. *Research in the Teaching of English, 27*(3), 265–271.

Fahnestock, J. (1999). *Rhetorical figures in science*. New York, NY: Oxford University Press.

Fahnestock, J., & Secor, M. (1988). The stases in scientific and literary argument. *Written Communication, 5*, 427–443.

Fahnestock, J., & Secor, M. (1991). The rhetoric of literary criticism. In C. Bazerman & J. Paradis (Eds.), *Textual dynamics of the professions: Historical and contemporary studies of writing in professional communities* (pp. 77–96). Madison: University of Wisconsin Press.

Farris, C. (1992). Giving religion, taking gold: Disciplinary cultures and the claims of writing across the curriculum. In J. A. Berlin & M. J. Vivion (Eds.), *Cultural studies in the English classroom* (pp. 112–122). Portsmouth, NH: Boynton/Cook.

Fish, S. (1985). Anti-professionalism. *New Literary History, 17*(1), 89–108.

Fish, S. (1994). *There's no such thing as free speech and it's a good thing, too.* New York, NY: Oxford University Press.

Fleming, B. (2000). What is the value of literary studies? *New Literary History, 34*, 459–476.

Flower, L. (1989). Taking thought: The role of conscious processing in the making of meaning. In E. P. Maimon, B. F. Nodine, & F. W. O'Connor (Eds.), *Thinking, reasoning, and writing* (pp. 185–212). New York, NY: Longman.

Flower, L. (1994). *The construction of negotiated meaning: A social cognitive theory of writing.* Carbondale: Southern Illinois University Press.

Foucault, M. (1972). The discourse on language (R. Swyer, Trans.). In *The archaeology of knowledge* (1st American ed.) (pp. 215–237). New York, NY: Pantheon Books.

Francoz, M. J. (1999). Habit as memory incarnate. *College English, 62*(1), 11–29.

Franklin, P. (1978). English studies in America. *American Quarterly, 30*, 21–38.

Franklin, P. (1984). English studies: The world of scholarship in 1883. *PMLA, 99*(3), 356–370.

Frantzen, A. J. (1990). *Desire for origins: New language, Old English, and teaching the tradition.* New Brunswick, NJ: Rutgers University Press.

Franzak, J. K. (2008). On the margins in a high-performing high school: Policy and the struggling reader. *Research in the Teaching of English, 41*(4), 466–505.

Freed, R. C., & Broadhead, G. J. (1987). Discourse communities, sacred texts, and institutional norms. *College Composition and Communication, 38*(2), 154–165.

Freedman, A. (1993a). Show and tell? The role of explicit teaching in the learning of new genres. *Research in the Teaching of English, 27*(3), 222–251.

Freedman, A. (1993b). Situating genre: A rejoinder. *Research in the Teaching of English, 27*(3), 272–281.

Freedman, A., Adam, C., & Smart, G. (1994). Wearing suits to class: Simulating genres and simulations as genre. *Written Communication, 11*(2), 193–226.

Freedman, C. (1994). Theory, the canon, and the politics of curricular reform: A response to Gerald Graff. In W. E. Cain (Ed.), *Teaching the conflicts: Gerald Graff, curricular reform, and the culture wars* (pp. 53–66). New York, NY: Garland.

Freire, P. (1993). *Pedagogy of the oppressed* (M. B. Ramos, Trans., 20th anniversary ed.). New York, NY: Continuum.

Fulwiler, T. (1988a). Evaluating writing across the curriculum programs. In S. H. McLeod (Ed.), *Strengthening programs for writing across the curriculum* (pp. 61–75). San Francisco, CA: Jossey-Bass.

Fulwiler, T. (1988b). Writing across the curriculum: Implications for teaching literature. *ADE Bulletin, 88*, 35–40.

Fulwiler, T. (1992). Writing and learning American literature. In A. J. Herrington & C. Moran (Eds.), *Writing, teaching, and learning in the disciplines* (pp. 156–173). New York, NY: Modern Language Association.

Gallagher, Catherine. (2000). A history of the precedent: Rhetorics of legitimation in women's writing. *Critical Inquiry, 26*(2), 309–327.

Gamer, M. (1995). Fictionalizing the disciplines: Literature and the boundaries of knowledge. *College English, 57*(3), 281–285.

Gamer, M. (1999). Authors in effect: Lewis, Scott, and the Gothic drama. *ELH, 66*(4), 831–861.

Geisler, C. (1991). Toward a sociocognitive model of literacy: Constructing mental models in a philosophical conversation. In C. Bazerman & J. Paradis (Eds.), *Textual dynamics of the professions: Historical and contemporary studies of writing in professional communities* (pp. 171–190). Madison: University of Wisconsin Press.

Geisler, C. (1994). *Academic literacy and the nature of expertise: Reading, writing, and knowing in academic philosophy.* Hillsdale, NJ: Erlbaum.

Geyh, Paula E. (2001). Triptych time: The experiential historiography of Meridel Le Sueur's *The Dread Road. Criticism, 43*(1), 81–101.

Gibbons, M., Limonges, C., Nowotny, H., Schwartzman, S., Scott, P., & Trow, M. (1994). *The new production of knowledge: The dynamics of science and research in contemporary societies.* London, England: Sage.

Gigante, Denise. (1999). Forming desire: On the eponymous *In Memoriam* Stanza. *Nineteenth-Century Literature, 53*(4), 480–504.

Gigante, Denise. (2000). Milton's aesthetics of eating. *Diacritics, 30*(2), 88–112.

Gilbert, Sandra M. (1999). "Rats' Alley": The Great War, modernism, and the (anti)pastoral elegy. *New Literary History, 30*(1), 179–201.

Gilbert, Sandra M. (2001). Widow. *Critical Inquiry, 27*(4), 559–579.

Giroux, H. A. (1983). *Theory and resistance in education: A pedagogy for the opposition.* New York, NY: Bergin & Garvey.

Graff, G. (1987). *Professing literature: An institutional history.* Chicago, IL: University of Chicago Press.

Graff, G. (1992). *Beyond the culture wars: How teaching the conflicts can revitalize American education* (1st ed.). New York, NY: Norton.

Graff, G. (1995). Afterword. In A. Young & T. Fulwiler (Eds.), *When writing teachers teach literature: Bringing writing to reading* (pp. 324–333). Portsmouth, NH: Boynton/Cook.

Graff, G. (2003). *Clueless in academe: How schooling obscures the life of the mind.* New Haven, CT: Yale University Press.

Graff, G., & Phelan, J. (Eds.). (1995). Adventures of Huckleberry Finn: *A case study in critical controversy.* Boston, MA: Bedford Books.

Graff, G., & Phelan, J. (Eds.). (2000). The Tempest: *A case study in critical controversy.* Boston, MA: Bedford Books.

Gross, A. (1988). On the shoulders of giants: Seventeenth-century optics as an argument field. *Quarterly Journal of Speech, 74*, 1–17.

Guerin, W. L., Labor, E., Morgan, L., Reesman, J. C., & Willingham, J. R. (2005). *A handbook of critical approaches to literature* (5th ed.). New York, NY: Oxford University Press.

Haas, C. (1994). Learning to read biology: One student's rhetorical development in college. *Written Communication, 11*, 43–84.

Habermas, J. (1991). *The structural transformation of the public sphere: An inquiry into a category of bourgeois society* (T. Burger & F. Lawrence, Trans.). Cambridge, MA: MIT Press.

Halasz, J., Brinckner, M., Gambs, D., Geraci, D., Queeley, A., & Solovyova, S. (2006). Making it your own: Writing fellows re-evaluate faculty "resistance." *Across the Disciplines: Interdisciplinary Perspectives on Language, Learning, and Academic Writing, 3*(3). Retrieved from http://wac.colostate.edu/atd/articles/halasz2006.cfm

Halloran, S. M. (1984). The birth of molecular biology: An essay in the rhetorical criticism of scientific discourse. *Rhetoric Review, 3,* 70–83.

Hamel, F. (2003). Teaching understanding of student understanding: Revising the gap between teacher conceptions and students' ways with literature. *Research in the Teaching of English, 38*(1), 49–84.

Hamel, F., & Smith, M. W. (1998). You can't play if you don't know the rules: Interpretive conventions and the teaching of literature to students in lower-track classes. *Reading & Writing Quarterly, 14*(4), 355–378.

Hare, V. C., & Fitzsimmons, D. A. (1991). The influence of interpretive communities on use of content and procedural knowledge in a writing task. *Written Communication, 8*(3), 348–378.

Harkin, P. (1987). Arguing a history: Gerald Graff's *Professing Literature. Critical Exchange, 23,* 77–90.

Harris, J. (1989). The idea of community in the study of writing. *College Composition and Communication, 40*(1), 11–22.

Hayton, H. R. (1999). "Many privy thinges wimpled and folde": Governance and mutual obligation in Usk's *Testament of Love. Studies in Philology, 96*(1), 22–41.

Hedley, J., & Parker, J. E. (1991). Writing across the curriculum: The vantage of the liberal arts. *ADE Bulletin, 98,* 22–28.

Herndl, C. G. (1993). Teaching discourse and reproducing culture: A critique of research and pedagogy in professional and non-academic writing. *College Composition and Communication, 44*(3), 349.

Herrington, A. J. (1981). Writing to learn: Writing across the disciplines. *College English, 43*(4), 379–387.

Herrington, A. J. (1985). Writing in academic settings: A study of the contexts for writing in two college chemical engineering courses. *Research in the Teaching of English, 19,* 331–361.

Herrington, A. J. (1988). Teaching, writing, and learning: A naturalistic study of writing in an undergraduate literature course. In D. A. Jolliffe (Ed.), *Advances in writing research, volume two: Writing in academic disciplines* (pp. 133–166). Norwood, NJ: Ablex.

Herrington, A. J. (1992). Composing one's self in a discipline: Students' and teachers' negotiations. In M. Secor & D. Charney (Eds.), *Constructing rhetorical education* (pp. 91–115). Carbondale: Southern Illinois University Press.

Herrington, A. J., & Curtis, M. (2000). *Persons in process: Four stories of writing and personal development in college.* Urbana, IL: National Council of Teachers of English.

Horsman, R. (1981). *Race and manifest destiny: The origins of American racial Anglo-Saxonism.* Cambridge, MA: Harvard University Press.

Howard, R. M. (1999). *Standing in the shadow of giants: Plagiarists, authors, collaborators.* Stamford, CT: Ablex.

Hyland, K. (2000). *Disciplinary discourses: Social interactions in academic writing.* Harlow, England: Longman.

Infante, D. A. (1971). The influence of a topical system on the discovery of argument. *Speech Monographs, 38*(2), 125–128.

Jacobus, L. A. (1996). *Literature: An introduction to critical reading*. Upper Saddle River, NJ: Prentice Hall.

James, M. A. (2008). The influence of perceptions of task similarity/difference on learning transfer in second language writing. *Written Communication, 25*(1), 76–103.

Johns, A. M. (1997). *Text, role, and context: Developing academic literacies*. Cambridge, England: Cambridge University Press.

Joseph, M. (2002). *Against the romance of community*. Minneapolis: University of Minnesota Press.

Kaufer, D., & Geisler, C. (1989). Novelty in academic writing. *Written Communication, 6*(3), 286–311.

Kaufer, D., & Young, R. (1993). Writing in the content areas: Some theoretical complexities. In L. Odell (Ed.), *Theory and practice in the teaching of writing: Rethinking the discipline* (pp. 71–104). Carbondale: Southern Illinois University Press.

Kennedy, G. A. (1999). *Classical rhetoric and its Christian and secular tradition from ancient to modern times* (2nd, rev., and enlarged ed.). Chapel Hill: University of North Carolina Press.

Kent, T. (1991). On the very idea of a discourse community. *College Composition and Communication, 42*(4), 425–445.

Kinneavy, J. L. (1983). Writing across the curriculum. *Profession*, 13–20.

Kirch, A. (1996). A basic writer's topoi for timed essay tests. *Journal of Basic Writing, 15*(2), 112–124.

Kirszner, L. G., & Mandell, S. R. (Eds.). (2001). *Literature: Reading, reacting, writing* (4th ed.). Fort Worth, TX: Harcourt College.

Knoblauch, C. H., & Brannon, L. (1983). Writing as learning through the curriculum. *College English, 45*(5), 465–474.

Langer, J. (1992). Speaking of knowing: Conceptions of understanding in academic disciplines. In A. Herrington & C. Moran (Eds.), *Writing, teaching, and learning in the disciplines* (pp. 69–85). New York, NY: Modern Language Association.

Larochelle, G. (1999). From Kant to Foucault: What remains of the author in postmodernism. In L. Buranen & A. M. Roy (Eds.), *Perspectives on plagiarism and intellectual property in a postmodern world* (pp. 121–130). Albany: State University of New York Press.

Lave, J., & Wenger, E. (1991). *Situated learning: Legitimate peripheral participation*. Cambridge, England: Cambridge University Press.

LeCourt, D. (1996). WAC as critical pedagogy: The third stage? *Journal of Advanced Composition, 16*(3), 389–406.

LeFevre, K. B. (1987). *Invention as a social act*. Carbondale: Southern Illinois University Press.

Leff, M. C. (1983). The topics of argumentative invention in Latin rhetorical theory from Cicero to Boethius. *Rhetorica: A Journal of the History of Rhetoric, 1*(1), 23–44.

Lentricchia, F., & McLaughlin, T. (1995). *Critical terms for literary study* (2nd ed.). Chicago, IL: University of Chicago Press.

Lindemann, E. (1993). Freshman composition: No place for literature. *College English, 55*(3), 311–316.

Lingard, L., & Haber, R. (2002). Learning medical talk: How the apprenticeship complicates current explicit/tacit debates in genre instruction. In R. M. Coe, L. Lingard, & T. Teslenko (Eds.), *The rhetoric and ideology of genre: Strategies for stability and change* (pp. 155–170). Cresskill, NJ: Hampton.

Lynch, Jack. (2000). "The ground-work of stile": Johnson on *The History of the Language*. *Studies in Philology, 97*(4), 454–472.

Macbeth, K. P. (2006). Diverse, unforeseen, and quaint difficulties: The sensible responses of novices learning to follow instructions in academic writing. *Research in the Teaching of English, 41*(2), 180–207.

MacDonald, S. P. (1987). Problem definition in academic writing. *College English, 49*(3), 315–331.

MacDonald, S. P. (1989). Data-driven and conceptually driven academic discourse. *Written Communication, 6,* 411–455.

MacDonald, S. P. (1992). A method for analyzing sentence-level differences in disciplinary knowledge making. *Written Communication, 9*(4), 533–569.

MacDonald, S. P. (1994). *Professional academic writing in the humanities and social sciences.* Carbondale: Southern Illinois University Press.

MacDonald, S. P., & Cooper, C. R. (1992). Contributions of academic and dialogic journals to writing about literature. In A. J. Herrington & C. Moran (Eds.), *Writing, teaching, and learning in the disciplines* (pp. 137–155). New York, NY: Modern Language Association.

Magnotto, J. N., & Stout, B. (1992). Faculty workshops. In S. H. McLeod & M. Soven (Eds.), *Writing across the curriculum: A Guide to developing programs* (pp. 32–46). Newbury Park, CA: Sage.

Mahala, D. (1991). Writing utopias: Writing across the curriculum and the promise of reform. *College English, 53*(7), 773–789.

Mahala, D., & Swilky, J. (1994). Resistance and reform: The function of expertise in writing across the curriculum. *Language and Learning across the Disciplines, 1*(1), 35–62.

Malinowitz, H. (1998). A feminist critique of writing in the disciplines. In S. C. Jarratt & L. Worsham (Eds.), *Feminism and composition studies: In other words* (pp. 291–312). New York, NY: Modern Language Association.

Manlove, C. N. (1989). *Critical thinking: A guide to interpreting literary texts.* New York, NY: St. Martin's.

Martin, J. R., Christie, F., & Rothery, J. (1987). Social processes in education: A reply to Sawyer and Watson (and others). In I. Reid (Ed.), *The place of genre in learning: Current debates* (pp. 58–82). Geelong, Australia: Deakin University Press.

Mathieson, M. (1975). *The preachers of culture: A study of English and its teachers.* Totowa, NJ: Rowman and Littlefield.

Mathison, M. (1996). Writing the critique, a text about a text. *Written Communication, 13*(3), 314–354.

Matz, Robert. (1999). Slander, Renaissance discourses of sodomy, and *Othello. ELH, 66*(2), 261–276.

May, Brian (2001). Memorials to modernity: Postcolonial pilgrimage in Naipul and Rushdie. *ELH, 68*(1), 241–265.

Mazzola, Elizabeth. (1999). Brothers' keepers and Philip's siblings: The poetics of the Sidney family. *Criticism, 41*(4), 513–542.

McCann, Sean. (2000). The imperiled republic: Norman Mailer and the poetics of anti-liberalism. *ELH, 67*(1) 293–336.

McCarthy, L. P. (1987). A stranger in strange lands: A college student writing across the curriculum. *Research in the Teaching of English, 21*(3), 233–265.

McHugh, Susan. (2000). Marrying my bitch: J. R. Ackerley's pack sexualities. *Critical Inquiry, 27*(1). 21–41.

McKeon, R. (1987). Creativity and the commonplace. In M. Backman (Ed.), *Rhetoric: Essays in invention and discovery* (pp. 25–36). Woodbridge, CT: Ox Bow.

McMahan, E., Day, S. X., & Funk, R. (1996). *Literature and the writing process* (4th ed.). Upper Saddle River, NJ: Prentice Hall.

McMurtry, J. (1985). *English language, English literature: The creation of an academic discipline.* Hamden, CT: Archon Books.

Meyer, M. (2001). *Thinking and writing about literature* (2nd ed.). Boston, MA: Bedford/St. Martin's.

Miller, C. R. (1984). Genre as social action. *Quarterly Journal of Speech, 70*, 151–167.

Miller, C. R. (1987). Aristotle's "special topics" in rhetorical practice and pedagogy. *Rhetoric Society Quarterly, 17*(1), 61–70.

Miller, C. R. (1992). Kairos in the rhetoric of science. In S. P. Witte, N. Nakadate, & R. D. Cherry (Eds.), *A rhetoric of doing: Essays on written discourse in honor of James L. Kinneavy* (pp. 309–327). Carbondale: Southern Illinois University Press.

Miller, C. R. (1994). Rhetorical community: The cultural basis of genre. In A. Freedman & P. Medway (Eds.), *Genre and the new rhetoric* (pp. 67–78). London, England: Taylor & Francis.

Miller, C. R. (2000). The Aristotelian *Topos*: Hunting for novelty. In A. G. Gross & A. E. Walzer (Eds.), *Rereading Aristotle's* Rhetoric (pp. 130–146). Carbondale: Southern Illinois University Press.

Miller, C. R., & Selzer, J. (1985). Special topics of argument in engineering reports. In L. Odell & D. Goswami (Eds.), *Writing in nonacademic settings* (pp. 309–341). New York, NY: Guilford Press.

Miller, T. P. (1999). Will English departments become the classics departments of the twenty-first century? Retrieved October 31, 2000, from http://www.gened.arizona.edu/tmiller/rhetoric/englishdepartments.htm. Updated 2005 at http://tmiller.faculty.arizona.edu/will_english_departments

Moretti, F. (2005). *Graphs, maps, trees: Abstract models for a literary history.* London, England: Verso.

Myers, G. (1985). The social construction of two biologists' proposals. *Written Communication, 2*, 219–245.

Nadeau, R. (1964). Hermogenes' *On Stases*: A translation with an introduction and notes. *Speech Monographs, 31*(4), 361–424.

Nagy, Andrea R. (1999). Defining English: Authenticity and standardization in seventeenth-century dictionaries. *Studies in Philology, 96*(4), 439–456.

Nelson, J. (1990). This was an easy assignment: Examining how students interpret academic writing tasks. *Research in the Teaching of English, 24*, 362–396.

North, S. (2005). Disciplinary variation in the use of theme in undergraduate essays. *Applied Linguistics, 26*(3), 431–452.

Ohmann, R. (1996). *English in America: A radical view of the profession.* Hanover, NH: Wesleyan University Press.

Parker, W. R. (1981). Where do English departments come from? In G. Tate & E. P. J. Corbett (Eds.), *The writing teacher's sourcebook* (pp. 3–19). New York, NY: Oxford University Press.

Patton, M. D., Krawitz, A., Libbus, K., Ryan, M., & Townsend, M. A. (1998). Dealing with resistance to WAC in the natural and applied sciences. *Language and Learning across the Disciplines, 3*(1), 64–76.

Paul, D., Charney, D., & Kendall, A. (2001). Moving beyond the moment: Reception studies in the rhetoric of science. *Journal of Business and Technical Communication, 15*(3), 372–399.

Perelman, C., & Olbrechts-Tyteca, L. (1969). *The new rhetoric: A treatise on argumentation.* Notre Dame, IN: University of Notre Dame Press.

Perloff, Marjorie. (1999). Language poetry and the lyric subject: Ron Silliman's Albany, Susan Howe's Buffalo. *Critical Inquiry, 25*(3), 405–434.

Peskin, J. (1998). Constructing meaning when reading poetry: An expert-novice study. *Cognition and Instruction, 16*(3), 235–263.

Pope, R. (2003). Re-writing texts, re-constructing the subject: Work as play on the critical-creative interface. In A. Dean & T. Agathocleous (Eds.), *Teaching literature: A companion* (pp. 105–124). New York, NY: Palgrave Macmillan.

Popper, K. R. (1966). *The open society and its enemies* (5th ed., Vol. 2). Princeton, NJ: Princeton University Press.

Prelli, L. (1989). *A rhetoric of science: Inventing scientific discourse.* Columbia: University of South Carolina Press.

Prior, P. (1995). Tracing authoritative and internally persuasive discourses: A case study of response, revision, and disciplinary enculturation. *Research in the Teaching of English, 29*(3), 288–325.

Prior, P. (1998). *Writing/disciplinarity: A sociohistoric account of literate activity in the academy.* Mahwah, NJ: Erlbaum.

Prior, P., Hawisher, G. E., Gruber, S., & MacLaughlin, N. (1997). Research and WAC evaluation: An in-progress reflection. In K. B. Yancey & B. Huot (Eds.), *Assessing writing across the curriculum: Diverse approaches and practices* (pp. 185–216). Greenwich, CT: Ablex.

Pullman, G. L. (1994). Rhetoric and hermeneutics: Composition, invention, and literature. *Journal of Advanced Composition, 14*(2), 367–387.

Purcell-Gates, V. (1995). *Other people's words: The cycle of low literacy.* Cambridge, MA: Harvard University Press.

Richardson, A. (2000). The eugenization of love: Sarah Grand and the morality of genealogy. *Victorian Studies, 42*(2), 227–254.

Richter, D. H. (1994). *Falling into theory: Conflicting views on reading literature.* Boston, MA: Bedford Books.

Roberts, E. V. (1983). *Writing themes about literature* (5th ed.). Englewood Cliffs, NJ: Prentice Hall.

Roberts, E. V. (1999). *Writing about literature* (9th ed.). Upper Saddle River, NJ: Prentice Hall.

Roberts, E. V., & Jacobs, H. E. (1998). *Literature: An introduction to reading and writing* (5th ed.). Upper Saddle River, NJ: Prentice Hall.

Roberts-Miller, T. (2003). Discursive conflict in communities and classrooms. *College Composition and Communication, 54*(4), 536–557.

Roozen, K. (2009). "Fan fic-ing" English studies: A case study exploring the interplay of vernacular literacies and disciplinary engagement. *Research in the Teaching of English, 44*(2), 136–169.

Roozen, K. (2010). Tracing trajectories of practice: Repurposing in one student's developing disciplinary writing processes. *Written Communication, 27*(3), 318–354.

Ross, T. (1996). The emergence of "literature": Making and reading the English canon in the eighteenth century. *ELH, 63*, 397–422.

Russell, D. R. (1995). Activity theory and its implications for writing instruction. In J. Petraglia (Ed.), *Reconceiving writing, rethinking writing instruction* (pp. 51–77). Mahwah, NJ: Erlbaum.

Russell, D. R. (2001). Where do the naturalistic studies of WAC/WID point? A research review. In S. H. McLeod, E. Miraglia, M. Soven, & C. Thaiss (Eds.), *WAC for the new millennium: Strategies for continuing writing-across-the-curriculum programs* (pp. 259–298). Urbana, IL: National Council of Teachers of English.

Russell, D. R. (2002). *Writing in the academic disciplines: A curricular history* (2nd ed.). Carbondale: Southern Illinois University Press.

Russell, D. R., & Yañez, A. (2003). "Big picture people rarely become historians": Genre systems and the contradictions of general education. In C. Bazerman & D. R. Russell (Eds.), *Writing selves/writing societies: Research from activity perspectives* (pp. 331–362). Fort Collins, CO: WAC Clearinghouse and Mind, Culture, and Activity.

Rymer, J. (1988). Scientific composing processes: How eminent scientists write journal articles. In D. Jolliffe (Ed.), *Advances in writing research* (Vol. 2, pp. 211–250). Norwood, NJ: Ablex.

Schaub, Melissa. (2000). Queen of the air or constitutional monarch? Idealism, irony, and narrative power in *Miss Marjoribanks. Nineteenth-Century Literature, 55*(2), 195–225.

Schilb, J. (2002). Composing literary studies in graduate courses. In D. R. Shumway & C. Dionne (Eds.), *Disciplining English: Alternative histories, critical perspectives* (pp. 135–148). Albany: State University of New York Press.

Schmersahl, C. B., & Stay, B. L. (1992). Looking under the table: The shapes of writing in college. In M. Secor & D. Charney (Eds.), *Constructing rhetorical education* (pp. 140–149). Carbondale: Southern Illinois University Press.

Scholes, R. E. (1985). *Textual power: Literary theory and the teaching of English.* New Haven, CT: Yale University Press.

Scholes, R. E. (1998). *The rise and fall of English: Reconstructing English as a discipline.* New Haven, CT: Yale University Press.

Schroeder, C., Fox, H., & Bizzell, P. (Eds.). (2002). *Alt dis: Alternative discourses and the academy.* Portsmouth, NH: Boynton/Cook.

Scott, M. (2002). Cracking the codes anew: Writing about literature in England. In D. Foster & D. R. Russell (Eds.), *Writing and learning in cross-national perspective* (pp. 88–133). Urbana, IL: National Council of Teachers of English.

Secor, M. (1984). Perelman's loci in literary argument. *PRE/TEXT, 5*(2), 97–110.

Secor, M., & Walsh, L. (2004). A rhetorical perspective on the Sokal hoax: Genre, style, and context. *Written Communication, 21*(1), 69–91.

Segal, J., Paré, A., Brent, D., & Vipond, D. (1998). The researcher as missionary: Problems with rhetoric and reform in the disciplines. *College Composition and Communication, 50*(1), 71–90.

Seitz, J. E. (1999). *Motives for metaphor: Literacy, curriculum reform, and the teaching of English*. Pittsburgh, PA: University of Pittsburgh Press.

Shamoon, L., & Burns, D. H. (1999). Plagiarism, rhetorical theory, and the writing center: New approaches, new locations. In L. Buranen & A. M. Roy (Eds.), *Perspectives on plagiarism and intellectual property in a postmodern world* (pp. 183–192). Albany: State University of New York Press.

Shaughnessy, M. (1977). Some needed research on writing. *College Composition and Communication, 28*(4), 317–320.

Shoulson, Jeffrey S. (2000). The embrace of the fig tree: Sexuality and creativity in Midrash and in Milton. *ELH, 67*(4), 873–903.

Showalter, E. (2003, January 17). What teaching literature should really mean. *Chronicle of Higher Education*, p. B7.

Shumway, D. R. (1992). Integrating theory in the curriculum as theorizing—a postdisciplinary practice. In M.-R. Kecht (Ed.), *Pedagogy is politics: Literary theory and critical teaching* (pp. 93–110). Urbana: University of Illinois Press.

Shumway, D. R. (1994). *Creating American civilization: A genealogy of American literature as an academic discipline*. Minneapolis: University of Minnesota Press.

Slomkowski, P. (1997). *Aristotle's* Topics. Leiden, The Netherlands: Brill.

Smith, M. W. (1989). Teaching the interpretation of irony in poetry. *Research in the Teaching of English, 23*(3), 254–272.

Smith, M. W. (1992). Effects of direct instruction on ninth graders' understanding of unreliable narrators. *Journal of Educational Research, 85*(6), 339–347.

Sosnoski, J. J. (1994). *Token professionals and master critics: A critique of orthodoxy in literary studies*. Albany: State University of New York Press.

Sosnoski, J. J. (1995). *Modern skeletons in postmodern closets: A cultural studies alternative*. Charlottesville: University Press of Virginia.

Spanos, W. V. (1993). *The end of education: Toward posthumanism*. Minneapolis: University of Minnesota Press.

Spellmeyer, K. (1989). A common ground: The essay in the academy. *College English, 51*(3), 262–276.

Spellmeyer, K. (1996). Inventing the university student. In L. Z. Bloom, D. A. Daiker, & E. M. White (Eds.), *Composition in the twenty-first century* (pp. 39–44). Carbondale: Southern Illinois University Press.

Staten, Henry. (2000). Is *Middlemarch* ahistorical? *PMLA, 115*(5), 991–1005.

Sternberg, R. J. (1999). What do we know about tacit knowledge? Making the tacit become explicit. In R. J. Sternberg & J. A. Horvath (Eds.), *Tacit knowledge in professional practice: Researcher and practitioner perspectives* (pp. 231–236). Mahwah, NJ: Erlbaum.

Sternberg, R. J., Okagaki, L., & Jackson, A. S. (1990). Practical intelligence for success in school. *Educational Leadership, 48*(1), 35–39.

Sternglass, M. S. (1997). *Time to know them: A longitudinal study of writing and learning at the college level*. Mahwah, NJ: Erlbaum.

Sullivan, P. (1991). Writing in the graduate curriculum: Literary criticism as composition. *Journal of Advanced Composition, 11*(2), 283–299.

Swales, J. M. (1990). *Genre analysis: English in academic and research settings*. Cambridge, England: Cambridge University Press.

Swales, J. M. (1998). *Other floors, other voices: A textography of a small university building*. Mahwah, NJ: Erlbaum.

Swanson-Owens, D. (1986). Identifying natural sources of resistance: A case study of implementing writing across the curriculum. *Research in the Teaching of English, 20*(1), 69–97.

Swilky, J. (1992). Reconsidering faculty resistance to writing reform. *WPA: Writing Program Administration, 16*(1–2), 50–60.

Thaiss, C. (2001). Theory in WAC: Where have we been, where are we going? In S. H. McLeod, E. Miraglia, M. Soven, & C. Thaiss (Eds.), *WAC for the new millennium: Strategies for continuing writing-across-the-curriculum programs* (pp. 299–325). Urbana, IL: National Council of Teachers of English.

Thaiss, C., & Zawacki, T. M. (2002). Questioning alternative discourses: Reports from across the disciplines. In C. Schroeder, H. Fox & P. Bizzell (Eds.), *Alt dis: Alternative discourses and the academy* (pp. 80–96). Portsmouth, NY: Boynton/Cook.

Thaiss, C., & Zawacki, T. M. (2006). Engaged writers and dynamic disciplines: Research on the academic writing life. Portsmouth, NH: Boynton/Cook.

Theisen, Bianca. (2000). The four sides of reading: Paradox, play, and autobiographical fiction in Iser and Rilke. *New Literary History, 31*(1), 105–128.

Tompkins, J. P. (1985). *Sensational designs: The cultural work of American fiction, 1790–1860.* New York, NY: Oxford University Press.

Toulmin, S. E. (1964). *The uses of argument* (1st paperback ed.). Cambridge, England: Cambridge University Press.

Toulmin, S. E., Rieke, R. D., & Janik, A. (1979). *An introduction to reasoning.* New York, NY: Macmillan.

Trimbur, J. (1995). "Taking English": Notes on teaching introductory literature classes. In A. Young & T. Fulwiler (Eds.), *When writing teachers teach literature: Bringing writing to reading* (pp. 15–22). Portsmouth, NH: Boynton/Cook.

Tyson, L. (1999). *Critical theory today.* New York, NY: Garland.

Vanderbilt, K. (1986). *American literature and the academy: The roots, growth, and maturity of a profession.* Philadelphia: University of Pennsylvania Press.

Villanueva, V. (2001). The politics of literacy across the curriculum. In S. H. McLeod, E. Miraglia, M. Soven, & C. Thaiss (Eds.), *WAC for the new millennium: Strategies for continuing writing-across-the-curriculum programs* (pp. 165–178). Urbana, IL: National Council of Teachers of English.

Wagner, R. K., & Sternberg, R. J. (1985). Practical intelligence in real-world pursuits: The role of tacit knowledge. *Journal of Personality and Social Psychology, 49*(2), 436–458.

Waldo, M. L. (2004). *Demythologizing language difference in the academy: Establishing discipline-based writing programs.* Mahwah, NJ: Erlbaum.

Walsh, L. (2010). The common topoi of STEM discourse: An apologia and methodological proposal, with pilot survey. *Written Communication, 27*(1), 120–156.

Walvoord, B. E. (1992). Getting started. In S. H. McLeod & M. Soven (Eds.), *Writing across the curriculum: A guide to developing programs* (pp. 12–31). Newbury Park, CA: Sage.

Walvoord, B. E. (1996). The future of WAC. *College English, 58*(1), 58–79.

Walvoord, B. E. (1997). From conduit to customer: The role of WAC faculty in WAC assessment. In K. B. Yancey & B. Huot (Eds.), *Assessing writing across the curriculum: Diverse approaches and practices* (pp. 15–36). Greenwich, CT: Ablex.

Walvoord, B. E., Hunt, L. L., Dowling Jr., H. F., & McMahon, J. D. (1997). *In the long run: A study of faculty in three writing-across-the-curriculum programs.* Urbana, IL: National Council of Teachers of English.

Walvoord, B. E., & McCarthy, L. P. (1990). *Thinking and writing in college: A naturalistic study of students in four disciplines.* Urbana, IL: National Council of Teachers of English.

Wardle, E. (2009). "Mutt genres" and the goal of FYC: Can we help students write the genres of the university? *College Composition and Communication, 60*(4), 765–789.

Warner, M. (1990). *The letters of the republic: Publication and the public sphere in eighteenth-century America.* Cambridge, MA: Harvard University Press.

Warren, J. E. (2006). Literary scholars processing poetry and constructing arguments. *Written Communication, 23*(2), 202–226.

Watkins, E. (1989). *Work time: English departments and the circulation of cultural value.* Stanford, CA: Stanford University Press.

Wenger, E. (1999). *Communities of practice: Learning, meaning, and identity* (1st paperback ed.). Cambridge, England: Cambridge University Press.

Wentworth, M. (1987). Writing in the literature class. *Journal of Teaching Writing, 6*, 155–162.

White, Paul A. (1999). The Latin men: The Norman sources of the Scandinavian kings' sagas. *Journal of English and Germanic Philology, 98*(2), 157–169.

Wilder, L. (2002). "Get comfortable with uncertainty": A study of the conventional values of literary analysis in an undergraduate literature course. *Written Communication, 19*(1), 175–221.

Wilder, L. (2005). "The rhetoric of literary criticism" revisited: Mistaken critics, complex contexts, and social justice. *Written Communication, 22*(1), 76–119.

Wilder, L. (2006). "Into the laboratories of the university": A rhetorical analysis of the first publication of the Modern Language Association. *Rhetoric Review, 25*(2), 162–184.

Wilder, L., & Wolfe, J. (2009). Sharing the tacit rhetorical knowledge of the literary scholar: The effects of making disciplinary conventions explicit in undergraduate writing about literature courses. *Research in the Teaching of English, 44*(2), 170–209.

Williams, J. (1999). The new belletrism. *Style, 33*(3), 414–442.

Williams, R. (1977). *Marxism and literature.* Oxford, England: Oxford University Press.

Williams, R. (1983). *Keywords: A vocabulary of culture and society.* New York, NY: Oxford University Press.

Winsor, D. (1996). *Writing like an engineer: A rhetorical education.* Mahwah, NJ: Erlbaum.

Winsor, D. (1999). Genre and activity systems: The role of documentation in maintaining and changing engineering activity systems. *Written Communication, 16*(2), 200–224.

Wolfe, J. (2003). A method for teaching invention in the gateway literature class. *Pedagogy, 3*(3), 399–425.

Young, A., & Fulwiler, T. (Eds.). (1995). *When writing teachers teach literature: Bringing writing to reading.* Portsmouth, NH: Boynton/Cook: Heinemann.

Young, R. (1980). Arts, crafts, gifts, and knacks: Some disharmonies in the new rhetoric. *Visible Language, 14*(4), 341–350.

Zamir, Tzachi. (2000). Upon One Bank and Shoal of Time: Literature, Nihilism, and Moral Philosophy. *New Literary History, 31*(3), 529–551.

Index

power relations, 8–9, 13, 26; in classroom, 13, 56–57; divide between
domain knowledge and rhetorical
processes, 62–63, 69–70, 109–13,
131–32, 201; expertise, denying, 62–63;
professional power within discipline,
192–93; resistance, 56–57; student
creativity and expression and,
154–55, 157–58. *See also* disciplinary
discourse communities; discourse
communities
practical criticism, 142
*Practicing Theory in Introductory Col-
lege Literature Courses* (Cahalan and
Downing), 56
predisciplinary pedagogy, 57–58, 61, 65,
76, 169, 176; professionalization concerns, 181, 188, 189
Prelli, L., 19
prewriting activities, 69, 165, 171, 182
Prior, P., 7, 11–12, 13–14, 15, 20
procedural display, 15
procedural knowledge, 19, 22, 26, 64, 73,
109, 123–25, 146, 151; studies, 113–16
procedural strategies, 124–25
*Professional Academic Writing in the
Humanities and Social Sciences* (Mac-
Donald), 3
professionalism, 5–6, 194–95
professionalization, 176, 181, 188, 189
proposal stasis, 17, 31, 32–33
*Publications of the Modern Language
Association (PMLA)*, 20–21, 22, 32, 53;
1886 issue, 22, 27–28, 33, 54
public writing, 2
Pullman, G. L., 20, 116, 117
Purcell-Gates, V., 112

"Queen of the Air or Constitutional
Monarch? Idealism, Irony, and Nar-
rative Power in *Miss Marjoribanks*"
(Schaub), *30*, 41, 48

Ramus, Peter, 191
"'Rats' Alley': The Great War, Modern-
ism, and the (Anti)Pastoral Elegy"
(Gilbert), *29*, 36, 39, 45–46

reading: activist practices, 40–41;
privileged over writing, 70–72, 182;
theories, 37
reflexive consciousness raising, 123
reliability curriculum, 115
"Rereading Faulkner: Authority,
Criticism, and *The Sound and the
Fury*" (Burton), *29*, 33, 38, 41, 46,
48–49
Research in the Teaching of English
(Freedman), 110
resistance, as term, 175. *See also* faculty
resistance to WAC/WID
resolution, lack of, 47–48
revision stage of writing, 64, 121
rhetoric: ancient, 15–17; formalist current-
traditional theories, 15; of literary
criticism, 20–23
rhetorical community, 10, 11
rhetorical processes, 73–74, 114; divide
between domain knowledge and,
62–63, 69–70, 109–13, 131–32, 201
rhetoric and composition, 5, 9, 19, 112,
184, 200–201; emergence of as field, 1,
3; professionalization, 176
Richards, I. A., 142
Richardson, Angelique, *30*, 32, 42–43, 45,
49, 51
Richter, D. H., 56
Rieke, R. D., 18, 54
Rilke, Rainer Maria, 37, 39
Roberts, E. V., 57–58, 66
Roberts-Miller, T., 13
Roozen, K., 11, 12
Rushdie, Salman, 38, 44
Russell, D. R., 13, 63, 113, 121, 133, 153, 197

Satanic Verses, The (Rushdie), 38
"Saying Yes and Saying No: Individualist
Ethics in Ellison, Burke, and Emer-
son" (Albrecht), *29*, 34, 45
Schaeffer, J. D., 185, 191–92
Schaub, Melissa, *30*, 41, 48
Schilb, J., 22–23
Schmersahl, C. B., 78, 170
Scholes, R. E., 55, 187
school discourse community, 154, 168

Laura Wilder is an assistant professor of English at the University at Albany, State University of New York, and has published essays in *Research in the Teaching of English*, *Rhetoric Review*, and *Written Communication*.